40 ON JUSTICE

The Prophetic Voice
on Social Reform

OMAR SULEIMAN

KUBE
PUBLISHING

40 on Justice: The Prophetic Voice on Social Reform

First Published in England by
Kube Publishing Ltd
MCC, Ratby Lane, Markfield
Leicestershire, LE67 9SY,
United Kingdom
Tel: +44 (0) 1530 249230
Email: info@kubepublishing.com
Website: www.kubepublishing.com

Copyright © Omar Suleiman 2021
All rights reserved.

The right of Omar Suleiman to be identified as the author and translator of this work has been asserted by him in accordance with the Copyright, Design and Patents Act, 1988.

CIP data for this book is available from the British Library.

ISBN: 978-1-84774-144-8 *casebound*
ISBN: 978-1-84774-143-1 *paperback*
ISBN: 978-1-84774-145-5 *ebook*

Editor: Zenab Shahid
Cover Design: Jannah Haque
Typesetting: Nasir Cadir
Printed by: Elma Basim, Turkey

CONTENTS

	Foreword	vii
1.	The Gravity of Injustice in Islam	1
2.	God is More Capable Than Us	10
3.	From the Scrolls of Ibrahim	19
4.	To Seek or Not to Seek Leadership	26
5.	We Will be Asked About Our Potential	36
6.	A Word of Truth in the Face of an Oppressor	46
7.	The Ruling on Silence and Injustice	53
8.	The Right to Food, Water and Shelter	63
9.	Responding to Evil with Good	71
10.	Everybody Else Does It	78
11.	The Comprehensiveness of *Tatfeef* (short-changing)	85
12.	Whoever Deceives is Not From Us	94
13.	Corrupt Lawyers and Unserved Justice	105
14.	Elitist Privilege	112
15.	Building a Coalition of Justice: the Fiqh of *Hilf al-Fadool*	119
16.	A Show of Strength	125
17.	Finding and Channelling Your Righteous Anger	131
18.	The Rights of the Neighbour	139
19.	The Definition, Categorisation and Prohibition of Torture in Islam	146
20.	Prophetic Guidance on Work Conditions and Employee Treatment	153
21.	The Characteristics of a Pious Employee	159

22.	Greed – The Root of all Social Injustice	168
23.	Why is Usury (*riba*) Prohibited?	171
24.	Insurance Companies and Vulnerable Citizens: The Concept of Uncertainty (*gharar*) in Islam	179
25.	Justice Between Parents and Children	185
26.	The Sin of Favouritism: Be Just with your Children	192
27.	How Rights Work in Marriage	199
28.	The Rights of Extended Family	209
29.	The Rights of the Elderly Within Society	206
30.	Islam's Position on Slavery	224
31.	Islamic Ethics Regarding Asylum, Refugees and Migration	231
32.	Racism, Supremacism and True Patriotism	237
33.	Stereotyping and Collective Guilt	249
34.	Gender Equity in Islam – Regard for Women	257
35.	How the Prophet Muhammad ﷺ Treated Those with Mental Illness, Disabilities and Special Needs	266
36.	Doctors of the Prophet ﷺ and Islam's History of Healthcare	276
37.	When Animals Indict Humans for Cruelty	283
38.	Environmentalism	293
39.	Without Justice, There Can Be No Peace	300
40.	Gradual Change versus Radical Reform	306
	Endnotes	317
	Index	320

بسم الله الرحمن الرحيم

FOREWORD

ISLAM AS A religion is exemplified more than any other virtue by the quality of *rahma*, a word that is difficult to translate into English. The customary translation of "mercy" suggests hierarchy, but this is not necessarily the case in the Arabic original. The *Oxford Dictionary of English* defines mercy as: "Compassion or forgiveness shown towards someone whom it is within one's power to punish or harm." Scholars of Arabic have suggested that while this may be an appropriate way to understand how God relates to human beings, it is not suitable for characterising how humans relate to each other. In the latter case, they point out that a more appropriate way of understanding *rahma* is that it means tenderness (*riqqa*) towards others. The Turkish scholar, Recep Sentürk, prefers to translate *rahma* as love, a word that seems to do justice to its meaning and whose semantic range in English renders it appropriate for both human beings and their Creator Who describes His relationship with the believers in the Qur'an as being of mutual love—"*He loves them and they love Him*" (al-Maiida 5: 54).

In a millennium old tradition, the ulama frequently begin their teaching of a new cohort of students with the Hadith of *rahma* that, as part of this tradition, is the first Hadith a student narrates from his teacher. The Hadith reads in Arabic:

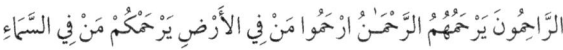

In light of the fact that *rahma* may be rendered as "love," this Hadith can be translated as follows:

> "The people who exemplify love are loved
> by the All-Loving One (al-Rahman).
> Love those on the earth, may the One in the heavens love you."[1]

Justice as Love

But what does love have to do with justice? Love and mercy are often seen as the opposite of justice. We can either seek justice, or show mercy. But what if the two are in fact inseparable? The African-American philosopher Cornel West, offers us a different way of looking at the relationship between justice and love. In a pithy but powerful phrase, he declares: "Justice is what love looks like in public, just like tenderness is what love feels like in private." The message rings true from an Islamic perspective, and our pursuit of justice as Muslims must be spurred by our love for our fellow human beings and our desire for their good. As the Prophet ﷺ said, "None of you truly believes until they love for their brother [and sister] what they love for themselves."[2] We all desire to be treated with justice and fairness, and so we should try to make this a reality for our fellow human beings, whoever they are.

We live in an age in which, perhaps more than any time in the past, we can witness with our own eyes the injustices perpetrated by the powerful against the weak on a global scale. The Qur'an describes us as a community (*ummah*) that stands up for justice, even if it is against our own selves and our families (al-Nisa' 4: 135). While *rahma* is the defining quality of our religion, the love and mercy it exemplifies cannot truly manifest without a concerted effort on our part to uphold justice. Ultimate justice is not to be had until the next life, but confronting injustice (*dhulm*) in this world is repeatedly enjoined in the Qur'an. The concept of *dhulm* is frequently coupled in the Qur'an with the worst of sins in Allah's eyes, namely worshipping anything aside from Allah (*shirk*). The Qur'an describes all sins as forgivable except *shirk* (al-Nisa' 4: 48). Elsewhere in the Qur'an, we are told that the Muslim *ummah* is one that is concerned with commanding right and forbidding wrong (Al 'Imran 3:104). As the Prophet ﷺ explains, this is required at every level of our behaviour, even at a psychological level. He informs us: "Whoever sees a wrong, let them set it aright with their hands. If they are unable to, then let them set it aright with their tongues (by speaking out against it). If they are unable to do even this, then let them set it aright with their hearts (by recognizing that it is wrong), and that is the lowest level of faith."[3]

The scholars have recognised that each and every Muslim has the responsibility to correct the wrongs of their own behaviour, but also of those around them and their societies. However, this is not to be demonstrated by an unreflective and self-righteous anger or disdain towards those who perpetrate these wrongs. Rather, as the Prophet ﷺ himself exemplified over the many years of his Prophetic mission, the righting of wrongs, and the rectifying of injustice in the world requires a great deal of patience, wisdom, and indeed love and compassion. As the Prophet ﷺ once counselled our Mother, 'Aisha, "Gentleness is never found in something except that it beautifies it, and it is never removed from something except that it renders it shameful."[4] Yet, when upholding justice required it, the Prophet ﷺ could demonstrate fortitude in pursuing justice even in just war. The Prophet ﷺ was the best example of the just human being and his actions are our guide to how we can confront injustice.

An age of injustice

We live in a time that is characterised by extremes of injustice on an epic scale. For the last several decades, we have witnessed major imperial wars and proxy wars by global powers with imperial ambitions. These in turn have given rise to great horrors in parts of the world in the form of rapacious regimes that are willing to kill hundreds of thousands of people in the quest to stay in power alongside an international order whose most powerful states either simply act as observers or actively support such bloodshed. Elsewhere, in the supposed name of fighting terrorism, emerging powers like China have recreated the worst horrors of the last century in the form of concentration camps for potentially millions of Uighur Muslims. Concentration camp like conditions are found in the effective Indian annexation and sealing off of Kashmir, and the decades old settler colonial project represented by the illegal Israeli occupation of Palestine. All of these myriad injustices have given rise to a massive refugee crisis that has witnessed thousands of human beings drown in the

Mediterranean and the Bay of Bengal while the "civilized" world doesn't simply look on, but its leaders often vilify those desperately trying to escape devastation and tragedy. Closer to home, in the West, and for many centuries rather than decades, the twin crimes of racism and colonialism have legitimated the dehumanisation of black and brown bodies in the Transatlantic slave trade and the colonial subjugation of more than eighty per cent of the globe by Western powers.

Besides this, humanity faces a climate crisis that is the inevitable product of a nihilistic global economic order whose systemic injustices have left no part of the world unscathed and produced massive inequality both within the populations of countries, and also between the Global North and South. Such inequality reflects not the just deserts of hard working rich countries over lazy poorer nations, but a global system of economic privilege that systematically redirects wealth from poorer nations to richer ones, and in the latter, siphons wealth into the top zero point one per cent who, in turn have the ability to corrupt democracies through lobbying politicians to perpetuate their privileged status while dispossessing some of society's most vulnerable.

In these otherwise dark times, we can find solace and guidance in Prophetic teachings and the Prophetic example. Imam Omar Suleiman has for many years demonstrated his commitment to standing up for justice while drawing on the Prophetic example in guiding his personal practice and his advocacy on behalf of the dispossessed. In keeping with the Muhammadan example that Allah exhorts us to follow in the Qur'an, he has joined broad coalitions of activists dedicated to working towards a more just society. The present work grows out of a series of Hadith commentaries he has written and presented within his community at the Valley Ranch Islamic Centre in Dallas, Texas, alongside online broadcasts in partnership with the Yaqeen Institute for Islamic Research.

Yaqeen is a pioneering institution, of which Imam Omar is president, that seeks to address the intellectual challenges faced by Muslims in the modern world through a recognition that Islam possesses rich resources for addressing the concerns of humanity in an age of extremes and widespread injustice. Imam Omar's exemplary leadership, spiritual, intellectual, communal and societal is exemplified in his myriad engagements in both his teaching and his activism which can inspire a new generation of Muslim leaders who recognise their duty to the Prophetic imperative to speak truth to power. He seeks to channel the Prophetic voice to enlighten our minds, hearts and souls so that we can be better prepared to confront injustices in our spiritual lives, our personal relationships, in wider society, and globally. We would do well to heed his call.

وَصَلَّ اللَّهُمَّ عَلَى سَيِّدِنَا مُحَمَّدٍ وَعَلَى آلِهِ وَصَحْبِهِ وَسَلِّم

Usaama al-Azami
University of Oxford
January, 2021

1

THE GRAVITY OF INJUSTICE IN ISLAM

On the authority of Abu Dharr al-Ghifari (may Allah be pleased with him) from the Prophet ﷺ is that among the sayings he relates from his Lord (may He be glorified) is that He said: O My servants, I have forbidden oppression for Myself and have made it forbidden amongst you, so do not oppress one another.

I WANT TO BEGIN this chapter by starting off with a wonderful quote by Syed Ja'far Raza, who authored a book called *The Essence of Islam*: "If I am asked to summarise the principles of Islam and the essence of Islam, I would say it is justice. Islam is synonymous with justice. Justice to the Creator by worshipping Him and obeying His injunctions and mandate. He is Justice. Justice to the Prophet Muhammad ﷺ by following him as he represents the authority of God on earth.

Justice to oneself by keeping it secure from sinfulness and egotism. Justice to the body by keeping it healthy and free from undue exertion and illness. Justice to the soul by keeping it pure with piety.

Justice in the matrimonial sphere, justice to the parents as they have been instrumental in gifting our existence. Justice to the spouse who shares the burden of raising a family. Justice to the offspring as they are the extensions of our own lives and motivating them to take the right decisions in life. Justice to our neighbours by sharing with them in their moments of trial.

Justice to the sick by assisting them in restoring their health. Justice to the downtrodden and poor by supplementing their basic needs.

Justice to the motherland by enjoying the fragrance of its soul and loving and promoting its prosperity and being ready to sacrifice for it. Justice to humanity by contributing to its development. Justice to knowledge by spreading it far and wide for by enabling mankind to enjoy its fruits without discrimination. Justice therefore is the foundation of Islamic principles and occupies a place next to the Oneness of God."

I find that this quote gives a comprehensive view of the importance of justice in Islam and how it encompasses everything we do on a daily basis. It is a fitting way to introduce the subject that we will cover in this chapter: the gravity of social injustice.

This topic is based on a Hadith Qudsi (the strongest form of Hadith; narrated directly by the Prophet Muhammad ﷺ on behalf of Allah).

Abu Dharr reported that the Prophet Muhammad ﷺ said, "Allah Almighty said: Oh my servants, I have forbidden oppression for myself and I have forbidden oppression amongst you, so do not oppress one another."[5]

This Hadith powerfully conveys that any form of oppression is not accepted by Allah – for Himself or for His creation.

Imam Ahmad, may Allah have mercy on him, went on to say regarding this Hadith that it is the most noble Hadith that was ever narrated by the people of Shaam (Syria, Palestine, Jordan and Lebanon are all part of Shaam). He also mentioned that when some scholars such as Abu Idris used to narrate this Hadith, they would be on their knees as a means of showing humility and vulnerability in the sight of Allah. The Hadith itself sets a paradigm of God being good with us, therefore we are expected to be good to one another.

There are also many other lessons that we can learn from this Hadith, in addition to the obvious message of oppression being forbidden, as we will cover below:

- If anyone was to have the right to wrong, it would be Allah. Nobody can set limitations or restrictions upon Him. Allah is infinite in His power.

Who can mandate anything upon Allah except Himself? He chooses not to oppress, He has forbidden oppression for Himself; He has forbidden Himself from wronging any of His creation. And in His glory, He has only mandated two things for Himself. One is for Him and His Angels to send their peace and blessings *(salawat)* upon the Prophet Muhammad ﷺ. And as this is mandated upon Allah and His Angels by Himself, we are also expected to send peace and blessings upon the Messenger ﷺ; it is a strong statement that puts Allah's mandates in perspective for us. We cannot have any argument against sending *salawat* upon the Prophet Muhammad ﷺ. And the second is that which has already been mentioned: Allah has forbidden oppression for Himself and forbidden us to oppress one another.

Ibn Rajab explains to us that there are three approaches to any situation: transgression, justice and grace. Allah has denied Himself transgression; even when dealing with the worst of His creation (for example the Pharaoh who wronged an entire nation!)

As for justice, Allah uses it and will use it when necessary. On the Day of Judgement for example, those who will be receiving punishments will be dealt with complete justice; there will be no element of transgression or extra punishment. They will be punished accordingly for the wrong that they have committed – Allah will not wrong anyone of that Day, nor will He allow the wrongdoing that was done against anyone to be forgotten.

And lastly, grace is something that Allah loves. Allah gives extra grace to those who are righteous and aim to obey Allah as best they can. He has made it easier for us to multiply our rewards with our good actions, all thanks to His Grace.

There is a Hadith narrated in Abu Dawud in which the Prophet Muhammad ﷺ sums this up perfectly: "If Allah were to punish all of the inhabitants of the heavens and the earth, then He would punish them without being unjust to them and if Allah shows mercy to them, then His Mercy is always better than their deeds."

Although we may initially be taken aback by the words "if Allah were to punish all of the inhabitants of the heavens and the earth," it is important to remember that the Prophet Muhammad ﷺ was explaining to us that we cannot match what Allah does for us, yet Allah has chosen not to punish everyone.

- Another lesson we can derive from this is the meaning of oppression (*dhulm*) and what Islam says about it. The word *dhulm* in the technical meaning within the Arabic language means injustice, and in Islam it means to misplace rights. Or in other words, putting something in a place in which it does not belong.

Linguistically, *dhulm* is of two types: going too far or excess, or withholding too much or deficiency. The first could be going too far in a dispute for example and resulting in violence or other forms of oppression, whilst the second could be withholding the rights of the spouse. There may not be violence or continuous fighting in a marriage, but not showing compassion towards your spouse is a form of oppression as Allah has mandated compassion for us in the marriage contract.

Islamically, the greatest form of oppression is to associate a partner with Allah, as Allah has mentioned in *Surah Luqman*, verse 13 Allah has created us; therefore, it is His right to be worshipped. To associate someone with Him is to put the creation in the place of the Creator. This goes to show that the concept of justice and injustice is deeply embedded in our theology.

- We learn the reasons behind Allah referring to us as *ya ibadi* (oh my slaves) in the Hadith Qudsi.

Firstly, it puts into perspective our relationship with Allah; if we do not properly understand the reality of our relationship with our Creator, then it becomes difficult to understand our relationship with society.

Secondly, the words *ya ibadi* show love from Allah. He calls upon us in a compassionate way to help us connect with Him better as well as to humble us. The one who is oppressing someone else is losing the spirit of love, or *muhabbah*, as it is known in Arabic. Our *fitrah*, or natural disposition, is one of kindness, compassion and mercy and not of cruelty or harshness. And it is in the way that Allah addresses us in this Hadith that we are truly able to understand the importance of compassion.

Similarly, if we were to admonish someone sharply for being harsh or committing wrong towards others, then that person would probably become harsher and make the problem worse. Allah knows this, so He shows us the correct way to give advice to one another whilst at the same time giving us advice not to oppress one another.

Thirdly, Allah is reminding us through the words "Oh my slaves," that He has created us to worship Him and that we were sent to Earth to serve and fulfil His purpose. We are mere slaves of Allah and we do not have the right to act arrogantly in the world. Allah will say on the Day of Judgement that He is the King, and He will call upon those who claimed that they were kings and all-powerful on Earth. This admonition is drilling home the truth that we have not been given the authority to wrong others. Allah gives us countless blessings, and going against what He asks of us is equal to ingratitude and disobedience. If Allah has blessed us with certain advantages, we cannot use them to cause injustice to others.

Fourthly, scholars say that it shows ingratitude on our part if we oppress others. Allah gives us blessings, yet we use those blessings as a means to oppress or wrong somebody else. We would have to be in a certain position in order to cause injustice to someone, and this phrase "Oh my slaves" is a reminder that we must not be ungrateful with the blessings that Allah bestows upon us, and we should never use them to commit evil.

Lastly, Allah does not address Muslims alone, He addresses all human beings through the words *ya ibadi*. It is not just Muslims who are slaves of Allah, but all of humanity, and He has ordered everyone to deal justly with one another.

At the end of *Surah Fatihah* we are asking Allah to *"not let us be amongst those who have earned Your Wrath nor those who have gone astray."* However, this supplication is negated when we transgress through our deeds as Allah also says in the Qur'an that He does not love the oppressors. By oppressing others, we sacrifice the love (*muhabbah*) of Allah. We cannot be guided by Allah if we mistreat His creation!

- The Prophet Muhammad ﷺ warned us against oppression as it is a form of darkness. Oppression will not only cause darkness in the oppressors' hearts, but also cause darkness for them on the day of Judgement. Allah says regarding the Day of Judgement in *Surah Ta-Ha*, verse 111 that, *"he will have failed who carries injustice."* This is the weight of injustice; anyone who has oppressed will bear the ultimate loss on the Day of Judgement.

The Prophet ﷺ also mentioned that on the Day of Judgement, people will witness the proceedings of the animals and the way in which Allah will deal with the injustice amongst animals. Such will be the justice of Allah, that even the horned goat that attacked the one that did not have horns will have its retribution. Watching the judgement of the animals will cause fear in the hearts of the oppressors and disbelievers who will wish that they could be reduced to dust before their own deeds are accounted for.

- The Prophet Muhammad ﷺ says in a Hadith reported by Safwan, may Allah be pleased with him: "Whoever wrongs someone we have a treaty with or who is under our protection, or diminishes his rights, or overburdens him beyond his capacity, or takes away something from him without his consent, then I will be his prosecutor on the Day of Judgement."[6]

    The weight of this Hadith is immense in that it clearly shows the seriousness of oppression in Islam. Causing oppression or injustice is such a grave sin, that the beloved Prophet ﷺ will stand against those from his own followers (*ummah*) who oppressed non-Muslims. If we will have our Prophet ﷺ arguing against us and asking Allah to punish us for the deeds that we committed against non-Muslims, then what hope do we have of making it to Paradise? The treaties that were made at the time of the Prophet Muhammad ﷺ may not exist anymore, but we still do not have a right to wrong anyone, be they Muslim or non-Muslim.

    As narrated by Abdullah ibn Amr ibn al-As, may Allah be pleased with him, the Messenger ﷺ said: "Whoever kills someone protected by Muslims will not smell the scent of Paradise; it is so strong that it can be smelt from a distance of forty years away."[7] Such are the grave consequences of causing injustice to others in this life. Being unjust leads us away from Paradise (*Jannah*), so far in fact that even smelling the beautiful scent of Paradise will not be possible for us.

Ibn al Qayyim said that the strongest verse in the Qur'an about justice is in *Surah al-Ma'idah*, Verse 8: *And do not let the hatred of others prevent you from being just. Be just, for that is closer to righteousness. And be mindful of Allah; indeed Allah is well aware of all that you do.*

We may dislike, or hate someone for a very good reason, yet Allah warns us not to let that hatred lead to wronging that person. It is better for us to act fairly and responsibly, whilst remembering Allah at all times.

- *"Allah loves those who act justly"* (*Surah al-Mumtahanah*, verse 8). The Prophet Muhammad ﷺ is the most beloved of Allah and he was constantly worried about the possibility of wronging someone. A fine example of this can be found in Sahih Bukhari where it is narrated that the Prophet Muhammad ﷺ sent Mu'adh ibn Jabl, may Allah be pleased with him, to be the governor of Yemen with the following words: "Fear the supplication of the oppressed, for there is no veil between that invocation and Allah, even if the one making the supplication is a disbeliever."

Yemen at the time was a very diverse place, with people of different religions co-existing together. Mu'adh, may Allah be pleased with him, was given a great responsibility, and he had to ensure that he dealt justly with all the inhabitants of Yemen – not just the Muslims. It is very clearly stated in the Hadith that if a non-Muslim made a supplication against Mu'adh because he wronged them, then it would be accepted by Allah.

Another powerful Hadith that reinforces the prayer of the oppressed is narrated by Abu Hurairah in which the Messenger of Allah ﷺ said: "There are three whose supplication is not rejected: the fasting person when he breaks his fast, the just leader, and the supplication of the oppressed person."[8]

However, the Prophet ﷺ was not just worried for his Companions and followers (*ummah*), he was so afraid of wronging someone himself that Umm Salamah, may Allah be well pleased with her, relates that he in fact never left the house without looking up at the sky and making a supplication to Allah, "Oh Allah, I seek refuge in You from being astray or leading someone else astray, or that I might slip or make someone else slip (off that path) or that I might be wronged or wrong someone, or that I would oppress or suffer oppression, or that I would do wrong or have wrong done to me."[9] If the Messenger ﷺ was so fearful of causing injustice to anyone, where does that leave us?

One particular incident that has been narrated was of a time when the Prophet ﷺ saw a young man laughing during an otherwise serious setting (one narration suggests it was the Battle of Badr), and he poked the shirtless young man in the stomach with a stick. The young man said to the Prophet, "You have harmed me, I want my revenge." The Prophet Muhammad ﷺ did not show any arrogance or anger, but instead bared his own stomach by lifting his shirt and asked him to poke him back with the stick to take revenge. The young man then kissed the Prophet's stomach and said, "That is all I wanted from you, oh Messenger of God."[10] Even in the midst of a battle, the Prophet's concern was not to have wronged this young man in the slightest.

Ibn Taymiyyah said that Allah will uphold a just nation even if it is a disbelieving nation, and Allah will destroy an unjust nation even if it is a believing nation. This statement is extremely powerful: it very plainly explains that Allah will allow just non-believers to thrive and unjust Muslims to fail. As mentioned by his student Ibn Qayyim, throughout the Qur'an, whenever Allah mentions the destruction of a nation, He says that He destroyed them because they were oppressive, they transgressed and were aggressive towards the Prophets and their followers. It wasn't simply because of their choice to reject the message the Prophets brought, but it was also punishment for their unjust acts.

Yet if associating equals with God (*shirk*) is the most unforgiveable of sins, how can Allah reward the unbelievers who are just in this world? A central and agreed-upon legal maxim (*qa'ida*) in Islam is 'if the right of the Creator and the rights of the creation are in conflict, fulfil the right of the creation.' This may seem confusing, but there are credible reasons for and examples of this. For instance, if the month of Ramadan has arrived, but you are too ill to fast, the right of your body takes precedence over Allah's right upon you. He allows you to recover your health and fast later to make up for it. Allah is the Most Merciful and Most Just; He does not want His creation to suffer and He has given us these dispensations.

If God is the Greatest and Most Worthy of worship, then how do we reconcile this with the legal maxim that in case of conflict the rights of creation are preferred over the rights of Allah? The scholars make three arguments here:

Firstly, Allah continues to grant us respite, delays His punishment and allows us the opportunity to turn back to Him in repentance until our moment of death. That is not to say that we should deliberately delay our repentance, but Allah's Grace is such that He will continue to give us chances up until our time of death.

Secondly, Allah is not in *need* of rights as He is Independent and the Greatest, but we, His slaves, are in need of our rights. His Mercy is encompassed within the scope of legislation; one such example is that if we wish to perform Hajj but we also have a debt to pay, then we must pay the debt back first. Allah does not need our Hajj at that point, but the person who we borrowed money from has the right to their money back before we consider fulfilling the rights of Allah. Allah has forgone His rights to ensure that the rights of His people are fulfilled.

Thirdly, Allah is the One who has given us these rights. Therefore, if we take the rights of people, it is a compounded offence because we not only wronged them but have also disobeyed Allah by dishonouring them when He honoured them with rights. That is why on the Day of Judgement we will see our acts of worship disappear, even if they were done for the sake of Allah, as they are given to anyone we have wronged, or withheld from, or harmed in some way without redress. This is the gravity of injustice in Islam.

May Allah protect us and save us from oppression (*dhulm*), allow us the grace to daily seek His protection from wronging anyone, and to never consciously wrong anyone, and to realise the gravity of injustice in this life and its consequences in the next. Amin.

2

GOD IS MORE CAPABLE THAN US

> *Abu Mas'ud al-Ansari reported: When I was beating my servant, I heard a voice behind me (saying): Abu Mas'ud, bear in mind Allah has more dominance over you than you have over him. I turned and (found him) to be Allah's Messenger . I said: Allah's Messenger, I set him free for the sake of Allah. Thereupon he said: Had you not done that, (the gates of) Hell would have opened for you, or the fire would have burnt you.*

AS WE CONTINUE to examine aspects of social justice in Islam, it is important here to remind ourselves that when people commit injustice or *dhulm*, they do it due to a false sense of power. However, it is Allah that is All-Powerful, and He is more capable than all of us to oppress – yet He has forbidden Himself from doing so.

The narration or Hadith that we will be covering in this chapter has three versions, two in Sahih Muslim and one in Abu Dawud:

- Abu Mas'ud al-Ansari reported: When I was beating my servant, I heard a voice behind me (saying): Abu Mas'ud, bear in mind Allah has more dominance over you than you have over him. I turned and (found him) to be Allah's Messenger ﷺ. I said: Allah's Messenger, I set him free for the sake of Allah. Thereupon he said: Had you not done that, (the gates of) Hell would have opened for you, or the fire would have burnt you. (Related by Muslim)

  - Abu Mas'ud al-Badri reported: I was beating my slave with a whip when I heard a voice behind me: "Understand, Abu Masud"; but I did not recognise the voice due to its intense anger. He (Abu Mas'ud) reported: As he came near me (I found) that he was the Messenger of Allah ﷺ and he was saying, "Bear in mind, Abu Mas'ud; bear in mind, Abu Mas'ud."

    He (Abu Mas'ud) said: I threw the whip from my hand. Thereupon he (the Holy Prophet ﷺ) said: "Bear in mind, Abu Mas'ud; verily Allah has more dominance over you than you have over your slave." I (then) said, "I never beat my servant after that." (Related by Muslim)

  - Abu Mas'ud al-Ansari said: When I was beating a servant of mine, I heard a voice behind me saying: "Know, Abu Mas'ud (Ibn al-Muthanna said this was said twice) that Allah has more power over you than you have over him." I turned around and saw that it was the Prophet ﷺ. I said, "Messenger of Allah! He is free for Allah's sake." He said, "If you had not done that (i.e., freed him), the fire would have burned you" or "the fire would have touched you." (Related by Abu Dawud)

There are a number of lessons that we can learn from these narrations:

1. The scholars have said that one of the best and most humble ways to give advice is by reflecting upon our own experiences, just like Abu Mas'ud has done in this Hadith. He embarrasses himself whilst teaching us, the *ummah*, a lesson. He admits that he did something unpleasant in the past before he gained knowledge from Prophet Muhammad ﷺ.

Another lesson to gain from this is that Abu Mas'ud mentions that he never hit a slave after this particular incident; he repented (made *tawba*) and never repeated the same mistake again.

As soon as Abu Mas'ud found that it was the Prophet ﷺ who was calling angrily to him, he immediately dropped the whip. However, the Prophet ﷺ didn't thank him for stopping and freeing the slave, he made it a point to say that had Abu Mas'ud not done so, he would have been punished by the Fire.

There are several pieces of wisdom behind this, the first being that Abu Mas'ud would narrate this incident to others in order for it to serve as a lesson to them. Another is that the Prophet ﷺ is teaching us to make up for our sins. And lastly, it is to show that Allah can give a greater punishment than what we give others. The Prophet ﷺ wanted it to be a life changing event for Abu Mas'ud and those that followed. Abu Mas'ud was not told by the Prophet ﷺ to free the slave, he was told to be aware of what he was doing and that was enough for Abu Mas'ud to understand that he must release the man.

Abu Mas'ud's example lets us understand that it is not enough to simply ask for forgiveness from Allah when it comes to undoing an act of injustice. True repentance will require us to right the wrong that we have committed to the best of our ability. For example, if we have been backbiting against someone and damaging their reputation, it is not enough for us to seek forgiveness from Allah, but we must seek forgiveness from that person, speak well of them to those whom we were backbiting to, and try to reverse the damage that we caused to their reputation.

2. An important point to note from these narrations is the use of the word *"e'lam,"* it does not just translate to "know" but it also translates to "beware" or "be careful." Abu Mas'ud in this Hadith explains that when he heard the word *e'lam*, he couldn't distinguish whose voice it was due to the angry tone. The Prophet ﷺ was extremely disappointed and angry when he witnessed the beating of the slave, it impacted his tone of voice, so much so that Abu Mas'ud who was so used to listening to the Prophet's voice on a regular basis could not recognise it.

Another well-known incident is that of a woman who was mourning someone loudly and inappropriately in a graveyard when the Prophet ﷺ

happened to be nearby, he told her to fear Allah and to be patient. The woman did not recognise the voice of the Prophet ﷺ due to the anger in it, and she answered back saying, "What do you know of my situation?"[11]

Aisha, may Allah be pleased with her, said that the Prophet Muhammad ﷺ did not get angry for himself, but he would become angry if the boundaries of Allah were transgressed. He would get angry for the sake of Allah. We cannot and should not portray the Prophet ﷺ as a man who was passive in the face of violence, passive in the face of aggression or oppression, passive in the face of wrongdoing. That was not the personality of our Messenger ﷺ. He became angry when the situation required him to, he raised his voice against transgressions against Allah and against injustice and oppression. Allah has made him a mercy to mankind but we do an injustice to the Prophet ﷺ by attributing more mercy to him than Allah gave him.

His anger was justified, and his anger terrified the Companions (*sahaba*) as they could see the severity of the actions that they had committed. The face of the Messenger ﷺ would become red, or his voice would become so different that they could not recognise it – like in Abu Mas'ud's narrations – but he would not abuse anyone through hitting or spitting or cursing.

However, returning to the word *e'lam*, to know or to beware, there are also many verses in the Qur'ran that begin with this word. Many scholars of *tafseer* (commentary on the Qur'an) – the first being Imam al Khurshaidi, may Allah be pleased with him – made a valuable point that each time Allah uses the word *e'lamu*, it indicates that the words or verse following it will be a call to action. It also indicates that Allah is making us aware of a serious matter that we must act upon with sincerity, or in other words, for every verse in the Qur'an that calls us to knowledge (*ilm*), the following verse calls us to action (*amal*).

3. I would also like to mention another Hadith here that ties in very well with Abu Mas'ud's:

    Umair, the freed slave of Abu'l-Lahm, said: "My master commanded me to cut some meat in to strips; (as I was doing it) a poor man came to me and I gave him some of that meat. My master came to know of that, and he beat me. I came to the Messenger of Allah ﷺ and narrated it to him. He (the Prophet) summoned him and said: Why did you beat him? He (Abu'l-Lahm) said: He gave away my food without being commanded to do so. Upon this he (the Prophet) said: The reward would have been shared by you both."[12]

What we learn here is that the Prophet Muhammad ﷺ did not justify the hitting of the slave, as no transgression justifies a transgression in response.

To further explain the point, there was a Sheikh who was speaking with a group of young men and said to them, "If you heard that a man was beating his wife what would be the first thing you would ask?" To which they replied, "What did she do to make him hit her?" This would not be the response of the Prophet ﷺ; he would not make an excuse or try to justify the act of beating. If there is oppression against someone, the reason why is irrelevant, the oppression in and of itself is wrong and needs to stop.

For all we know the slave may have done something terribly wrong when he was being beaten by Abu Mas'ud, but the Prophet did not start off by saying why are you beating him, his immediate response was to intervene and stop the oppression and this is teaching us that it is not acceptable to ask why or make an excuse. We must take responsibility for our actions, and no form of oppression (*dhulm*) is ever justified.

4. When someone commits a violation or act of injustice and gets away with it, they continue down the same route. When someone is abusive towards their spouse or any other family member, and nobody is able to stop them, they become more abusive. We unfortunately commit greater forms of oppression (*dhulm*) once we have gotten away with smaller acts of oppression. It creates a sense of power in the oppressor, they feel that they are in control of the situation, this power is intoxicating and deceives the oppressor into thinking that they are not accountable; the severity of the Hadith is reminding us that we have no control over the situation, we are powerless in front of Allah and we are accountable for each and every one of our actions.

Scholars mention that oppression (*dhulm*) has three varying degrees (*darakaat*).

- The first level of oppression is to oppress someone who has a great right over you, and the person who has the greatest right over us in this world is our mother – the very person who gave birth to us. She should be receiving good (*khair*) from us, and not any form of ill treatment. Allah orders us to be obedient to our parents, immediately after calling us to worship Him in *Surah Israa*, verse 23: *And your Lord has decreed that you worship none but Him and to parents good treatment.*

Imam Hasan al-Basri, may Allah be pleased with him, said, "I am amazed at a person who eats from his brother's food, who takes from his brother's money, who enjoys his brother's company, but in his absence reverts to nothing but cursing and backbiting him." Here he is explaining that when someone does good to us, but we respond with evil, then this injustice is the worst in the sight of Allah.

- The second level (*darakaat*) of oppression is to wrong someone who is beloved to Allah, as Allah says in a Hadith Qudsi: "Whosoever shows enmity to someone devoted to Me, I shall be at war with him. My servant draws not near to Me with anything more loved by Me than the religious duties I have enjoined upon him, and My servant continues to draw near to Me with voluntary deeds so that I shall love him."[13]

One of the scholars of Hadith has commented on this saying that we should notice that Allah mentions the obligatory actions and voluntary actions; we could do all of them, but if we do one form of injustice against someone who is beloved to Him, then all our deeds would be negated. And the difficult part of this is that we cannot know who is beloved to Allah as they have been hidden amongst us.

Yahya bin Maeen, may Allah be pleased with him, also went on to say, "Sometimes we curse people and they settled under the throne of Allah two hundred years ago." This is a powerful statement, teaching us not to curse anyone, for all we know they may already have been awarded

Paradise. We would not want Allah waging war upon us, and the solution for this is not to commit a sin against anyone – do not wrong anyone.

- The third and worst level is to oppress someone who has no protector besides Allah. These people include the orphans, the poor and the slaves. It is anyone who is already disadvantaged within society and yet we choose to wrong them due to their vulnerability. We cannot expect the mercy (*rahma*) of Allah upon ourselves if we take advantage of the weak and commit injustice towards them, and this ties in very well with the Hadith of Abu Mas'ud beating his slave.

There are some very beneficial lessons that we can learn from the incident of Abu Mas'ud, with several pieces of wisdom and Hadith coming to light once we begin to delve deeper.

One such account is narrated in Tirmidhi by Anas ibn Malik, may Allah be pleased with him, who said: "I served the Prophet ﷺ for ten years. He never said 'uff' and never blamed me by saying, 'Why did you do so?' or 'Why did you not do so?' And the Messenger of Allah ﷺ had the best character among all of the people."

The Prophet Muhammad ﷺ admonished his own children (without hitting them), yet never did so with Anas as he was a servant (*khaadim*)– someone who was in a more vulnerable position than the children of the Prophet ﷺ. And after the Prophet ﷺ had passed away, Anas, may Allah be pleased with him, used to see the Prophet ﷺ in his dream every night; this exemplifies the nature of the relationship that they had!

Additionally, Ibn Abbas also said, "The Companions were more afraid of wronging orphans than their own children." This is a short but extremely powerful statement given by Ibn Abbas, as he is telling us that the Companions (*sahaba*) were genuinely fearful of wronging orphaned children in any way. They would not even eat from the same food as them, even if they were living under the same roof due to them having taken the orphans under their care. This was due to the understanding that the orphans were at their mercy, they had no-one besides Allah and that they must be extra careful in the way that they dealt with them.

Allah hates it the most when we are in a position of advantage and we oppress someone who should be treated well by us. Even after a marriage has come to an end we must not seek further aggression against a spouse just because we are in a position to do so, as Allah describes in *Surah Nisaa*, verse 34, "*[if they return to you] do not pursue further means against them, indeed Allah is ever Exalted and forever Great.*"

There is also a wonderful Hadith narrated by Ma'rur in Bukhari which depicts the importance of treating those less advantaged than us with the best of manners:

"I saw Abu Dharr wearing a fancy garment (*burda*) and his slave too was wearing the same garment, so I said him, 'If you take this (burda of your slave) and wear it, you will have a nice outfit and you may give him another garment.' Abu Dharr said, 'There was a quarrel between me and another man whose mother was a non-Arab and I called her bad names. The man complained about me to the Prophet ﷺ. The Prophet ﷺ said, 'Did you abuse Bilal?' I said, 'Yes.' He said, 'Did you call his mother bad names?' I said, 'Yes.' He said, 'You still have the traits of ignorance.'

I said. '(Do I still have ignorance) even now in my old age?' He said, 'Yes, slaves and servants are your brothers, and Allah has put them under your command. So, the one under whose hand Allah has put his brother, should feed him of what he eats, and give him clothes from what he wears, and should not ask him to do anything beyond his capacity. And if he asks him to do a hard task, he should help him with it.'"

This was the attitude of the Companions towards the teachings of the Prophet ﷺ. The fear of disappointing Allah by causing injustice to others would fuel their extra caution. Again, it shows that if we are in a position of authority over someone, if someone is under our care or is vulnerable, then we need to fear Allah even more with regards to how we treat them.

Umar ibn al-Khattaab, may Allah be pleased with him, was a true man of justice. When Umar was Khalifa, Amr ibn Al 'As was the governor of Egypt, and his son Muhammad was a famous horseman. Muhammad ibn Amr once raced a Coptic Christian slave and was beaten by the Christian. Muhammad ibn Amr felt shamed by his loss and hit the slave with a whip saying 'are you going to beat me? I am the son of the noble ones'. The Christian slave was advised by people to report this incident to Umar and so he made his way to Madinah to issue his complaint to the Khalifa.

Upon hearing the complaint, Umar ordered for Amr and his son to also travel to Madinah and in the meantime provided accommodation for the Christian. When they arrived, Umar called for the Christian and said, "Behind you is my stick, take it and hit the son of the noble ones (Muhammad ibn Amr)." The Christian then picked up the stick and hit

Muhamad ibn Amr on the head, after which Umar told him to put (not hit) the stick on the bald head of Amr. This made the Christian confused, to which Umar replied, "This person did not hit you except by the power of that person."

Umar did not find it enough for the Christian to exact his revenge on the son, but he wanted to teach Amr that just because he was governor it did not give his son the right to oppress others.

In conclusion, we have learnt that whenever someone takes advantage of someone who is vulnerable, Allah is more capable of showing them what true vulnerability is. However, when we choose to take care of and honour those less advantaged than us, Allah will not allow us to feel vulnerable on the Day of Judgement.

May Allah protect us from deceiving ourselves with a false sense of power, may Allah allow us to use any advantage that He blesses us with for doing good towards others, and may Allah show us any wrongdoing that we have done so that we may repent and that He does not hold us accountable on the Day of Judgement for the actions that were not apparent to us. Amin.

3

FROM THE SCROLLS OF IBRAHIM

It is narrated by Abdullah ibn Umar, may Allah be pleased with him: "The Messenger of Allah said, 'The just will be seated upon pulpits of light on the right side of the Merciful (Ar-Rahman). Those who are fair with regards to their judgement and with their families and anything they undertake.'"

I WOULD LIKE TO begin this chapter by quoting a Hadith regarding the Scrolls of Ibrahim, may Allah be pleased with him, as it will help us in understanding the main Hadith that I will be covering. This Hadith is narrated in Sahih Ibn Hibban, and there is some dispute regarding its authenticity amongst some scholars like Imam Albani, however the message that it gives is undoubtedly authentic and extremely profound.

Abu Dhar, may Allah be pleased with him, narrated: "I said, 'Oh Messenger of Allah, what were the Scrolls of Ibrahim?' He said, 'They were parables,' (and he recited one of the parables that were revealed to Ibrahim): 'Oh king who has been entrusted with authority and who has been tested with that authority and who has been deluded by that authority; I did not send you to this world to amass the fortunes of it. Rather I sent you to avert from Me the call of the oppressed for I do not reject the call of the oppressed even if it comes from a disbeliever.'"

This Hadith is covering the same theme that we have discussed so far in the book, however, it is interesting to note that there is a consistency in the message that Allah has sent to His Messengers and Prophets, may peace be upon them all. Every single Prophet preached the same social values and creed; the only differences that occurred were in the legislation (*tashr'ee*). Allah has emphasised the importance of justice from the very beginning, and He has made it the purpose of the ones entrusted with authority to ensure that they deal with all matters in a just manner, as we can see in the following quote from the Hadith: "I sent you to avert from Me the call of the oppressed."

Allah says that He did not send us to the world to amass the fortunes of it, yet this is one of the main causes for people to be unjust and oppressive towards others. In current times, capitalism is one of the greatest reasons for oppression and inequality in the world – a limited number of people are accumulating huge sums of wealth whilst the poor get poorer and weaker. It is the obsession with this world that leads to injustice.

Now that I have given an introduction, we can move on to the main Hadith that we will be covering in this chapter. It is narrated by Abdullah ibn Umar, may Allah be pleased with him: "The Messenger of Allah ﷺ said, 'The just will be seated upon pulpits of light on the right side of the Merciful (*Ar-Rahman*). Those who are fair with regards to their judgement and with their families and anything they undertake.'"[14]

Once again, there are several lessons to be learned from the above Hadith:

1. The Hadith specifically mentions the *muqsiteen*; people who are put in a position to judge, govern, arbitrate or distribute. Whilst it may at first seem as though the Hadith is referring to those in a high position of power, it is actually casting a broad net that can cover all of us. It includes those who are

just in governance, those that are just with their families and those that are just in anything that they undertake.

2. The Prophet ﷺ mentions pulpits of light on the Day of Judgement for these people, and these pulpits are located beside Allah, on His right side. This is on a Day that we will all be struggling to find shade, yet Allah will assign pulpits for people who dealt justly in their lives.

This is the opposite of the oppressor (*dhaalim*) about whom scholars have said that he is power hungry in this world and so Allah humiliates him. As mentioned in the first chapter, the Prophet ﷺ said that oppression is darkness, upon darkness, upon darkness on the Day of Judgement – this is the outcome for the oppressor (*dhaalim*). Those who deal justly (*muqsiteen*) on the other hand do not let a quest for power allow them to be unjust, and so Allah elevates their rank on the Day of Judgement.

3. Thirdly, we learn that Allah loves the *muqsiteen* and does not love the *dhaalim*:
    Surah al-Imran, 3:140: *"And Allah does not love the oppressors."*
    Surah al-Hujurat, 49:9: *"Indeed Allah loves those who act justly."*

The scholars have clearly stated that the person who has authority but chooses not to wrong those who they have authority over, will find a sense of security (*al aman*) in this world. It is through this sense of security that people who are just are given an affirmation of their reward in the Hereafter, as the Prophet ﷺ mentioned in a Hadith related by Tirmidhi: "The most beloved person to Allah on the Day of Judgement and the closest to Him in status is the just ruler. And the most hated of people on the Day of Judgement and the farthest from Him is the oppressive leader."

4. The Prophet ﷺ also mentioned in a well-known Hadith that there will be seven groups of people who will be shaded by the throne of Allah on the Day of Judgement, and whilst different narrations have the seven groups ordered

differently, one thing that remains consistent in all of the narrations is that the first type to be mentioned is the just ruler.

Scholars such as Sufyan ath-Thawri have said that the just ruler is always mentioned first because if a society has a just leader, it sets the stage for that society to be engaged in righteousness and justice. A just ruler makes it easier for people to give charity, to go to the masjid and to love each other for the sake of Allah. Sufyan ath-Thawri, may Allah be pleased with him, also stated: "There are two groups of people that if they are righteous, people will be righteous, and if they are corrupt, people will be corrupt. They are the scholars and the rulers."

He has made a very clear distinction of the two groups of people that hold a lot of responsibility on their shoulders to keep themselves and people away from corruption. A ruler is someone who is in charge of worldly affairs, whilst the scholar is someone who deals with and guides with regards to religious affairs, and even if one of them becomes corrupt, it usually affects the other and then in turn affects the people who they have authority over.

Furthermore, the scholars have commented that a just ruler will not only be in the shade of Allah's throne, but they will also be seated upon pulpits of the light. They are the best of the seven mentioned in the Hadith and will receive the best reward.

5. The Prophet ﷺ talks about people in general in order to make it clear that authority is not just limited to leaders or governors, we have authority over others in a variety of capacities. Ibn Hajr explained this very well when he said, "The father is the leader (*imam*) of the children, the mother is the leader (*imamah*) of the household, the teacher is the leader of the students, the *imam* is the leader of the congregants (for prayer), and the employer is the leader of his employees."

In addition to Ibn Hajr's explanation, there is also a wonderful Hadith reported by Ibn Umar, may Allah be pleased with him: The Prophet ﷺ said: "All of you are guardians and all of you will be questioned about your flock. The ruler is a guardian of his society, the man is a guardian of his family, the woman is a guardian and is responsible for her husband's house and offspring; and so all of you are guardians and are responsible for your subjects."[15]

We are all given some form of authority in some capacity by Allah, and it is our duty to ensure that we establish justice within the flock that we are responsible for. The bigger the flock that we have authority over, the bigger our responsibility.

The Prophet ﷺ governed the *ummah* (Muslim community) with utmost justice and he advised each and every one of us to be upright in our responsibility to Allah and to be upholders of justice.

In another authentic Hadith related in *Sunan Bayhaqi*, the Prophet ﷺ said: "There is not a single person who has been entrusted with ten people except that he will be brought with those ten people on the Day of Judgement and his hands will be chained to his neck. Justice will cause his hands to be released, oppression will cause him to perish."

Here we learn that being in authority over even ten people (that could be ten employees, or ten family members or relatives, or ten people in the mosque), will put us in an extremely vulnerable position. If we did not act justly, we will have destroyed our chances of being granted respite and entry into Paradise; whilst if we feared Allah and were just in all our actions, we will be released and given respite.

The Prophet Muhammad ﷺ also said: "Indeed Allah is with the judge (*qadi*) as long as he is not unjust. When that person becomes a tyrant, Allah abandons him and 'sticks' a devil (*Shaytan*) to him."[16]

Imam Al-Qutayba, may Allah be pleased with him, commented on this Hadith and said: "Nothing hardens a heart like oppression. Once someone becomes oppressive in some capacity, the punishment for that person is that other forms of oppression become easy for them."

Both the Hadith and the commentary here are extremely compelling and frightening. We can very easily lose the guidance of Allah through one act of oppression and become stuck with Satan as our companion. However, if we want to soften our hearts we must act upon the teachings of the Prophet ﷺ; we must act justly and support the most vulnerable in society such as the orphans and the poor, and we must repent and reverse the oppression that we committed that set off the downward spiral.

Another worrying situation for us to be in is when we wrong someone who has authority over us, but they have not wronged us in any way. In regard to this, Abu Hurairah narrated that the Messenger of Allah ﷺ said: "There are three people whose supplications are not turned back: A just ruler, a fasting person until he breaks his fast, and one who has been wronged."[17]

If we wrong someone who has authority over us, their supplication (*du'a*) is answered for two reasons; despite having authority over us, they have been just towards us and we have decided to wrong them despite their good attitude.

On a more personal level, I would like to mention an incident that occurred with a brother whom I know and who has given me permission to share it, as it is a powerful example of a supplication being accepted. This brother was arguing with his mother who had always been just and good towards him, and after throwing things around during the argument he picked up his phone and his mother said, "May Allah burn your hands." And Allah answered her supplication right there and then; his phone caught fire in his hands and he still has the scar from the burn on his hand. This is precisely why we must always be aware of our actions. A parent, a mother, who is just towards her children whilst in a position of authority will have double the reason for her supplication (*du'a*) to be accepted due to her being wronged whereas she has not wronged anyone.

There is also a wonderful account of Umar, may Allah be pleased with him, during his reign as Caliph. Hurmuzan, the ruler of Persia, arrived in Madinah with an important diplomatic matter to discuss with Umar, and upon arrival he asked where he could find the Caliph. Such was the simplicity of Umar, may Allah be pleased with him, that Hurmuzan found him to be asleep under a tree with his head resting upon his shoes, with no bodyguards or weapons nearby. This was the complete opposite to how the Persian rulers were, as they had extravagant lifestyles with many bodyguards.

After seeing Umar sleeping peacefully under the shade of a tree, he spoke his famous words: "Oh Umar! You ruled. You were just. Thus you were given security, and thus you slept."

Umar, may Allah be pleased with him, was known for his honesty and justice. He had nothing to fear because he *knew* that he had not wronged anyone and was blessed with a sense of security (*al aman*) during his time.

Authority, quite literally, is something that will either make you or break you on the Day of Judgement. Allah will not speak to those who oppressed others nor will He purify them on the Day of Judgement, whereas He will reward the just person immensely and justice could be in the simplest of forms.

One example of this, that I would like to end this chapter on is mentioned by Imam al-Bayhaqi who said that a mother visited Aisha, may Allah be pleased with her, and was given three dates by Aisha. She gave one date each to her two children, who then looked to her for the last date. The mother then split the last date in half and gave it to her children. Aisha related this incident to the Prophet ﷺ who praised the woman and said that she has entered Paradise because of her just and merciful actions. The fact that she did not differ between the children that she was given authority over was enough for her to be rewarded with Paradise. Iman al- Bayhaqi points out that this woman comes under the umbrella of a just leader, she dealt with those under her with justice and mercy. The point being that all of us in one capacity or another have authority over someone else and our dealings in that capacity have implications.

May Allah give us pulpits of light on the Day of Judgement, may He not allow us to wrong anyone who is under our authority in any capacity. May Allah forgive us for our shortcomings with them, ourselves and our duties towards Him. May Allah protect us from oppression and allow us to be in the company of the Prophet ﷺ on the Day of Judgement. Amin.

4

TO SEEK OR NOT TO SEEK LEADERSHIP

It has been narrated on the authority of Abu Dhar who said: I said to the Prophet ﷺ: Messenger of Allah, "Will you not appoint me to a public office?" He stroked my shoulder with his hand and said: "Abu Dhar, you are weak and authority is a trust. And on the day of judgment it (worldly authority) is a cause of disgrace and remorse except for one who fulfills its obligations and (properly) discharges its duties."

IN THIS CHAPTER we will look into another Hadith narrated by Abu Dhar, may Allah be pleased with him. Abu Dhar was a Companion who would frequently ask the Prophet ﷺ questions and has narrated many Hadiths for us to benefit from. Abu Dhar, may Allah be pleased with him, was a very special Companion of the Prophet Muhammad ﷺ. He belonged to a tribe named Ghiffaar which was known for its thugs and robbers; it was a notorious tribe that nobody wanted to get on the wrong side of. Abu Dhar went out in public to announce his acceptance of Islam at a time when it was extremely dangerous for Muslims and they were being physically beaten. When he was attacked by the people for reciting the Qur'an al-Abbas, may Allah be pleased with him, came out and warned the people that they were hitting a man of the Ghiffaar, immediately they stepped away and stopped.

Another inspiring piece of information regarding Abu Dhar, may Allah be pleased with him, is that the Prophet ﷺ testified the following about him: "The earth has not carried, nor has the sky covered a man more trustworthy and truthful than Abu Dhar."[18] However, when comparing this statement to the Hadith that we are about to cover, it is easy to feel confused, but let us first have a look at the Hadith:

Abu Dhar said, "I said to the Prophet ﷺ: 'Messenger of Allah, will you not appoint me to a public office?' He stroked my shoulder with his hand and said, 'Abu Dhar, you are weak, and authority is a trust. And on the Day of Judgement, it (worldly authority) is a cause of disgrace and remorse except for one who fulfils its obligations and properly discharges its duties.'"[19]

An important thing to note here is that Abu Dhar did not ask this question for egotistical reasons as the Prophet ﷺ had already confirmed his internal purity and truthfulness. Abu Dhar was genuine in his intention and wanted to be able to do more for the sake of Allah. However, despite his integrity and purity, the Prophet ﷺ advised him against seeking a role of leadership and power.

In another Hadith, Abu Dhar said about the Prophet ﷺ: "He said to me, 'I see you to be a weak man. I love for you what I love for myself. Don't ever find yourself in a position where you oversee two people. And don't ever be entrusted with the wealth of an orphan.'"[20]

Whilst at first it may seem as though the Prophet ﷺ was being harsh towards Abu Dhar, the truth is that the Messenger of Allah ﷺ was not demeaning him or insulting him. In fact, he made it a point to mention that he loved for Abu Dhar what he loved for himself, meaning that he wanted Abu Dhar to attain a place in Paradise. There was wisdom behind the advice of the Prophet ﷺ, as he knew why a position of leadership wouldn't be suitable for Abu Dhar.

It is interesting to compare the advice and decisions of the Prophet ﷺ between Mu'adh – whom he sent to be governor of Yemen – and Abu Dhar, whom he advised not to even find himself in charge of two people.

Why would the Prophet ﷺ – who said he loved both of his Companions – then make such different choices for them? There are several reasons behind the advice given by the Prophet Muhammad ﷺ as we will learn in the following points:

1. The Messenger of Allah ﷺ told us that the first form of injustice we need to fight is the injustice of our own self. We need to protect ourselves from being in a place of injustice as it will cause difficulty for us on the Day of Judgement. If we are in a position where it is our responsibility to solve the issues of other people, but this causes us to become problematic ourselves, the injustice that we cause will ruin our hereafter (*akhira*). It could not be clearer that we should avoid any circumstance that will lead us to be unjust in any way; no glory in the world is worth humiliation on the Day of Judgement.

2. The scholars have said that there are two explanations as to why the Prophet referred to Abu Dhar as weak:

    - One is that Abu Dhar did not belong to a powerful tribe (instead he belonged to a tribe known to be thugs), so he may not have been taken seriously enough by other Companions. However, this explanation isn't convincing because the Prophet ﷺ did on several occasions appoint Companions to a position of leadership whilst they also did not belong to powerful tribes.

    - The second explanation is that the Prophet ﷺ has mentioned in other Hadith that the strong person is not the one who is able to overcome his opponents, but the strong person is the one who can control himself in a time of anger. Abu Dhar was known to have gotten himself into arguments at times, and so the Prophet ﷺ was worried about him compromising his status in the Hereafter due to Abu Dhar not having the restraint necessary for a position of leadership.

3. The Prophet ﷺ told Abu Dhar: "You will live alone. You will die alone. And you will be raised on the Day of Judgement alone."[21] It is interesting to note that the Prophet ﷺ mentioned this to Abu Dhar as he was aware of Abu Dhar's personality; he was very strict with himself and would also be tough towards other Companions if he saw them becoming more wealthy as he believed they were selling themselves for this world. This strict attitude of his made it difficult for him to get along with everyone, hence why the Prophet ﷺ mentioned these three points to him. Abu Dhar will be raised up alone with his own special status on the Day of Judgement and the Prophet ﷺ wanted him to understand this profound statement and not become involved in any leadership positions.

4. A point that keeps on returning is that a just ruler allows society to follow suit and be filled with righteousness and justice. The Prophet ﷺ warned us that he does not fear poverty for his followers (*ummah*), but he worries that the world is open to us and that we will fight each other over it. People tend to fight for power more than wealth, and this is dangerous for us as an *ummah*. Islamic history itself can be summed up with two words: betrayal and conquest. Most of the problems we have had to deal with in the *ummah* have been due to betrayal and the pursuit of power. Scholars and people of knowledge, or those who pose as such, are also subject to their egos. It is their ego that causes them to pursue power or to envy others and try to bring them down and everyone suffers as a result of it. It is destructive to our spirituality as individuals and destructive to our community collectively.

5. Leadership is incredibly important; in a Hadith the Messenger ﷺ was asked, 'When is the Day of Judgement?' he said 'When trust is lost, then await the Hour.'[22] They asked him how trust was lost and he replied when leadership is placed with those who do not deserve it, and a position of trust is in the wrong hands. Leadership has been called a

trust. He knew better than Abu Dhar did, and it was for Abu Dhar's own benefit that he advised him not to seek a role of leadership. This also brings back the statement made by Sufyan ath-Thawri in which he said that the two categories of people that set the tone for the rest of society being righteous or corrupt are the scholars and the rulers.

Here we learn that there is an important distinction between leadership as a goal and leadership being a means to achieve another goal:

- The messengers, may peace be upon them all, were protected from their egos and were given leadership as a means of calling people towards righteousness. Leadership then as a means is praiseworthy. For example, the Prophet Sulayman asked Allah to grant him a kingdom that would not be given to anyone after him; not for his enjoyment of power, but as a means to establish righteousness throughout the world.

  The Prophet Ibrahim also taught us a wonderful supplication in which he asked Allah to make our spouses and our offspring the coolness of our eyes and make us collectively as *imams*, as people that lead the way. The point that he is making here is that he was not personally seeking a position, but he was seeking an institution of justice throughout the world. He wanted the goodness (*khayr*) that he had worked for and brought about to continue long after he had passed away. These examples highlight leadership as a means towards a goal rather than the goal itself, and in this form it is praiseworthy.

- Comparatively, wanting a position of leadership as a goal in and of itself is problematic. The issue arises when we pursue leadership for the sake of worldly gain or praise. We must disconnect ourselves from the desire of being elevated in this world and aim for Jannah instead.

  Allah says in the Qur'an, *Surah Al-Qasas*, 28:83: *"That home of the Hereafter [Jannah] We assign to those who do not desire exaltedness upon the earth or corruption. And the [best] outcome is for the righteous."*

A great example is of how Umar ibn Abdul Aziz was appointed Caliph without his prior knowledge. Sulayman ibn Abdul Malik left a will that Umar would be his successor but knowing that Umar would reject the position of leadership had he asked him, Sulayman wrote it down and had a witness to this will. After Sulayman passed away, Raja'a bin Khaiwa from Gaza delivered this will to Umar bin Abdul Aziz.

Umar began to cry and said that he did not ask for this leadership position, neither privately nor publicly. He did not want to be put in a position which could involve making wrong decisions and putting himself at risk in the Hereafter. When he stepped on the pulpit (*mimbar*) to make his inauguration speech, he also declared his resignation. He said that he had been given the Caliphate, but he was giving it up and that the people should choose someone else from amongst themselves. As he stepped off, the people put him back on the pulpit and said, "We want you." Umar was so afraid of this responsibility that he tried to run away from it, but the people knew he was extremely capable of making a good Caliph and so he gave in. Reluctantly, he accepted the leadership and asked Allah for protection and told people to hold him accountable for his actions.

He was only Caliph for two and a half years before he passed away at the age of 37. Being made Caliph at such a young age, Umar could have easily been driven by his ego, especially as he came from a family of leaders. Yet, he chose to lead with steadfastness and righteousness. At the time of his death, his face lit up and he said, "Welcome to these beautiful faces that don't belong to humans or jinn." He could see angels entering upon him; his reward in the Hereafter was already beginning and he died reciting verse 83 of *Surah Al-Qasas*. He did not want the position of leadership, but he embraced it and led the *ummah* to a golden era that will not be seen again until the time of the Prophet Isa.

There have been and will continue be times when someone may be forced into a leadership position without wanting it. Uthman, may Allah be pleased with him, was told by the Prophet ﷺ, "There will come a time when people will ask you to resign from your position and Allah gave you that position – do not take off a garment that Allah dressed you with."[23] This was the wisdom of the Prophet Muhammad ﷺ; he made it clear that if you are put in a position rightfully, and people try to take it away from you wrongfully, you must remain in that position. Do not abandon your post even though you may not want it, because Allah has entrusted that position upon you.

How can we then ensure that we protect ourselves from taking a wrong step? It comes down to our intentions and our actions. In regards to protecting oneself, Umar ibn al-Khattaab gave a very important and sound piece of advice to Sa'ad ibn Abi Waqas when he appointed him as the governor of Kufa in Iraq: "Guard your prayers." He told Sa'ad to guard his *salah* and private worship; if we lose our prayer, we will lose everything.

One of the biggest tricks that satan plays on our minds, is that he can make us believe that our public work makes us immune and that we do not have to worry about our private spiritual practices anymore. It is for this very reason that Umar cautioned Sa'ad about guarding his prayers (*salah*) as our connection with Allah must remain. If our connection with Allah is severed, then our leadership will become about us – it will no longer be for the sake of Allah. Sa'ad was a very successful governor, but when turmoil broke out in the community (*ummah*), disputes over leadership began, he shunned everything as he did not want anything to do with the rebellion (*fitnah*). He left his position of leadership and raised sheep in the mountains, and even went as far as China to spread the message of Islam, after which he built the first mosque in China. He remembered the words of the Prophet Muhammad ﷺ who said that Allah loves a person who is pious and fears Allah (*taqi*), is hidden from public sight (*khafi*) and who is self-sufficient and does not need anybody except Allah (*ghani*). And it was due to these words that he went so far away from his position as governor to avoid being involved in any type of *fitnah* because he knew that the quest for leadership can ruin one's spirituality.

1. In Sahih Muslim, there is a chapter dedicated to the prohibition of desiring a position and actively seeking it; Abu Dhar wasn't the only person that the Prophet ﷺ advised against seeking a position of leadership. Another

Companion named Abdur Rahman ibn Samra, may Allah be pleased with him, also asked the Prophet ﷺ if he could be made in charge of his tribe or area, to which the Prophet ﷺ replied that never ask to be in a position of leadership because Allah would abandon you in that position of leadership and would not support you. Whereas, if you are given a position of leadership without asking for it, you will maintain the support of Allah throughout. We can see this through the example of Umar ibn al-Khattaab who was the most successful Caliph due to him despising the leadership position, and Allah supporting him throughout it.

2. The only times it is permissible to seek leadership is if people find you qualified and ask you to lead them. In such a circumstance, we should ask Allah for protection and then take up the role (unless we know that there is a valid reason for us not to, such as hidden corruption or something within ourselves that would hinder us from being a good leader). Or, we must ask people we trust to be sincere in their advice about whether we would make a good and just leader. The Prophet ﷺ was sincere in his advice to Abu Dhar, he advised against leadership due to his love for Abu Dhar – he knew what would be best for him.

The Prophet ﷺ was asked by Uthman ibn Abi al-Aas to be made the leader (*imam*) of his people, to which the Prophet ﷺ replied, "You are their *imam*."[24] Whilst this may seem contradicting to the previous point of not actively seeking leadership, the Prophet ﷺ was aware of the character of Uthman and was also aware that he was already being followed by his tribe. This was then a validation that he was indeed the leader of his tribe, rather than a request for leadership without any experience.

3. Imam al-Ghazali said that nothing should cause you to take on a position other than the truth, and nothing should cause you to hold back from taking on a position other than the truth. It is truth that should be the motivator for both holding back and moving forward.

This statement brings forward two questions we must ask ourselves:

- Would we only do the work if we were in a position of leadership? If we are not committed to the actual cause regardless of the position, then the reality is that we only want the leadership for our own ego. If, however we are concerned with the cause then we will find ways to carry out work for the sake of Allah.

A very recent example I can give is of a brother I know who was involved in a mosque that I was *imam* of in New Orleans. Nobody knew that he was not on the board but they assumed that he was as he was always working extremely hard to do what he could for the mosque and the community.

- Is the position beautifying you or are you beautifying the position? This question is derived from a poem by Bilal ibn Abi Burda about Umar ibn Abdul Aziz, in which he said: "If the Caliphate has nobility to it, you made it more noble." There are people who make irrelevant titles relevant due to the effort that they put in and the good that they bring with their work.

Another important point to make here is that sometimes the most qualified person for a certain position may not necessarily be the most religious. On the other hand, Abu Dhar, may Allah be pleased with him, was known for his piety and truthfulness, yet he was not qualified enough to take on a leadership role – even for two people. In some instances, it may be due to personality issues (flaws) or other obligations that can prevent someone from being a good leader. The Prophet ﷺ chose people perfectly for their given positions; he knew where everyone belonged – Khalid belonged in the battlefield, whilst Mu'adh belonged in Yemen as a governor.

I would like to conclude this chapter with a very fitting Hadith related by Bukhari, in which the Prophet ﷺ walked by some people who were planting trees and he gave them a suggestion on how to plant the trees which they accepted and followed. Some time had passed and the Prophet ﷺ passed by their garden again and saw that the trees had died, and he asked what had happened, to which they replied that they followed his advice, but their trees had died. The Prophet ﷺ then said that they are more knowledgeable than him in regards to their worldly affairs, he was not giving this advice as a Prophet but as someone with his own experience of planting, they should not feel compelled in worldly affairs.

What we learn here is that we should be aware of our capabilities. The Messenger of Allah ﷺ also said, "May Allah have mercy on a person who knows his limits."[25] People may assume that you are qualified for something by virtue of your God-consciousness (*taqwa*) or your nobility, but you must be able to admit to them that you are not fit for that position, you may not be the most experienced or most knowledgable.

May Allah always put us in positions that are pleasing to him, and may He not allow our egos to obstruct the truth in regards to our own affairs and those of others. May Allah allow us to fulfil any responsibility that He has entrusted upon us, and may He forgive us for any shortcomings and not let us be deluded by the temporary pleasures and wealth of this world. Amin.

5

WE WILL BE ASKED ABOUT OUR POTENTIAL

Narrated by Malik ibn Murthad from his father who said: Abu Dhar said, "I said, Oh Messenger of Allah ﷺ, 'What are the things that protect a person from the Hell-Fire?' He said, 'Faith in Allah.' I said, 'What are the actions that accompany faith?' He said, 'He should spend from (the small amount) that Allah has provided him.' I said, 'What if that person is too poor and he cannot find anything to give?' He said, 'Then he should enjoin good and forbid evil.' I said, 'Oh Messenger of Allah, what if that person is in a position in society where they are too vulnerable to be able to enjoin good and forbid evil?' He ﷺ said, 'Assist someone who is skilled or do something for the one who has no skill.' I said, 'Oh Messenger of Allah, what if this person has no skill and knowledge?' He said, 'He should support someone who is oppressed.' I said, 'What if that person is weak and oppressed himself?' He said, 'You aren't going to leave any good for your brother to do? The prophet then said, 'He should restrain his evil from people.' I said, 'If that is all he does then will he enter into Jannah? The prophet ﷺ said: There is no believer that pursues any one of these things except that on the Day of Judgement it grabs his hand until it enters him into Jannah.'"

IN THIS CHAPTER we will look at the third and final Hadith narrated by Abu Dhar that has been selected for this book. This Hadith is mentioned in several different books of Hadith and has various different wordings; however, the essence of the Hadith remains the same.

Narrated by Malik ibn Murthad from his father who said: Abu Dhar said, "I said, 'Oh Messenger of Allah ﷺ, what are the things that protect a person from the Hell-Fire?' He said, 'Faith in Allah.' I said, 'What are the actions that accompany faith?' He said, 'He should spend from the small amount that Allah has provided him.' I said, 'What if that person is too poor and he cannot find anything to give?' He said, 'Then he should enjoin good and forbid evil.' I said, 'Oh Messenger of Allah ﷺ, what if that person is in a position in society where they are too vulnerable to be able to enjoin good and forbid evil?' He said, 'Assist someone who is skilled or do something for the one who has no skill.' I said, 'Oh Messenger of Allah ﷺ, what if this person has no skill or knowledge?' He said, 'He should support someone who is oppressed.' I said, 'What if that person is weak and oppressed himself?' He said, 'You aren't going to leave any good for your brother to do?' Then the Prophet ﷺ said, 'He should restrain his evil from people.' I said, 'If that is all he does then will he enter into Paradise?' The Prophet ﷺ said, 'There is no believer that pursues any of these things except that on the Day of Judgement it grabs his hand until it enters him into Paradise.'"[26]

Abu Dhar, may Allah be pleased with him, was known for his inquisitive nature. He always wanted to know more, the Prophet ﷺ gave him a very short simple answer to begin with (having faith in Allah), knowing that Abu Dhar would ask further questions. Imam As-Safarini mentioned that this was not like the case of the Bedouin in which the Prophet ﷺ taught him about the five pillars, since Abu Dhar was beyond that point and at a different level.

The following points cover the different deeds that the Prophet ﷺ taught Abu Dhar in the above Hadith:

1. Abu Dhar asked what actions accompany faith, and the Prophet ﷺ responded by saying that a person should spend from the small amount that Allah has provided him. The word specifically used in this Hadith is *radkh*, as opposed to the word *yunfiq*, while both mean 'to spend' *radkh* clearly carries the meaning of 'a very small amount'.

The Prophet ﷺ used this word in order to tell Abu Dhar that he understood that Abu Dhar wasn't rich, and that charity is not limited to those who are well-off. Those who have little should still try to give a very small amount in the way of charity, as it is a way for an individual to purify themselves and their wealth and a means of bringing them closer to Allah.

A consistent message in Hadiths is that the Messenger of Allah ﷺ always spoke about simple people doing simple deeds that became their ticket to Paradise. Whether it be the woman who gave water to the thirsty dog or the man who removed something harmful from the road; they were not rich themselves, but their deeds were rich and well-appreciated by Allah. However, scholars have said that Uthman, may Allah be pleased with him, was the exception. He was just, very wealthy and every time that he was called to action, he went above and beyond the expectation of him.

Poverty is discussed in many Hadiths as a type of injustice, because it is very often inflicted upon people. Poverty is not a result of certain people being lucky and others being unlucky; there are unjust actions that cause it, usually through some form of exploitation or oppression. Even in current times we can see that eighty-five per cent of the world's wealth is owned by a small handful of people and things such as racism, oppression, and exploitation have caused this great imbalance in the distribution of wealth. Some political scientists have also stated that economic injustice is the unfinished business of the civil rights movement. It is this injustice that puts people in an economically disadvantaged position and can often lead them down a dark path.

Furthermore, Allah mentions that the first trait of the people of excellence (*ihsaan*) is that they spend in both their good times and their bad times. Even when there is no expectation from them to give in charity, they still choose to do so within their capacity as they place that expectation upon themselves. Allah says about these people in the Qur'an that they prefer others to themselves, even when they are in need of that which they are giving. The Prophet ﷺ also told us that the best charity is the one that is given when a person fears poverty.

2. The advice that the Prophet ﷺ gave Abu Dhar was extremely important in the sense that it provides us with the next step that we can take when physically spending money is not a

possibility. If one finds themselves in a position that they cannot give even half a date in the way of charity, then they should work to enjoin good and forbid evil as these are forms of charity (*sadaqah*) that do not involve monetary spending. The Messenger ﷺ mentioned that every time a person calls to good or forbids evil, it is a form of charity on their part. Ibn Hajr, may Allah be pleased with him, also said that a person could be involved in the process that leads to the act of charity and still end up with the same reward as the person who actually gave the charity. This could mean that a person is simply delivering the charity or facilitating that charity or inviting someone to perform that act of good.

Abdullah ibn Mas'ud, may Allah be pleased with him, mentioned that it is more difficult to forbid evil and thus it becomes more beloved to Allah. Enjoining or doing good is the easier of the two, as it is often done in response to some evil, but if we were to remove the cause of that evil then that would be better. He also made another point stating that a person who works to forbid evil will face more opposition and consequences as a result of doing so. This is due to the reason that when a person does good, it is unlikely that they will receive any backlash for it. However, when that person challenges the evils in society, it is more likely that they will face opposition for taking a stand.

3. Abu Dhar, may Allah be pleased with him, then goes on to ask what if it is too dangerous for a person to enjoin good and forbid evil? What if that person is in a very vulnerable position and they are unable to perform these free acts of charity? Abu Dhar himself was in that very position when he accepted Islam in the early days of Makkah. The Prophet Muhammad ﷺ told him and others not to proclaim their acceptance of Islam publicly as it posed a serious threat to their lives. Abu Dhar however could not contain himself and announced his Islam publicly but was also nearly beaten to death because of it. Ibn Masud, may Allah be pleased with him, also had a similar encounter when he proclaimed his acceptance of Islam in public; his collar bone had been broken and he was beaten unconscious.

The Prophet ﷺ understood that people have different capacities (*aqsaam*) and that some people may not have the authority to enjoin good and forbid evil, which brought him to give the following advice to Abu Dhar with regards to his question:

- Assist someone who is skilled or do something for the one who has no skill. If you are not in a position to enact change then find someone who is in a position to enact that change and help them. One example of this could be that someone you know is a good public speaker or even policy maker, but they do not have enough knowledge to convey the required message or information properly, so you assist them by sharing what you know. You may not be a good public speaker or in a position of authority, but you are able to help facilitate a change through assisting someone i.e. by providing them with information and facts.

It is important to remember that not everyone in a position of authority has all the required knowledge all of the time. Everyone has weaknesses, and on many occasions a person with some level of power in society can make what seem like easily avoidable mistakes, but our advice to them could change that for the better. If we are able to influence the influencers, then they will be able to carry out righteous tasks and agendas on our behalf.

In regards to this, the Prophet Muhammad ﷺ mentioned that the one who guides to something good is just the like the one who performs that act of good, and whoever establishes a good tradition, they gain the reward (*ajar*) of anyone who acts upon it.

- Scholars such as Ibn Hajar have also commented on this Hadith and said: "Sometimes the injustices that those who are labourers (working class) face are less obvious than those who are overtly disadvantaged." To make this clearer, he quoted Ibn ul Muneer as saying that "the Hadith indicates helping the skilled takes precedence over the unskilled." This in other words means that people who have disabilities and are known to be unskilled are understood to be in need of assistance, but sometimes those who are labourers or are known to have some sort of skills (such as trade skills) are neglected and they are not helped through charitable means.

An example of this could be of when we visit the Holy mosques of Makkah and Madinah (*Haramain*); we will automatically be inclined to help those that we see on the street, but we will not give much thought to those who are working in the mosques. We may assume that because they are receiving a salary they are not in need of any assistance. However, it is mostly the working class that is overlooked, gets caught in between and suffers as a result of this injustice and negligence.

- Another piece of wisdom (*faida*) that we can take from this Hadith is that it is better to teach someone a skill rather than to provide for them, as in the famous saying of teaching a man to fish versus giving a hungry man a fish. The wording that the Prophet ﷺ used in this Hadith gives more depth to his advice of assisting others. For example, we may know someone who is inherently disadvantaged and the best thing that we can do for that person is to teach them a skill that will allow them to be in a position to provide for or help themselves within society in the long-term.

- Following this, Abu Dhar continued to ask the Prophet ﷺ about what else a person could do if he had no skills to offer either, and the answer he received was to support a person who is oppressed or is dealing with a misfortune or distressing situation.

A wonderful example of this is of Ibn Abbas, may Allah be pleased with him, who was sitting in the mosque of the Prophet ﷺ during the last ten nights of Ramadan and saw a man walk into the masjid who looked visibly distressed. Ibn Abbas approached the man and asked him what was wrong, the man replied that he was in debt, but he had no money to pay it off and was afraid to confront his lender. Ibn Abbas himself did not have the financial means to help pay the debt of this man, but he offered to speak to the lender to ask if he would be willing to extend the time of repayment.

There are two lessons that we learn from this example:

- Ibn Abbas may not have been able to help pay off the debt, but he did what he could. He offered support and solidarity to his brother in Islam

- Even if Ibn Abbas returned unsuccessful with the lender refusing to offer a grace period, the fact that he tried to help, in whatever capacity he could, would offer a lot of emotional assurance to the debtor that Ibn Abbas noticed his difficulty and tried to help him.

The Prophet ﷺ here was teaching Abu Dhar that even if we are unable to make a difference in circumstances, offering support can make a positive difference to a person's mental wellbeing. We may not be able to give charity, we may not be able to enjoin good (*Da'wah*), we may not be able to stand up to a form of injustice, and we may not even be able to offer to equip someone with skills or knowledge so that they can change circumstances for themselves or society, but we can offer support to those who are in a difficult situation.

Another Hadith that supports this very well is one in which the Prophet ﷺ said, "If anyone protects a believer from a hypocrite, Allah will send an angel who will guard his flesh on the Day of Resurrection from the fire of Hell (*Jahannam*)."[27]

Protecting or supporting someone who is being oppressed is not considered a small act, as the reward it brings is so great in terms of the Hereafter – we will be protected ourselves by an angel from the Hellfire.

The Prophet ﷺ also said, "Whoever responds on behalf of a believer when he is not present, Allah has made it a right upon Him to protect him from the fire."[28] What is meant here is that a person or a group of people could be backbiting about someone else and you defend that person. Protecting someone in their absence whilst they are being wrongly or negatively targeted earns you protection from the Hellfire.

Muslims are brothers to one another, and this means that we cannot wrong one another, nor can we betray one another. It is upon us to defend our brothers and sisters if we witness wrongdoing towards them.

- Lastly, Abu Dhar asks what to do if a person is weak or oppressed themselves and cannot help anybody else. Before giving his answer, the Prophet ﷺ said to Abu Dhar, "You aren't going to leave any good for your brother to do?" This was to ask if he was really that incapable of doing any of the acts mentioned before. He then followed on to say, "He should restrain his evil from people." In other words, the Prophet ﷺ was saying that if we cannot do any good for people, then the least we can do is refrain from harming them in any way.

The following Hadith ties in well with this particular piece of advice, "Whoever believes in Allah and the Last Day should speak good or remain quiet."[29] If you do not have anything positive or productive to contribute, whether it be in person or online , then it is best to remain quiet. If we cannot offer support to someone or if we cannot defend someone, then we must stay quiet or better – get up and leave. One of the greatest Companions Abu Dujana, may Allah be pleased with him, took part in all the battles alongside the Prophet, but he did not depend on his involvement in the battlefield to earn him a place in Paradise. Abu Dujana said that the one thing that he depends on with Allah is that he never used his tongue to curse a believer or to say anything bad about anyone.

As mentioned in an earlier chapter regarding the character of Abu Dhar, he found it difficult to get along with people due to the fact that he was harsh towards them in regard to their material belongings. And it was due to Uthman ibn Affan, may Allah be pleased with him, reminding him of the Prophet's ﷺ advice that he withdrew himself from interacting with people. He understood that the solution was to simply not speak, as his speech would be counterproductive.

We find that this last piece of advice was what Abu Dhar actually wanted to hear. He kept asking the Prophet ﷺ for simpler, easier actions that could allow one to enter Paradise (*Jannah*), and after receiving the last piece of advice, he asked, "If that is all he does then will he enter into Paradise?" To which the Prophet ﷺ replied, "There is no believer that pursues any one of these things except that on the Day of Judgement it grabs his hand until it enters him into Paradise." This closing statement is very profound as it explains that our charity will come and take us by the hand, our spoken word of truth will come and take us by the hand, our act of help for our fellow Muslim will come and take us by the hand, our act of defence towards someone who is being wronged will come and take us by the hand and lead us to Paradise.

It is beneficial here to mention another Hadith narrated by Abu Dhar in which he complained to the Prophet Muhammad ﷺ that the emigrants from Makkah (*muhaajireen*), who were poor, were being beaten in good deeds by the rich Companions as they are able to give money towards charity whilst the poor could only pray and fast. The Prophet ﷺ said has not Allah given you something to give charity with too? Abu Dhar asked, 'What?' and the Prophet replied 'Allahu Akbar' 'Alhamdulillah', every (*tasbeeh*) is a charity (*sadaqa*) and taught him that reciting the *tasbeeh* after prayers is also charity. Abu Dhar then went back to the poor Companions and told them to recite the *tasbeeh*, which the rich Companions also found out about and started reciting too. After this Abu Dhar returned to the Prophet ﷺ once again to complain about the rich Companions to which he was told that it is the bounty of Allah and He gives it to whomever He wishes.[30]

We can clearly see the personality of Abu Dhar in this Hadith as he always wanted to do more, and he always wanted to learn of ways that he could gain rewards despite not being able to spend money like those richer than himself.

It is important for us to learn and remember that our issue is not the things that we wish we could do, but the issue is that we fail to act on the things that are within our capability. Allah gives us all opportunities to do good deeds and earn Paradise, but we must recognise this potential within us and use it.

We do not need to be constantly searching for 'big actions,' small acts of kindness can be much bigger than we initially think. For example, Abdullah ibn Mubarak said that "to cover a child from the cold at night is more beloved to Allah than fighting in the battlefield." We don't need to be in a position of authority or power to do good for people; we can build up good deeds by doing little things such as teaching others how to read Qur'anic Arabic, driving people places, helping elderly or disabled people – these small acts of kindness should not be neglected.

The bigger message behind the Prophet's ﷺ advice to Abu Dhar and his followers (*ummah*) in the Hadith that we have covered in this chapter, is that it is a sign of insincerity if we do not do what we are capable of doing. Allah will ask us regarding how we utilised our abilities to do good. However, at the same time we have also been told not to take the easier option if we have the potential to carry out a more difficult task.

Abu Bakr, may Allah be pleased with him, used to go to the outskirts of Madinah and clean the homes of elderly women when he was Caliph, just as he did before he was given this position of authority.

I would like to end this chapter with a beautiful example set by Umar ibn Abdul Aziz, he was found crying by his wife Fatima bint Malik after he had finished praying. She asked him why he was crying, to which he replied, "I was given this position without any interest for it on my part. So I started to think about the hungry orphan, the direly destitute, the widow, the needy, the elderly parents with many children and little wealth, and I realised that my Lord will ask me about them on the Day of Judgement and that my opponent and their defender will be the Prophet ﷺ."

Umar knew about these people before he became Caliph, but now after being given a position of power, he had the means to act for these people. He was afraid of the responsibility and him not being able to carry it out properly.

May Allah employ us to carry out good for His religion, His creation and may Allah spread righteousness through us. Amin.

6

A WORD OF TRUTH IN THE FACE OF AN OPPRESSOR

The Prophet ﷺ said, "The best form of jihad (striving) is to speak a word of truth (haqq) in the face of an oppressor."

IN THE PREVIOUS CHAPTER we covered a Hadith in which the Prophet ﷺ told Abu Dhar what actions one can do based on their capacity in order to attain Paradise. The Prophet ﷺ gave different levels of actions and at the end he said that if we cannot do any of the actions mentioned before, then we must refrain from doing any sort of harm. This Hadith is also similar to the more famous Hadith in which the Messenger of Allah ﷺ said: "Whoever amongst you sees evil, let him change it with his hands, and if he cannot do that then with his tongue, and if he cannot do that then hate it in his heart. And that is the weakest of faith."

Speech is something that can easily influence good or evil; both usually start with the tongue and end with the tongue. There is a famous narration of Luqman Hakeem, the Abyssinian slave, may Allah be pleased with him, in which he was told by his master to cook the best part of a sheep and bring it to him. Luqman cooked the tongue and brought it to his master, after which he was asked to go and cook and the worst part of the sheep and bring it to him, and once again he brought the tongue. His master asked why he had brought the tongue on both occasions and he answered, "When the tongue is used for good, it is the best part of the body. And when the tongue is used for evil, it is the worst part of the body."

What we learn from the above is that our tongue will play a big role in whether we enter Paradise or the Hellfire. The Prophet ﷺ mentioned in numerous different Hadiths that we often do not consider our words to be actions. Underestimating our words and the impact they can have, can lead us to underestimate the sinfulness of them. If we do not understand the harm that our tongue can cause, then we put ourselves in a difficult position that could result in eternal punishment in the Hereafter.

This brings us to the Hadith that we will be covering in this chapter. It has two narrations from Abu Sayeed al-Khudri, may Allah be pleased with him:

1. The Prophet ﷺ said, "The best form of struggle (*jihad*) is to speak a word of truth (*haq*) in the face of an oppressor."[31]

2. He ﷺ said, "A word of justice (*'adl*) in the face of an oppressor is the best form of striving (*jihad*)."

The word truth (*haq*) is more general than the word justice (*'adl*), and we must look at it in the context of this Hadith as truth can mean many things. The second narration of the Hadith helps us to understand further, a word of justice is a very particular type of truth; the Prophet ﷺ here meant for us to use our tongue to challenge oppression in the face of a tyrant.

These Hadiths can be seen as a reverse of the Hadith covered in chapter two, in which the Prophet ﷺ saw a Companion beating his slave to which he said that Allah is more able than you to cause harm. We are reminded that oppression usually stems from a false illusion of power, when a person forgets that real power is with Allah. Here the equation has switched, if someone speaks a word of justice to an oppressive ruler, it shows that one who is powerless is able to speak up against a powerful person through their firm belief in the ultimate power of Allah over everyone. Having belief that Allah is in charge of change, one can and should muster up the courage to speak a word of justice in the face of an oppressor. What is important is that we put in the effort, Allah will do the rest and He will not hold us accountable if the oppressor does not change their ways.

There are different ways to speak a word of truth to an oppressor:

1. The first involves giving advice (*naseeha*) to someone in a position of authority that they do not have the right to wrong others. The advice should involve reminding them of the error of their ways so that they may rectify them. The ultimate goal here is not to be celebrated as someone who has challenged the oppressor, but to rid society of oppression.

2. The second way is to speak a word of truth as a form of objection in order to remind the oppressor that they must be held accountable. Abu Bakr Siddiq, may Allah be pleased with him, said: "Obey me as long as I obey Allah and the Messenger ﷺ and rectify me when I do not obey Allah and the Messenger ﷺ." He was making it clear to people that they must correct him; they must advise him if they see him make a decision that goes against the laws of Islam (*Shari'ah*) and the life practices of the Prophet (*Sunnah*).

Umar al-Khattab, may Allah be pleased with him, also said: "Let not one of you see a fault on my part except that they expose that fault."

There are also a number of other lessons that we can derive from the Hadith narrated by Abu Sayeed:

- Why has it been called the greatest struggle (*jihad*)?

- Imam Khattabi said that when two people are fighting on the battlefield, they are generally fighting on equal grounds. However, when it comes to speaking the truth to an oppressor, it is not a level playing field. The oppressor is in a position of authority, and is capable of causing more harm, whilst the one speaking against oppression has nothing except courage and faith in Allah.

- A group of scholars argued that it is the best form of struggle (*jihad*) because if one is able to rectify the ruler or person in authority, it will benefit all of society at once and save them from bloodshed and the ill effects of war.

- Another group of scholars mentioned that the greatest form of striving (*jihad*) is in fact the personal *jihad* or struggling against our own ego (*nafs*). Our weaknesses and fears are able to overcome us due to a lack of trust (*tawakul*) in Allah, and this can become a disease of the heart. Struggling against ourselves to defeat this disease is thought of very highly; the Prophet ﷺ called it the best struggle (*afzal-ul-jihad*) as it involves striving against oneself and striving against the oppressor. This struggle has the ability to benefit on an individual level and potentially on a societal level. We may not be able to make the oppressor change their ways with our words, but we may inspire others to voice the truth and they could be more successful. Speaking up can also make the current ruler or their successor realise that their acts of injustice will be called out and they will be questioned. We may not have an immediate impact, but the fact that we spoke the truth is still meaningful and beneficial.

- Speaking the truth to those in authority is not praiseworthy if it is done recklessly, or in an unwise manner, or if it is done for the intention of being praised and perceived as brave. It is only praiseworthy when it is done with the correct intentions and is beneficial. We must be willing to disregard ourselves for the sake of a noble cause. In the light of this scholars have also said that in some circumstances it is better to remain silent in order to advance the cause of justice, even if we are called cowards in the process.

  Appeasing the masses is not in any way less insincere than appeasing those in positions of authority. Just as there are scholars of the rulers (*ulema sultan*), there are also scholars of the people (*ulema awaam*). Choosing to say something for the sake of it being convenient rather than it being true becomes an issue as it is not done with the right intention.

This also coincides with another issue of selectively choosing to speak the truth, which can actually be worse than not speaking at all. Choosing to condemn something because we can get away with it and choosing not to condemn another matter because we assume or know that we won't be able to get away with it, is hypocritical and it is better to not speak at all. We must be consistent when speaking the truth (*kalimatul haq*), otherwise we should remain silent.

We must show wisdom (*hikmah*) when speaking, we should be calculated and controlled in our speech. The word *hikmah* comes from the Arabic word meaning 'reins,' as it requires us to know when to hold back. Wisdom is to know when to say something, how to say it and when to refrain from speaking altogether. Our goal must be to advance the truth, not ourselves as a spokesperson. And this ultimately requires us to take into consideration aspects such as time and place in order to ensure that our speech can help a noble cause, instead of speaking in such a way that can cause further damage. Recklessness does not equate to bravery, and it is important to make this distinction between the two.

- Ambiguity with injustice is not acceptable under any circumstances. One clear example of this is of Hajjaj bin Yusuf who was a tyrant ruler. The Companions took different approaches against Hajjaj's oppression. Abdullah bin Zubair, may Allah be pleased with him, was a blessed Companion who received *tahneek* (date mixed with saliva) directly from the Prophet Muhammad ﷺ when he was a baby, he took an aggressive stance against Hajjaj. Abdullah bin Zubair revolted against Hajjaj as he believed that it would be beneficial to take a physical stance against him.

However, Abdullah bin Umar, may Allah be pleased with him, believed in a different approach. He was not passive or ambiguous about the oppression, but he used his tongue to clearly call out and condemn Hajjaj regarding his oppression. Abdullah bin Umar called out to Hajjaj when he was giving a speech and said, "Oh enemy of Allah, we don't want to hear your voice, we are done with you." He challenged him verbally, in front of everyone, which resulted in Hajjaj poisoning him. This shows that Hajjaj was threatened just as much by the tongue of Abdullah bin Umar as he was by the physical stance of Abdullah bin Zubair.

The two may have differed over their methodology of how to stand up to the injustice, but they were not ambiguous about where they stood on the matter of injustice. We should never be ambigious about where we stand on the question of oppression

Fear plays a big role in stopping many people from speaking up against oppression. Let's have a look at the different types of fear:

- The greatest form of fear is the fear of persecution; about which the Prophet ﷺ said that the greatest form of struggle (*jihad*) is speaking the truth despite having this fear. The thought or fear of enduring physical harm may make someone think twice before speaking out against an oppressor, yet if they still speak out, they can expect a wonderful reward in the Hereafter.

- There are also more subjective fears – those that involve our feelings. An example of this could be that a person may fear being mocked by others or losing friends if they speak the truth. There is a Hadith narrated by Abu Saeed that is well-suited here: "The Messenger ﷺ said, 'Let not one of you belittle himself.' The Companions asked him, 'How do we belittle ourselves?' So, he said, 'A person sees something that they should speak about, but they don't speak about it. Allah will say to that person on the Day of Judgement, 'What stopped you from speaking about such and such?' The person will say, 'Fear of people.' And Allah will say, 'And I am more deserving of being feared than people.'"[32]

    We learn here that we will be held to account if we do not speak the truth and call out injustice due to the fear of people.

- There is also another Hadith narrated by Abu Saeed, in which the Prophet ﷺ said, "Do not let the fear of people prevent you from speaking the truth if you see something that deserves to be spoken about. Doing so will not cause your lifespan to be shortened and it will not decrease your wealth."[33]

In this Hadith, the Messenger ﷺ is saying we should fear the consequences of disappointing Allah rather than being afraid of people. The root cause of us failing to speak up against oppression is that we do nott take into consideration the importance and might of Allah over people.

Lastly, in another Hadith, the Prophet Muhammad ﷺ mentioned to Abdullah b. Amr, "If my followers (*ummah*) come to a time when a person cannot say to an oppressor, 'Oh oppressor,' then you might as well walk away from them."[34] It is important to understand here that the Prophet ﷺ was not saying abandon or walk away from the Muslim Community (*ummah*). Rather, the Prophet ﷺ was telling us that there could be no good left in them for matters to reach such a point that a Muslim cannot call out a blatant oppressor, allowing the oppressor to freely carry out acts of injustice.

We ask Allah to protect us, put courage in our hearts and truth on our tongues. May Allah bless us with the sincerity to speak the truth at the times and in the way that He is most pleased with. Amin.

7

THE RULING ON SILENCE AND INJUSTICE

From Qays ibn Abi Hazm who said I heard Abu Bakr (may Allah be pleased with him) say, "O you people! I hear you reciting this verse: 'O you who believe! Worry about your own selves. If you follow the (right) guidance [and enjoin what is right (Islamic Monotheism and all that Islam orders one to do) and forbid what is wrong (polytheism, disbelief and all that Islam has forbidden)] no harm can come to you from those who are in error.' (5:105) But I heard the Messenger of Allah ﷺ say: "Indeed when people see an oppressor but do not prevent him from (doing evil), it is likely that Allah will punish them all."

IN THIS CHAPTER we will look at the rulings on silence as it is not often addressed in a comprehensive manner. We will cover three Hadiths regarding this matter, and I'll begin with a Hadith narrated by Qays bin Abi Hazm, may Allah be pleased with him, who said:

"I heard Abu Bakr, may Allah be pleased with him, say, 'Oh you people! I hear you reciting this verse: *'Oh you who believe! Worry about your own selves. If you follow the right guidance, no harm can come to you from those who are in error.'* (al-Ma'idah 5:105) But I heard the Messenger of Allah ﷺ say: 'Indeed when people see an oppressor but do not prevent him from doing evil, it is likely that Allah will punish them all.'"[35]

Abu Bakr made a very important point here in mentioning that there are verses that are often recited and given improper explanations, or they are applied to contexts that have meanings contradictory to the actual intent of the verse (*ayah*). We should note here that Abu Bakr, may Allah be pleased with him, said these words to a generation that was very close to the revelation of the Qur'an, yet they were still applying or interpreting the verses incorrectly.

My father-in-law, Shaykh Abul Abed made a very profound statement that I believe elaborates very well on the above: "Any explanation (*tafseer*) that departs from the reasons of revelation (*asbab an-nuzul*) and the *Sunnah* context of those *tafseer* is bound to go astray." This is because departing from the original contexts makes it susceptible to the agenda of the one doing the explanation (*tafseer*), which can in turn do harm to the original meaning of the verses.

Going back to the Hadith itself, Abu Bakr was reminding the people that Allah is not saying that we should be silent in the face of injustice. He therefore went on to mention what the Prophet Muhammad ﷺ said in this regard; the Prophet ﷺ is the one through whom we learn the true meaning of the Qur'an, and naturally his life practice (*Sunnah*) is the explanation (*tafseer*).

Whilst it may at first seem as though there is a contradiction between the statement of the Prophet Muhammad ﷺ and the verse (*ayah*), Allah is in fact talking about those people who have already exhausted their options in trying to change others around them. They become saddened by their inability to correct the wrong in society, and it is because of this that Allah has said that no harm will come from those who are in error.

These people feel paralysed by their lack of success in stopping oppression, similar to the Prophet Muhammad ﷺ who felt great empathy towards his people and was saddened over the fate of the people around him. Allah talks about this nature of His Messenger ﷺ in *Surah al-Kahf*, 18:6: *"Then perhaps you would kill yourself through grief over them,*

[O Muhammad], *if they do not believe in this message, and out of sorrow."*
The Prophet ﷺ even described himself as being like a man who's trying to catch flies as they are jumping into the fire; meaning to say that he was so saddened by people around him and he was trying to 'rescue' them all from a fiery fate but it was not always possible.

What we take from this is that Abu Bakr, may Allah be pleased with him, was saying that the *ayah* from *Surah al-Ma'ida* can not be used as an excuse for complacency or laziness towards speaking out against injustice. Another point to be aware of is that if his own generation was misinterpreting the ayah over 1400 years ago, we must exercise even more caution in understanding and implementing the Qur'an.

The second Hadith is that of the Prophet Muhammad ﷺ in which he asked his Companions of the strange things they encountered in Abyssinia. Jabir, may Allah be pleased with him, narrated:

"When the emigrants who had crossed the sea came back to the Messenger of Allah, he said, 'Tell me of the strange things that you saw in the land of Abyssinia.' Some young men among them said, 'Yes oh Messenger of Allah. While we were sitting, one of their elderly nuns came past carrying a vessel of water on her head. She passed by some of their youth, one of whom placed his hand between her shoulders and pushed her. She fell on her knees and her vessel broke. When she stood up, she turned to him and said, 'You will come to know oh foolish young man, that when Allah sets up the Footstool and gathers the first and the last, and hands and feet speak of which they used to earn, you will come to know your case and my case in His presence soon.' The Messenger of Allah said, 'She spoke the truth, she spoke the truth, she spoke the truth. How can Allah purify any people (of sin) when they do not protect their weak against their strong?'"[36]

The Companions who related their experience to the Prophet ﷺ did not get involved in the situation as they were refugees in Abyssinia and were in no position to intervene. They even wanted to defend Najashi when there was internal conflict and rebellion against him, but they could not due to being observers and people under protection. However, we can see from this Hadith that this experience had left a profound impact on them and made them feel uncomfortable as they knew it was wrong, and this was due to the lessons (*tarbiyyah*) that the Prophet ﷺ had given them beforehand. Muhammad ﷺ had instilled traits in them which unnerved them when they witnessed transgression and injustice.

Upon relating this incident, the Messenger of Allah ﷺ blamed society as a whole, and not just the young man who had oppressed the nun. The blame was to be put on the society that had allowed such behaviour to normalise, it was society's fault that the young man could freely push an old woman without being held accountable. The young oppressor was a product of a facilitating institution.

The third Hadith that we will cover in this chapter is from the mother of believers, Zainab Bint Jahsh, may Allah be pleased with her:

"I asked the Prophet ﷺ: Will we be destroyed even if we have righteous people amongst us? The Messenger ﷺ said, 'Yes, if filth (base sins) becomes rampant.'"[37]

The Prophet ﷺ here was saying that even if there are righteous people amongst us, but sins are allowed to thrive in society without anyone speaking up against them, then everyone suffers as a result. Furthermore, when looking at all three Hadith, essentially the moral of all three is that if people do not speak up when evil is being committed, everyone will suffer.

Scholars have mentioned a few things regarding this matter:

1. All the nations that were destroyed before were not destroyed just because they were worshipping other than Allah (*shirk*), but for becoming oppressors (*dhaalim*). Nations were destroyed when they became aggressive and oppressive towards their messengers. The people of Shuaib, may the blessings of Allah be upon him, were destroyed for their polytheism (*shirk*) and cheating with weights/scales (*tatfeef*). Saeed bin Musayab, may Allah be pleased with him, commented on this and said that if you find a place where people do not cheat with their weights, settle in that land, and if you find that they do cheat, then leave as quickly as you can. When these types of things are normalised in society, the problems and suffering caused by them will affect everyone.

2. Umar bin Abdul Aziz commented on private sins versus public oppression and injustice. Allah would never punish an entire population even if everyone committed private sins, whereas if one person sins publicly, the entire population may become deserving of Allah's punishment.

3. Different scenarios call for different actions. The Muslims in Abyssinia were under an observer status and wanted to be able to practice their religion freely. The Muslims in Makkah were under persecution and had to hide their Islam and the Muslims in Madinah were in a place of authority. They were all in different positions, but they were all responsible for doing their part.

4. Allah also mentioned that people would be punished as a result of that which they used to do. If people wrong one another, they will also experience some of what that feels like.

Usually when people are punished, they are punished by the elements (nature), such as rain or wind. They are punished by things that they took for granted and did not see any threat in. Similarly, the people who are exploited do not see the threat in others in many situations. They are in a position of vulnerability, and many times that vulnerability is volunteered because they feel safe with them, but unfortunately, they are then taken advantage of and their vulnerability is violated.

Allah has placed a duty upon us of being upright and speaking the truth regardless of the circumstances, bringing us onto the rulings of silence.

Silence is prohibited (*haram*) when three conditions are met:

1. When we are certain of something being evil (*munkar*); there is no grey area. Musa, may the blessings of Allah be upon him, made an assumption when he saw the man from Bani Israel and the Egyptian fighting. It was not a clear situation (thus could be classed as a grey area). Shaykh Salman made an interesting observation; has said that if you notice Muslims being overzealous, they are usually so regarding things that are not a hundred per cent certain, but they will not be overzealous on matters that are completely indisputable and known to be wrong.

2. When we are sure that an evil was committed; not based on gossip or rumours, but strong evidence. Allah has stated clearly in the Qur'an in *Surah al-Hujurat 49:6*: *"Oh you who*

have believed, if a rebellious evil person comes to you with news, verify it…"

We must be certain, through witnessing it ourselves or a testimony from someone who had witnessed it first-hand.

3. When the greater likelihood is that speaking up will remove or reduce the evil being committed. Speaking out for the sake of Allah requires courage as we can expect both criticism and opposition by people, however, we must speak out against injustice for the sake of Allah, regardless of the people.

Imam al-Ghazali, may Allah be pleased with him, spoke regarding the major sins of the scholars (*ulema*): when a scholar is in the presence of an unjust ruler, they must speak about the injustice committed by the oppressive ruler.

Unfortunately, dictators or unjust rulers use scholars to legitimise the injustice that they carry out, and this even includes massacres that have occurred and are occurring currently. Exploiting the cloak of scholarship to justify ugly injustices is a very old propaganda technique that has been used by Christians such as Pope Urban II as well as Muslims. Thus, the silence of scholars in such situations is extremely sinful as they are religious authorities and must not be ambiguous towards acts of injustice.

Imam Abu Hanifa, may Allah be pleased with him, likened the army of Zayd bin Zain ul Abideen to the people of Badr. He was very forthcoming and was not ambiguous about where he stood on this matter. He was aware that with his position of leadership (*imamah*), came an even greater responsibility.

We also have the example of Imam Ahmad, may Allah be pleased with him, who was put in an extremely testing situation in which people were trying to force him to adopt a doctrine that was not from Islam. They were pushing him to say that the Qur'an was created and not the speech of Allah. Imam Ahmad was told by other scholars that he would be killing himself if he did not give them the statement that they wanted to hear. Imam Ahmad answered by pointing out of the window from his prison cell at the people, and said that if an average Muslim gets stopped in the street and gets forced to say such a statement or face death, he will not be sinful as he would be trying to protect his own life, whereas Imam

Ahmad himself would be sinful as his statement would be legitimising it. An average Muslim would be like Ammar bin Yasir, may Allah be pleased with him, when he cursed the Prophet ﷺ under duress and the Prophet ﷺ told him that if the oppressors threaten and pressurise him again, he should say it again as his statement would not be corrupting the religion or normalising anything as such. It is a means of escaping persecution, making it permissible for a person not in a position of authority to make such statements.

Another example is of Imam al-Haraawi, may Allah be pleased with him, who said: "I was subjected to the sword five times (threatened with execution), and I was not told to take back my position, rather I was told to be silent about the oppressors but I refused to be silent."

Saeed bin Jubair, may Allah be pleased with him, left a very powerful legacy. He showed no fear whatsoever in the face of the oppression by Hajjaj and it was his courage that drove Hajjaj crazy. He grew increasingly frustrated with Saeed bin Jubair as he was so at ease throughout his ordeal, forcing him to say to Saeed, "Don't you know that I will take your life?" To which Saeed bin Jubair replied, "If I thought you had the power to take my life, then I would have worshipped you instead of Allah."

Saeed bin Jubair was killed in prostration (*sujood*) and this haunted Hajjaj until the day he died of severe illness, at which point he was repeatedly saying, "Saeed has killed me, Saeed has killed me."

We can learn from these examples that sometimes silence becomes criminal, so much so that even backbiting (*gheebah*) can become obligatory (*fard*). Backbiting is something that is generally very sinful and looked down upon in Islam, yet when it comes to an oppressor who abuses others on a serial basis, it becomes obligatory to speak out (even through backbiting) in order to warn potential victims.

The Prophet Muhammad ﷺ told us to help our brother whether he is the oppressed or the oppressor; we help the oppressor by stopping him from oppressing others further. We do not sit back and allow the oppressor to carry on committing injustice and sins. Sometimes silence is violence; if we do not speak, we risk the lives of the oppressed. And what is worse, is to tell a victim of injustice, to remain silent. Unfortunately, it has happened and continues to happen on many occasions that a victim is shamed into remaining silent in the face of oppression. If someone is being wronged, they must speak, and if they are scared, we must encourage them to speak so that the oppressor does not wrong anyone else. We owe it not only to ourselves, but to everyone who is a potential victim.

It is important for us to realise here that silence in such situations enables oppression to continue, whether it be at a state level or an individual level. As mentioned earlier, backbiting is a sin in normal circumstances, and remaining silent whilst someone is wrongly being backbitten is enabling the wrongdoing.

By sitting there silently, we are essentially condoning sinful behaviour. The Prophet Muhammad ﷺ also said, "Whoever believes in Allah and the Last Day, let him not sit at a table where alcohol is being served."[38] It is best for us to avoid sitting with people who are involved in drinking alcohol, otherwise by sitting at the same table we are silently approving the serving and consumption of something prohibited (*haram*).

The rulings of jurisprudence (*fiqh*) are diverse and they also cover the permissibility of silence, which we will now be looking at. There are times when it is not good to speak, and silence becomes permissible (*halal*) or even mandatory (*fard*).

The following Hadith gives us a good insight into the permissibility of silence: Abu Saeed narrates that he heard the Messenger ﷺ say Allah will hold a servant accountable on the Day of Judgement, asking him/her, "What stopped you from calling out that evil when you saw it?" The servant says, "Oh my Lord, I had hope in you and I left the people."[39] This is a person who tried and was not successful and then withdrew themselves because they were incapable of making a change and was hopeful of Allah's forgiveness and so they will be forgiven.

What we can take from this Hadith is the fact that this person has a legitimate excuse for remaining silent. This person is not admonished by Allah because he had exercised his options but could not do anything to change the situation, unlike a person who chooses to remain silent without even trying. The scholars have also commented on this Hadith saying that this person had hope in the people and tried their best to make them understand the evil of their actions but was not successful so left them. They recognise their incapacity in this regard and turn to Allah in the hope that He will forgive them for leaving the people and will deal with the evil Himself.

Silence can also become mandatory upon us, but when? If evil (*munkar*) will increase with us speaking, it is important to remain silent and it is often a point that we fail to understand. Imam Ahmad, may

Allah be pleased with him, was severely tortured but they could not kill him because they knew that if they killed him, then the supporters of Imam Ahmad would seek revenge by killing them.

When Imam Hussain, may Allah be pleased with him, the grandson of the Prophet Muhammad ﷺ went out to fight, the Companions did not think he would be successful. The Companions sensed that the people would not support him; they did not think he was wrong, but they thought that he would not succeed. They tried to stop him because they were worried about his life – not because they thought his cause was wrong. However, Imam Hussain believed he could remove the evil (*munkar*). He did not go alone but was amassing an army to face Yazeed. He believed he had the means to undo and remove the evil, but other Companions believed that he would unknowingly cause more harm than good.

Sometimes speaking up is harmful and ineffective in removing evil and instead empowers an oppressor to commit more oppression and it is in these cases that it becomes mandatory to remain silent. Speaking in such circumstances can be reckless, making it important for us to consider withdrawing (*uzlah*) and deciding at which point we should withdraw from the situation.

Another Hadith narrated by Abu Saeed al-Khudri mentions that the Prophet Muhammad ﷺ said, "There will come a time when the best property of the Muslim will be a sheep and he will take that to the top of the mountain so he can flee with his religion from all of the afflictions (*fitnah*)."[40]

This Hadith is effectively saying that we can withdraw from society or certain situations in order to protect our faith, however we should only take the bare minimum of what we need. We must note that we cannot use this Hadith to try and avoid all forms of afflictions or tests (*fitnah*). The Companions of the Prophet ﷺ experienced many different and difficult trials, but they did not give up or run away. The Hadith is specifically talking about situations where we cannot speak out, or we are suffering persecution because of our faith or we are unable to practice our faith freely, then we should withdraw. In such a situation we must keep in mind that we should only take that which we can suffice ourselves with (not any luxuries), as moving away is purely for the sake of safeguarding our faith and family.

The Prophet ﷺ also mentioned in another Hadith that "The one who mixes with and tolerates people is better than the one who withdraws from people."[41] What is meant by this Hadith is that there are certain traits and qualities that we can learn by interacting with people. Our faith (*iman*) is put to the test when we interact with others as we learn to control our tongues, our anger and our gaze, as well as learn how to do business correctly. It is much easier to keep our gaze lowered if there is nobody around, but if we are in a certain situation and we lower our gaze, the reward from Allah is much greater. Umar bin Khattab, commented on this and said, "They are the people whose hearts were tested with *taqwa*."

Lastly, it is good to remind ourselves here about the Hadith narrated by Abu Dhar in which he asked the Prophet ﷺ several questions and at the end of the Hadith the Prophet ﷺ said that we should avoid doing harm and withhold our evil from people. If we are in a gathering and we cannot stop an act of injustice from happening, it is not enough to hate it in our heart and stay there, we must get up and leave that gathering. If we are not able to say anything against it, we should leave otherwise our silent presence means that we consent to the injustice.

We might be in a difficult situation with family members (especially those older than ourselves), and we are unable to stop them by saying it outright. We have to be careful not to cause further problems, and one of the best ways to direct them away from the injustice is to change the subject and talk about something that does not involve backbiting or gossip. By doing so we have done our part as we hate the act in our heart and we did our best to steer them away from committing more injustice. But if this does not work then we have the option to withdraw from that situation and leave.

May Allah grant us the courage to stand up to injustice and protect us from causing more harm. Amin.

THE RIGHT TO FOOD, WATER AND SHELTER

'Uthman bin 'Affan (May Allah be pleased with him) reported: The Prophet ﷺ said, "There is no right that the son of Adam is more entitled to other than these (four) rights: A home to live in, a garment to cover his nakedness, a piece of bread, and water."

FROM THIS CHAPTER onwards, we will begin looking at specific issues of injustice and how to deal with them. Very often we come across these issues, but we overlook or fail to realise that there is an entire lifetime of the Prophet (*Sunnah*) that addresses them, along with the priceless contributions from knowledgeable Muslims and the *fiqh* that is our jurisprudence based upon the life of the Prophet (*Sunnah*) itself.

We will begin with a Hadith narrated by Uthman bin Affan, may Allah be pleased with him, who said, "The Prophet ﷺ said, 'There is no right that the son of Adam is more entitled to other than these four rights: a home to live in, a garment to cover his nakedness, a piece of bread and water.'"[42]

Firstly, it is interesting to note that this particular Hadith was reported by Uthman bin Affan who also has his own story with regards to water which I would like to mention before going into detail with the above Hadith.

When the Muslims migrated to Madinah, they were in need of water but were struggling to get access to it. A non-Muslim resident of Madinah saw that they were in desperate need of water, and he raised the price of the water from his well even further to make it almost impossible for them to afford it. The Prophet Muhammad ﷺ approached the owner of the well and asked for a price on the well, to which the owner replied forty thousand dirhams. The Prophet ﷺ knew that this was a ridiculously high price, but he announced the price to the Muslim community and said that whoever purchases the well will be guaranteed a place in Paradise (*Jannah*). Uthman, may Allah be pleased with him, jumped at the opportunity.

After agreeing to purchase the well, Uthman went to the owner but he changed his mind about selling the well because he was able to make money off the migrants (*muhajireen*) by selling them water. Uthman, may Allah be pleased with him, then asked the owner to sell him half of the ownership of the well for twenty thousand dirhams. This meant that they would have access to the well on alternate days. Uthman would invite everyone in Madinah to come and take water for free from the well on his days. The man whom he bought half the ownership from became aware of this, as he was no longer receiving any customers, and went back to Uthman to say that he will sell the remaining ownership to him for a further twenty thousand. Uthman did not agree to paying another twenty thousand as he knew the man was trying to make an unfair profit but agreed to pay ten thousand dirhams instead.

This story is significant as water is one of the basic rights of a human being as narrated by Uthman himself from the Prophet Muhammad ﷺ. Uthman, may Allah be pleased with him, made the well an endowment (*waqf*) for the community of Madinah, it still exists today, allowing them to benefit from it.

Moving onto the Hadith itself, the Prophet Muhammad ﷺ mentioned that there are four specific things that the son of Adam is entitled to, those being a home, clothes, bread and water. What is interesting in this

Hadith is the language that the Messenger ﷺ has used, as he is talking about tangible physical rights that we as humans are entitled to. Allah also mentions in the Qur'an, *Surah al-Ma'arij* 70:24-25: *"And those within whose wealth is a known right, for the needy and the destitute"* – the needy is the one who asks, and the destitute is the one who is forbidden from asking, either through self-imposed reasons (such as shyness) or because of law and society. Allah wants us to understand that the wealth that He has blessed us with is not just for us, there are other people who also have rights over it. Allah is talking about the people of charity (*sadaqah*) in these verses and we must use our own initiative and search for those who are in need, to fulfil their rights, rather than waiting for people to approach us themselves.

There is also another Hadith narrated by Ibn Abbas in which the Prophet Muhammad ﷺ said, " Muslims are co-owners of three things: water, pasture and fire – and their price is unlawful."[43]

Scholars of Hadith have said there is an emphasis here on Muslims, which makes it more important for us to understand the rights of all Muslims. What is meant by water in this Hadith is public water, such as an open stream; it isn't referring, for example, to bottled water that a person is selling. Pasture is referring to things like herbage that grow naturally from lands that are accessible to everyone. And the scholars have commented on fire saying that it refers to firewood or similar items that can be collected to make fire. A Muslim cannot claim these things to be under their sole ownership and forbid others from using them, it becomes harmful to the community and this is not acceptable in Islam. However, scholars have also made it a point to say that if you do own something in a public setting, such as a garden and there is water that runs through it or there are fruit trees, you do have the first right but you should also make it available for the community to benefit from.

In the Qur'an, Allah has given us an example of people who were selfish and did not allow others to benefit from their garden; *Surah al-Qalam*, 68:17: *"Indeed We have tried them as We tried the companions of the garden, when they swore to cut its fruit in the early morning."*

This is in reference to a generous man who owned a garden and he would allow the surrounding community to come and harvest from his garden, however he had selfish and entitled children. They decided they would pick the fruit in the night before the people came in the morning. Allah destroyed the garden in order to teach them a lesson.

Another example is of Zubair and his dispute with an *Ansari* man regarding a stream at al-Harrah which they used to irrigate their date palms with as it ran through both of their plots of land. However, Zubair blocked the water off so it would stay in his plot, the *Ansari* approached the Prophet Muhammad ﷺ to complain about Zubair not letting the water flow to his plot of land. The Prophet ﷺ said to Zubair, "Oh Zubair! Water your land and then let the water flow to your neighbour." The *Ansari* was not satisfied with this and replied angrily, "Oh Messenger of Allah! Is it because he is your cousin?" The face of the Messenger of Allah ﷺ changed after hearing this and he said, "Oh Zubair! Water your land and withhold the water until it flows over your walls."[44]

The way in which the *Ansari* responded showed that there was a sense of greed in him and he wanted more than his fair share, and the scholars have commented on this saying that the one who owns the land has the most right to it, but they should not just restrict it to themselves. The owners should allow others to benefit too. Saeed bin Zubair further commented on this, saying that "Allah curses a man who has a wealthy plot of land with fruits, vegetation and water but he closes it off while people around him starve and go thirsty."

We should note that the Prophet emphasises water, but why is that? The scholars mentioned in the books of major sins that contaminating a water supply, or withholding or confiscating water from people that have a right over it is a severe sin. When we look into the explanation of verses (*tafseer*) about spending from the obligatory charity (*zakah*), the first right due is towards the poor and destitute. The scholars of *tafseer* will always mention water followed by food, clothing and shelter. The highest amount of stress is given to water, so much so that if a person visits your home and they asked for a glass of water, you cannot deny them a drink – it will be considered as something forbidden.

When the Prophet ﷺ emphasises water and that everyone has a right to it, we should think about those who have no access to safe, clean water and providing them with their right. It is so important that the Prophet Muhammad ﷺ said in a Hadith narrated by Jabir bin Abdullah, may Allah be pleased with him, "Whoever constructs a well of water, no human being, no jinn, no bird and no wild beast will drink from it except that Allah will give him reward for that on the Day of Judgement. And whoever builds for Allah a masjid even if it's the size of a bird's nest, or even smaller, Allah will build for him a house in Paradise."[45]

The scholars comment here that the Prophet ﷺ is mentioning both physical needs and spiritual needs. But what is interesting to note here is that providing for the physical needs of animals is also rewarded.

Next, we will look at the rights of housing and food. Having a roof over your head and food to eat are both fundamental rights that the Prophet ﷺ mentioned. An example of this can be found in the people of *Suffah*; a group of poor Companions who could not afford a home for themselves, so they lived at the back of the mosque (*masjid*). The Prophet Muhammad ﷺ used to spend on them and share his food with them, as the Prophet ﷺ himself knew very well the pain of hunger. If at anytime a gift came or some food came to him, he would call the people of *Suffah* and sit with them to share whatever he had received.

There is a wonderful account showcasing these traits of the Prophet Muhammad ﷺ, Abu Hurairah, may Allah be pleased with him, narrates that he was extremely hungry one day and he went out in the hope of finding food. He came across Abu Bakr, may Allah be pleased with him, and asked him a question regarding the Qur'an even though he knew the answer already, but he was hoping that Abu Bakr would notice his hunger. However, Abu Bakr answered his question and went on his way. Abu Hurairah then approached Umar, may Allah be pleased with him, but the same happened again. And then the Messenger of Allah ﷺ was passing by and he only had to look at the face of Abu Hurairah to realise that he was hungry, as the Prophet ﷺ had experienced extreme hunger himself and knew the pain that comes with it.

The Prophet Muhammad ﷺ asked Abu Hurairah to call his Companions of *Suffah* so that they could be fed, and the Prophet ﷺ went to fetch a pitcher of milk from his home. Abu Hurairah sat next to the Prophet Muhammad ﷺ whilst he passed it around the other way so that every single person could drink from it, and Abu Hurairah was afraid that there would be nothing left by the time the pitcher would reach him. When it did reach him, Prophet Muhammad ﷺ told him to go ahead and drink and he was surprised that the pitcher was still full. The Messenger ﷺ told him to keep drinking and he kept drinking until he could not drink anymore, thus witnessing a miracle of Allah through the Prophet ﷺ.[46]

When the Muslims migrated to Madinah, the Messenger of Allah ordered the indigenous community (*Ansar*) to establish a tie of brotherhood. He asked them to take the Muslims of Makkah, who were otherwise complete strangers to them, into their homes, giving them a roof over their heads and the same food and clothing as themselves, as well as providing avenues of work for the migrants. It was a big ask of the *Ansar*, who were newly entering Islam, to take people in to live in their homes and provide for them the same clothing and food as they did for themselves. Homelessness is described as being almost, if not more disastrous, than being an orphan by the scholars. Being homeless is essentially a feeling of being an orphan. And it is due to this that there is a high importance given to the act of reaching out to people who cannot afford a home, easing their burdens through providing a place to stay or feeding and clothing them at the least.

After housing, the Prophet ﷺ spoke about the importance of clothing. Anas bin Malik, may Allah be pleased with him, mentioned that nobody ever asked the Prophet ﷺ for a garment except that he took it off his back and gave it to them. This was to the point where he said that once the Messenger ﷺ was wearing a cloak that was gifted to him from Yemen, and a man began pulling it off him and said, "Give to me from what Allah gave you," and the Prophet ﷺ took it off and gave it to him. He also then asked Anas to take the man to the treasury and give him some charity. Here we can see that even though the man was quite rudely demanding from the Prophet Muhammad ﷺ, he didn't hesitate in taking the clothing off his back to give to the man.[47]

In another narration, Anas also mentioned that the Prophet ﷺ saw a non-Muslim tribe covering themselves with skins and he became angry with the people for not hastening to provide proper clothing for them. He commanded the community to go and provide clothing for the tribe. We can also see this in the jurisprudence (*fiqh*) on captives and how the Messenger ﷺ dealt with captives or prisoners of war. They were required to be clothed from the same clothing as the captors themselves. The Prophet ﷺ did not forbid people from dressing well, but he ordered that if they had a captive, they must provide for them the same clothing as they wore themselves. Scholars have said that clothing is the greatest signifier of wealth and social status, and that is why during hajj and *umrah*, pilgrims must wear *ihram*; they are all dressed in the same way with two plain white sheets so there is no indication of their social status.

We can also see this when Allah speaks about the freeing of slaves, He mentions clothing and feeding the needy directly afterwards. We find that Allah has tasked us with making people's lives easier; if we cannot free someone, we should at the very least clothe them and feed them.

Before concluding this chapter, I would like to mention a historical example of Zubaida, the wife of the Caliph Haroon ar-Rasheed, who took counsel from the scholars and did a lot for the advancement of Muslim society as a whole. Zubaida was known as being the most charitable woman of her generation and many of the traditions of hospitality began with her; when anyone would travel to Madinah, or Makkah or Iraq, she would make sure that they were taken care of properly. One of Zubaida's greatest accomplishments and favours upon the Muslim community was a road that she had built from Baghdad to Makkah – over twelve-hundred kilometres long! It was known as the 'Road of Zubaida'. Before the road was built, people travelling to Makkah for hajj or *umrah* would find it a very difficult journey to make, Zubaida had the entire way paved so people could travel with ease. And not only did she have a road built, she had set up forty stations along the course of the road that served as shelters for the travellers and stables for the animals. There were wells placed every ten or fifteen kilometres so that people could have access to safe drinking water throughout their journey. Zubaida had also set up pools so that people could cool down in the hot weather, guest houses and over fifty mosques. Security posts were also made, as well as minarets that lit the entire road, ensuring that people did not travel in pitch darkness. It was a tremendous feat that served the people (*ummah*) for over one thousand years; and if it was made today it would have cost several billions of dollars. The road has not been in service as a route for the past three-hundred years, but it can still be seen if you go on tour when in Makkah for Hajj or *umrah*.

The example of the Road of Zubaida helps us to understand the importance of helping others and giving them the fundamental rights that the Prophet Muhammad ﷺ mentioned in the Hadith narrated at the beginning of this chapter. It is deeply rooted in our tradition and we must endeavour to carry these traditions on. We should advocate for water to stay clean and accessible for all people; individually we may not all be able to take this up on a large scale, but we should at least do it locally. And another wonderful form of charity (*sadaqa*) is the constructing of wells, providing clean and safe water which can help save lives. Saad, may Allah be pleased with him, asked the Prophet ﷺ what would be the best form of *sadaqa* on behalf of his mother, who had passed away, and the Prophet ﷺ

responded "Water."[48] Saad then set up a water well on behalf of his deceased mother as charity (*sadaqa*).

May Allah allow us to play our part in giving people their fundamental rights, and may He give us the means to provide clean water for deprived communities, food for those who are hungry, clothing for those who are unclothed and shelter for those who cannot afford a home. Amin.

9

RESPONDING TO EVIL WITH GOOD

Jabir (ra) narrates that when verse 7:199 was revealed to the Prophet ﷺ he asked Jibril (as) "What is the meaning (taweel) of this verse and what are its implications?" So Jibril (as) said, "Allow me to ask my Lord and I will come back with more details on this matter." So he went and asked Allah (swt) and returned to the Prophet ﷺ and he said "Oh Muhammad, Allah commands you to forgive the one who wrongs you, to give to the one who withholds from you, and to maintain the ties of kinship with the one who cuts you off."

IN THIS CHAPTER I want us to look at a story that is narrated in the explanation (*tafseer*) of a well-known verse in *Surah al-A'raf* 7:199, *"Hold to forgiveness, enjoin what is good and turn away from the ignorant."* This particular verse is special as it involves many Hadiths and narrations from the Companions of the Prophet ﷺ.

We will begin with a narration given by Jabir, may Allah be pleased with him, who said that when this verse was revealed to the Prophet Muhammad ﷺ, he asked Jibreel "What is the meaning (*taweel*) of this verse and what are its implications?" So Jibreeel said, "Allow me to ask my Lord and I will come back with more details on this matter." He then went and asked Allah and returned to the Prophet ﷺ to say, "Oh Muhammad, Allah commands you to forgive the one who wrongs you, to give to the one who withholds from you, and to maintain the ties of kinship with the one who cuts you off."

So, after hearing this, the Prophet ﷺ stood up among the people and said, "Shall I not guide you to the most noble of characteristics in this world and in the Hereafter?" They (the Companions) said, "And what is that, Oh Messenger of Allah?" He replied, "That you forgive the one who wrongs you, you give to the one who withholds from you, and that you maintain the ties of kinship with the one who cuts you off."[49]

This is a very difficult Hadith; it is very easy to give this advice to someone else, but very difficult to put it into practice ourselves. We will almost certainly try to find a way to avoid doing any of these three things if we are in the position of having been wronged by someone, or having something withheld from us, or been cut off by a family member. It is important to remember that most acts of injustice are perpetuated because we fail to hold ourselves to higher standards, and when we are wronged by others we justify our reactions by saying, "Since I was wronged in this manner, my reaction is justified." This results in us justifying our lower standards of behaviour and injustice (*dhulm*) towards others, based upon injustice that was done to us, and this is something that we must be wary of as it sustains a sense and practice of injustice in society.

Now, moving onto the story about the revelation of this verse, it is narrated in Bukhari by Ibn Abbas, may Allah be pleased with him: al-Hurr bin al-Qayys was a young man who had memorised the Qur'an and was on the council (*shura'*) of Umar bin al-Khattab (those with whom he would consult). One day al-Hurr's cousin Uyaynah asked for permission to sit with Umar and Umar gave him permission to sit in on the meeting. Uyaynah sat down and began to scream at Umar saying, "Oh son of al-Khattab, beware, you neither give us sufficient provision nor do you judge amongst us with justice." This was a severe and unfounded accusation and it angered Umar, may Allah be pleased with him. Al-Hurr noticed that his cousin's accusations had made Umar angry and said, "Allah said to His Messenger ﷺ: *'Hold to forgiveness and enjoin that which is good and turn away from the ignorant.'* This man is ignorant so just turn away and ignore him." So, Umar turned away from him.

Ibn Abbas, may Allah be pleased with him, commented on this and said that Umar was a person who was always held by the book of Allah. He was conscious of the Qur'an and whenever he heard its verses, he would abide by them, and so even in this situation, his anger was immediately subdued on hearing this verse.

There is also another incident mentioned in *Al-Adab Al-Mufrad* (a collection of good mannerisms and characteristics), that Abdullah bin az-Zubair used to recite this verse (*ayah*) when he was Caliph and say on the pulpit, "By Allah, we are commanded by this *ayah* to accept the character of the people and I will accept their character as long as I am amongst them."

I would like to discuss how we can understand the meaning and implications of this important verse. The scholars of Qur'an say that every person that you meet will deal with you in one of two ways:

1. *Al-Ihsaan*; they will do more than what is required of them, or in other words, go above and beyond.

2. *At-Taqseer*; they will deal with you with deficiency, or in other words, do less than they should.

The scholars reflect on this verse and say that you should forgive the people of deficiency (*taqseer*), and with regard to your dealing with others, you should embody excellence (*ihsaan*) in every way possible. What they mean to say here is that there will be people who will give you a hard time despite you dealing with them in an excellent manner, but Allah has told us to turn away from them and to not allow them to drag us down to their level.

In addition to this, there is another famous Hadith in which we see how the Companions and their children nurtured themselves with the traditions of the Prophet ﷺ with regards to their dealings. Yusuf bin Malik al-Makki said that he used to undertake accounting for a group of orphans. There was one orphan who had been cheated out of a thousand dirhams. The orphans would work and the guardians would collect the money and then hand it to them. Yusuf was able to obtain two thousand dirhams from the guardian, but instead of taking this amount the orphan told him that the Prophet ﷺ said, "Honour the trust of the one who entrusted you with something and do not betray the one who betrays you." The orphan was essentially saying that because this person stole one thousand from him, it did not give him the right to take two thousand in return.[50]

This is mentioned in many different narrations and it poses many interesting issues of jurisprudence, as well as issues of social justice and how we understand transactions in Islam. There were times that the Prophet Muhammad ﷺ would allow people to take from someone when they were withholding from their rights. A well-known incident is of when Hind came to the Prophet ﷺ and complained that her husband was tight-fisted and did not give her enough money to cover expenses. The Prophet ﷺ told her that she could take her right, by taking what she needs for herself and her child but not anymore, in other words, take in a way that is reasonable. In this situation, there was an established right that was not being fulfilled. The Prophet ﷺ gave us permission in the jurisprudence (*fiqh*) that when there is no grey area, and someone withholds something that we are entitled to, we can take our right. However, we cannot take something that we are not entitled to as that involves treachery (*khiyana*), and we must not stoop to the level of the one who wrongs us.

Imam Ibn-Taymiyyah also commented on the narration of the orphan, saying that if someone is wronged, the first thing that they should do is go to the authorities to try and receive their rights; they should not attempt to take it back in an unlawful way such as stealing because it perpetuates problems in society.

When Uthman, may Allah be pleased with him, was assassinated, Ali, may Allah be pleased with him, emphasised that they needed to make sure that the people that killed Uthman were held accountable but to ensure that only those who were definitely and directly involved were punished. What we learn from this is that we should not become vengeful and become like the one who wronged us. On some occasions we may even be able to forgive the person, however, we should not enable their injustice. The first thing that the Prophet ﷺ mentioned in the Hadith was that we forgive the one that wrongs us, but this doesn't mean that we allow the one who wronged us to go unaccounted. If we do not hold that person to account, we are in essence enabling them to oppress others.

The Prophet ﷺ also said in the Hadith that we should spend on those who withhold from us. The scholars provided many different connotations to describe this:

1. If we find ourselves in a situation where we are in need and someone withholds from us, but then the situation changes and they are in need, we should not withhold from them.

2. Within the family dynamic a person who is responsible for others does not fulfil their obligation in the way that they should, but as time goes on, we find ourselves in the position of obligation, we should not withhold their rights.

3. We try to uphold the ties of kinship with someone who cuts us off, unless there is a fear that by maintaining the relationship, we open ourselves up to abuse.

The Prophet Muhammad ﷺ taught us these ideals and we see them exemplified in his life (*Sunnah*). One example is of trust (*amaan*); the Messenger ﷺ was entrusted with the possessions of Abu Jahl, Uqba bin Abu Moeet and Amr bin Aas, before he began calling to Islam. After he became a Prophet, they placed a bounty on his head and wanted him killed, however, when the Prophet Muhammad ﷺ was going to migrate to Madinah from Makkah, he ensured that his son-in-law Ali, may Allah be pleased with him, returned the possessions to their rightful owners. We should not betray the one who betrays us, nor should we deal with them in the way that they dealt with us.

A more recent example of these ethics is seen through Umar Mukhtar, the Libyan warrior who fought imperialism in the early twentieth century. They had captured two Italians during battle and one of his generals said to him, "Why don't we make an example of them like they do to us?" Umar Mukhtar replied, "We are not people who kill our prisoners." The general then said, "But they do it to us," to which Umar replied, "They are not our teachers." What he meant by this was that we do not learn our ethics from people who wrong us, if we did, we would become just like our enemies.

We also saw this when the Prophet ﷺ conquered Makkah and he stood upon Mount Safa with an army behind him; and the army consisted of the same Companions (*sahabah*) who had lost family members and much more at the hands of the *Quraysh*. The Prophet ﷺ asked the *Quraysh*, "What do you think I should do with you?" They did not have any real answer to give him, and the Prophet Muhammad ﷺ then told them, "Go, for you are free. There is no blame on you today."

Ibn Qayyim commented on this and said that by asking the *Quraysh* this question, the Prophet ﷺ first established the proof (*hujjah*) against them, and then he chose to pardon them, responding with excellence (*ihsaan*) by letting them know that they would not face any act of vengeance.

When reading or listening to such stories, many beautiful aspects get lost because we unfortunately have a habit of cutting to the chase. We do not look into the processes, such as why the Prophet ﷺ said certain things or did certain things, and thus we miss out on the profound wisdom behind his decisions that also highlight a lot about his character.

There is another wonderful story of a man named Ghawrath who held a sword over the head of the Prophet ﷺ and said, "Oh Muhammad, who will stop me from killing you?" The Prophet ﷺ replied confidently and said, "Allah." Ghawrath was extremely surprised by his fearlessness, and he dropped the sword. The Prophet ﷺ then picked the sword up and held it over Ghawrath and said, "And who will protect you from me?" Ghawrath replied, "Be generous," to which the Prophet ﷺ told him to go free.[51] This is yet another prime example of "they are not our teachers," as we should not drop to the level of those who have wronged us, we set higher standards for ourselves and provide lessons in good character.

Similarly, when Salahuddin had conquered Jerusalem, he set an example for the Muslims and non-Muslims alike by not treating the Crusaders in the manner that they had treated Muslims. He did not allow mutilation or rape or any such action against them. By choosing this approach, not only did he win Jerusalem, but he also won the hearts of everyone who heard about him.

Before we go on to conclude this chapter, it is fitting to mention here something that Ibn Qayyim said which is very deep. He said that sometimes a person wrongs you and you have no idea how or why they wronged you, and you may ask yourself what you did to that person to deserve such treatment. Ibn Qayyim then goes on to say that every person you have ever met or interacted with, has either been shown excellence (*ihsaan*) or deficiency (*taqseer*) from you, and it is possible that Allah is purifying you for a deficiency that you showed to someone else or an *ihsaan* that you took advantage of, by having deficiency shown to you in order to balance the scales. We never know how Allah is working to balance the scales, and we should be thankful to Him for keeping us away from major transgressions. Something that most of us can relate to is when parents say to their children that they did not behave in such a way when they were younger; however, when we think more deeply, the parents may have said or done something to displease their own parents when they were younger without a second thought at the time.

Thus, we have learned in this chapter that the Messenger of Allah ﷺ and his Companions suffered greatly at the hands of the *Quraysh*, but he did not treat them like for like. He taught us that we should never respond to injustice with injustice. Abu Jahl tortured and mutilated Sumayyah, may Allah be pleased with her, but Abu Jahl was not treated in the same way even in battle. As Muslims we must always take the higher moral ground. We cannot use an act of injustice that was done to us as an excuse to behave injustly towards others who are blameless, nor towards the person who wronged us. We cannot allow injustice (*dhulm*) that was done to us, to make us unjust (*dhaalim*).

May Allah protect us from becoming wrongdoers and oppressors, and from becoming like those that have harmed us. We ask Allah to allow us to choose the higher moral ground in all situations, so that we may do what is pleasing to Him. Amin.

10

EVERYBODY ELSE DOES IT

Hudhaifa narrated that the Messenger of Allah said: "Do not become 'yes-men' saying, 'If the people do good then we will do good, and if they do wrong then we will do wrong.' Instead, make up your own minds: if the people do good then you will do good, and if they do evil, then you will not behave unjustly."

WE SHOULD NOT be influenced by those who transgress; we cannot let someone with bad character teach us their ways, nor can we use their injustice towards us as an excuse to cause injustice to them. The Prophet ﷺ said that we should fulfil the trust of the one who entrusts us with something, to not betray the one who betrays us and to not deceive the one who deceives us. The idea of mercy and tolerance is to stop a person from stooping down to the level of the one who wrongs them, and this is one of the most profound lessons we learn from the biography of the Prophet Muhammad ﷺ.

The Hadith that we will cover in this chapter will highlight the point of not becoming involved in wrongdoing because everybody else around us is, and at the same time, not doing good while everybody else around is doing good.

Hudhaifa narrated that the Messenger of Allah ﷺ said, "Do not become 'yes-men' saying, 'If the people do good then we will do good, and if they do wrong then we will do wrong.' Instead, make up your own minds: if the people do good then you will do good, and if they do evil, then you will not behave unjustly."[52]

Most of the injustice that is committed in society is because that behaviour has become normalised with the concept of 'everyone else is doing it.' For example, if a society functions on bribes, then it is likely that everyone will think of it as normal despite it being impermissible (*haram*), the Prophet Muhammad ﷺ cursed the one who bribes and the one who accepts a bribe. However, it is unfortunate that people resign themselves to the notion of, 'if you can't stop them, join them'. Acts of injustice become far easier to justify when the majority of people are engaged in them. One such act is cheating with weights (*tatfeef*) which is a corrupt business practice that people are still involved in even today, so others around them think of it as acceptable too and do the same.

An example from recent history is that of Allen Brooks, a sixty-five-year-old black man from Dallas in America who was lynched publicly in 1910. A crowd gathered around him and took photos, which were then used as postcards. This was how normalised public lynching had become in the south of the United States; families would come out and have a picnic whilst watching someone being lynched. They had lost their sense of sympathy and empathy towards other humans and would not think of the oppression towards black people as an injustice. It shows that the standards of a society dictate the behaviour of the people living within it, causing evil to become normalised, and this is why the Prophet Muhammad ﷺ taught us that the least we can do is to hate acts of evil in our hearts.

Even if an evil is common in society (regardless of whether it is a moral sin or a transgression against someone else), our hearts should not be comfortable with it, nor should we conform to it. There may be a system that is based on interest (usury) which buries people in debts, and thus paves the way for more problems such as suicide or stealing; but this does not allow us as Muslims to accept it or to become a part of it. Yet, most people become affected by widespread sins and oppression and eventually cave in and say, "I will have to do this to get by".

Allah also says in the Qur'an in *Surah al-An'am* 6:116: *"And if you obey most of those upon the earth, they will mislead you from the way of Allah."*

This message is in our creed, but it also transfers into our daily practices. Our tongues can easily succumb to transgression; if those around us are involved in lying or backbiting, we could also fall into the same trap because it has become normalised behaviour.

Imam Ibn Qudama, may Allah be pleased with him, reiterated this in his book *Mukhtasar Minhaj al-Qasideen*: "Through frequent exposure, a person begins perceiving corruption as trivial, and its effect and gravity fades. Thus, whenever a person regularly sees another person committing a major sin, he belittles the minor sins he himself commits… Similarly, if a scholar is seen wearing a silk garment or a gold ring, the people would aggressively denounce that. Yet, they can watch him sit in a long gathering where he does nothing but backbite people, yet they are not offended by that. Backbiting is far worse than wearing gold, but because of how frequently it is witnessed, hearts become desensitised to it."

This is a powerful paragraph, clearly stating that we become so desensitised to major sins because of how commonly they are committed, whereas we pay attention to and passionately object to trivial things, or matters that are of doubt even if we are not entirely sure if they are prohibited (*haram*).

Ibn Mas'ud, may Allah be pleased with him, said: "You should accustom yourself so that if everyone on the face of the earth disbelieved, you should still believe." What is meant here is that we should get ourselves out of the mindset that if everyone else is doing something, we are free to do the same. We cannot let others set low standards for us, we must set higher standards and ideals for ourselves and not let ourselves get carried away by what surrounds us. Also we must not allow ourselves to get accustomed to seeing others being wronged, as that normalises such behaviour and enables it further in society.

There is another important Hadith that I would like to mention here, in which the Prophet Muhammad ﷺ said: "Beware of belittling sins. Imagine a group of people who descend into a valley and they each bring their sticks. They all begin to throw their sticks into a fire until the fire becomes so huge that it consumes them all."[53]

He used this metaphor to explain that when every person contributes a small sin (and deems it insignificant), the whole of society suffers as a result.

Ibn Abbas relates: "There is no major sin if you seek forgiveness for it and there is no minor sin if you insist upon it."[54] Allah can pardon major sins if you seek forgiveness from them, but if we insist and repeat minor sins then it becomes a bigger offence. We should not think of minor sins as irrelevant, as they add up and can cause more damage than a single major sin.

Furthermore, we allow evil to become common within society by enabling it to happen in the first place. And regarding this, Al 'Urs bin 'Amirat al-Kind narrated from the Prophet ﷺ: "When a sin is committed, he who saw it and disapproved of it will be like the one who was not present; but he who did not see it but approved of it will be like he who was present when it was committed."[55] This Hadith highlights the need to take a hard stance against injustice by at least condemning it, so we don't enable it in any way.

Abdullah bin Mas'ud, also narrated from the Messenger of Allah ﷺ: "The first defect that destroyed Banu Israel was that a man (of them) met another man and said, 'Oh so-and-so, fear Allah and abandon what you are doing, for it is not lawful for you. He then met him the next day and that did not prevent him from eating with him, drinking with him and sitting with him. When they did so, Allah mingled their hearts with each other."[56]

This Hadith shows that the man did not take a strong stance against the evil, his disavowal was not serious, and he took the sin lightly. We should not be like this man; instead, we should stand firmly against injustices and not allow ourselves to become desensitised to them.

When looking at it from a jurisprudence (*fiqh*) perspective, we may wonder if it is permissible to sometimes participate in something that is disliked in Islam, but has become common in the society that we live in. It is permissible; however, it is only permissible under certain conditions:

1. In times of dire need or necessity.

2. If our life is in danger.

3. To avert a greater evil. For example, you may be in a position where you have to choose between two evils, and you engage in the lesser evil.

4. If you cannot escape the evil entirely, so you only engage in it to the extent necessary and do not enthusiastically embrace it.

An example of this could be interest (*riba*); as Muslims we are prohibited from directly engaging in interest, but due to where we live, we may have to engage in that system to some extent, whether we like it or not.

Ibn Taymiyyah, may Allah be pleased with him, also said: "Hearing is not like listening." What this means is that we have no control over what is being said, but we can control whether we are paying attention to it or not and we can hate it in our heart like the Prophet Muhammad ﷺ told us to.

I would like to mention here a very interesting Hadith narrated by the Prophet Muhammad ﷺ about an event that took place before he received the revelation of the Qur'an:

Zayd bin Amr bin an-Nufayl never worshipped idols, he was a follower of Ibrahim, may the blessings of Allah be upon him. The Prophet Muhammad ﷺ said: "I remember sitting in a gathering where they would eat meat sacrificed for the idols and I would not partake of that meat." When they presented the food to Zayd, he stood up and said, "Allah created you, provides for you and for your animals and yet you sacrifice for other than him." The Prophet ﷺ was amazed watching Zayd take on the powerful people at that time. Similarly, when the Arabs were making tawaf around the Kaaba, Zayd would stand with his back to the Kaaba and say, "None of you is upon the religion of Ibrahim." He would also cry and say, "Oh Allah, if only I knew the best way to worship you I would, but I do not know."[57]

He died before Muhammad ﷺ received prophethood, but he died as a monotheist; he believed in Allah and was searching for the truth. However, Zayd's son Saeed became one of the first people to accept Islam and is one of the ten promised Paradise. Saeed, may Allah be pleased with him, asked the Prophet ﷺ about his father's fate, and the Prophet ﷺ replied, "On the Day of Judgement Zayd will be standing all by himself as his own nation." Zayd was the opposite of a 'yes-man' – he didn't care about the norms of society, he chose not to partake in their acts of ignorance and instead searched for the truth sincerely and earnestly. He is a noble example to whom we should look to for guidance in terms of not conforming to what everyone else may be doing in society without thinking about our words and actions.

The story of Zayd shows us how monotheism and natural inclination (*fitrah*) lead a person to justice. Ibn Abbas, may Allah be pleased with him, said that when the Arabs went to bury their daughters, Zayd would go to rescue the girls and bring them to his home to raise them until they reached the age of marriage, after which he would marry them off. Zayd was doing this before Allah revealed that female infanticide was prohibited (*haram*) and unjust; he knew this practice was wrong and he did not accept it. He took whatever action was necessary in order to stop innocent girls from being buried alive as he did not conform to the evil norms of his society, and the Prophet ﷺ praised him for this behaviour.

The Hadith narrated by Hudhaifa at the beginning of this chapter gives way to many different events and statements that enable us to understand the importance of not conforming to injustice. One very powerful statement is from Ibn Taymiyyah who said: "Whoever assists an oppressor will one day be tested by that same oppressor." (*Majmu Al-Fatwa*) We may enable a form of oppression because it is of benefit to us, but it will eventually come back and haunt us.

I would like to end this chapter by sharing another wonderful story with you that really hits home the message of the Hadith mentioned at the beginning of this chapter. It is narrated by Abdullah bin Zubair bin Aslam (Aslam was the son of Umar bin al-Khattab, and so Abdullah was Umar's great-grandson): "Aslam said, 'While I was in disguise with Umar bin al-Khattab in Madinah during one of his frequent night patrols to survey the condition of his people, we overheard a milkmaid refusing to obey her mother's order to dilute the milk with water and sell adulterated milk. When her mother insisted that Umar would be none the wiser, the girl replied, 'Oh mother! By Allah! I would never obey him in public and disobey him in private. For if Umar will not come to know it, the Lord of Umar surely knows!' Upon hearing this conversation, Umar gave instructions for the door of their house to be marked and for enquiries to be made as to who they were and if the daughter was married or not.' Aasim was the only son of Umar who was not married at that time.

The following morning, Umar said, 'Oh Aslam, pass by that house and purchase from the girl to see if she kept her resolve,' and so he did and learned that the milk was unadulterated as she had vowed. Umar summoned the girl and her mother to his court and told them what he had heard. As a reward, he proposed to marry the girl to his son Aasim.

She accepted and from this union a girl was born who was named Layla, who would in due course become the mother of Umar bin Abd al-Aziz."

We can clearly see here that the girl refused to do what everybody else was doing because she knew that Allah was watching, and it was wrong to cheat. Her piety and truthfulness had earned her a wonderful husband in the form of the son of the Caliph. She was rewarded with a place in the household of the head of the state after being in a poor situation, and she also went on to become the grandmother of another head of state. Our intentions and our actions can reap rewards in our life here on earth, and most certainly in the Hereafter.

May Allah grant us sincerity and piety, and allow us to resist the urge to conform to the evils in society. Amin.

11

THE COMPREHENSIVENESS OF *TATFEEF* (SHORT-CHANGING)

It was narrated that Ibn Abbas said, "When the Prophet ﷺ came to al-Madinah, they were the worst people in weights and measures. Then Allah, Glorious is He, revealed: "Woe to the mutaffifeen (those who shortchange others)," and they became the best of people in how they dealt with weights and measures after that."

IN THIS CHAPTER we will focus on a specific financial interaction that has been highlighted by the Prophet Muhammad ﷺ and broadening our understanding of how it applies to everyday life. Short-changing or cheating (*tatfeef*) has been addressed explicitly because of its ill effects on society. The Hadith that we are looking at is narrated in Ibn Majah:

It was narrated that Ibn Abbas said, "When the Prophet ﷺ came to Madinah, they were the worst people in weights and measures. Then Allah, Glorious is He, revealed: 'Woe to the *mutaffifeen* (those who short-change others),' and they became the best of people in how they dealt with weights and measures after that."

The language he uses here is very strong in referring to the people who cheat others as the worst of people. There was a reputation in the markets of Madinah of people who used to cheat with their weights and measures when selling, and so Allah revealed His disappointment with them. After the verse was revealed in *Surah al-Mutaffifeen*, Ibn Abbas mentioned that those same people became the best of people in terms of the way they dealt with their weights. People started to take very close account of how they would do business with one another, so as to ensure that nobody was being wronged.

There are two types, or aspects, to short-changing which we can understand further after looking at the following verses from *Surah al-Mutaffifeen* 83:1-3: *"Woe to those who give less (than due), those who, when they take a measure from people, take it in full. But if they give by measure or by weight to them, they cause loss"*:

1. The first is when someone takes or buys a product, they will take its measure in full.

2. The second is when that person is in the position of selling or distribution themselves, they cause loss to others by withholding from the full weight or measurement of the product.

A newer or more current example of this problem (taking maximum but giving the minimum) is seen in the concept of insurance. Whilst in Islam the concept of pooling money is acceptable, for example a group of fishermen pooling some money in order for it to be used when one of their boats is damaged, the concept of insurance today has an aspect of gambling to it as the insurance company ideally wants to give you as little as possible, but collect their full payment from you.

Looking into the explanation (*tafseer*) of the above verses, we come to learn that there was a man in Madinah named Abu Juhayna, who was a master salesman, about whom these verses were revealed. When he would collect his payments, he would tip the scales a little with his hand, and he became rich through this form of cheating which is known as *gharrah*.

Ibn Katheer, may Allah be pleased with him, said that *tatfeef* is to cheat or be stingy or to be unfair in the way that we collect and the way that we give back. He also made it a point to mention how Allah ends the opening passage of *Surah al-Mutaffifeen* 83:4-6: *"Do they not think that they will be resurrected, on a tremendous Day – the Day when mankind will stand before the Lord of the worlds?"* When everybody is gathered before Allah, the Lord of the worlds on the Day of Judgement, Allah will fulfil their rights as the scales of Allah are unlike any other scales. There can be no doubt that the scales of Allah will do the slightest form of injustice because our Lord is the Most Just.

It is narrated by Sulayman in Fath Al Bari that If you were to put the entire heavens and earth on the scales that Allah will use on the Day of Judgement, it would fit them and it would weigh them accurately. Allah will not cheat anybody on that day; rather, He may tip the scale, out of His Mercy, towards good but He will never tip the scale towards evil. Allah is Most Merciful and He does and will do the opposite of what He condemned in the opening passage of *Surah al-Mutaffifeen*. One example of His Mercy is that the declaration of faith, the *kalimah*, will weigh very heavily on the scales and will outweigh the bad deeds of some of His servants. We are inherently deficient and are incapable of giving Allah what He deserves, but when Allah gives, He gives us more than we deserve as He is *Ash-Shakoor*.

The goal is to exemplify the attributes of Allah when there is a possible human application of the same attributes; this is meaning to say that because Allah does the opposite of *tatfeef* with us, we should strive to behave similarly and in accordance to those attributes as that is the best way to fulfil the right of that attribute.

Furthermore, one point we should take into consideration is the fact that it is much easier to do *tatfeef* today than it was in the past. This is because trading with currency is now mostly done through computer systems, and a simple click or press of a button can cause huge financial implications. We also do not pay enough attention to the numbers and it becomes easier for people to cheat, for example rounding up for ourselves but rounding down for others.

This is something that must be given its due importance, as it was seen as a priority when the Prophet ﷺ had first arrived in Madinah. Allah did not wait to condemn this practice, and we must also take the act of shortchanging someone (*tatfeef*) very seriously.

Short-changing *(tatfeef)* itself is a very broad concept, we often tend to restrict it to the financial aspect, but it applies to several different contexts such as:

1. *Tatfeef* of your Lord

   - People try to cheat Allah, but in reality, they cheat themselves. A great example of this is of when Umar bin al-Khattab, may Allah be pleased with him, left after performing the *Asr* prayer and met a man who had not attended. Umar asked him what had kept him from the prayer, and even though the man gave a good reason, Umar replied to him, "You have short-changed yourself."[58]

   - There is also a Hadith, in which it has been reported that someone was rushing through their prayer and the Prophet Muhammad ﷺ told him that he had cheated in his prayer and made him redo it.[59] In every position of prayer, we should take a moment where our body settles in that position rather than rushing without any pauses; it is within those pauses that we can recite the supplications and appreciate the connection with our Lord. By rushing through the prayer, we are short-changing it and not giving its due – we must remember that this time is for Allah.

2. *Tatfeef* with regards to teachers and students

   - The scholars have said that the mannerisms of a student should include early arrival to their lectures or classes. By showing that they are prepared and enthusiastic, taking notes and being attentive, they give the knowledge that is being given to them its due right. Being distracted by a mobile phone or anything else whilst someone is trying to teach is also *tatfeef*.

   - The Prophet Muhammad ﷺ was once sitting with his Companions, he had a ring on his finger that he kept getting distracted by, and was not giving the Companions the attention that he normally would. As soon as he ﷺ noticed this he threw his ring aside and apologised to his Companions for not giving them his undivided attention. Not giving your students your full attention is also a form of short-changing them (*tatfeef*).

- If a teacher does not prepare properly in advance, it is a form of *tatfeef*. By arriving to teach unprepared, a teacher is short-changing their students by not teaching them properly even though they took out the time to come and learn.

- It is also *tatfeef* to favour some students over others, as you are not giving the other students their full right upon you. Being lenient to one student but unfair to another is cheating the student.

3. *Tatfeef* in the family context

- Giving preference to one child over another is *tatfeef*. Your children should be treated equally without preference.

- Misdirecting your anger towards your children is also *tatfeef*; becoming upset or angry at something or someone else and then taking it out on your child is unfair to the child. The child has done nothing wrong to deserve your anger and this is something we must be careful of.

- Arguing with your spouse in front of your children can also be a form of *tatfeef*, short-changing your children as they are made to suffer and witness the argument.

- Taking your full right but giving your spouse less than their full right is *tatfeef*. A beautiful example of this can be found with Ibn Abbas, may Allah be pleased with him, who said, "I love that I beautify myself for my wife just like I love that she beautifies herself for me. On the Day of Judgement Allah will ask me about the rights that were due upon me and the rights that I gave. I want the rights that I gave to be more than the rights I took so that Allah can fill that gap with *ihsaan*."

Allah also mentions in *Surah al-Baqarah* 2:228: *"And for them (the wives) is the like of that which is upon them"* – meaning to say that women have the same rights that are due upon them from men. Allah has legislated this equality in terms of fulfilment of marital rights.

If a husband makes a mistake and the wife says, "You have never done anything for me," this is *tatfeef* on her part as she is not acknowledging or appreciating the good that he has done for her in the past.

An interesting ruling with regards to equal rights is where Imam Uthaymeen was once asked by a woman about the permissibility of voluntary fasting without her husband's permission because he was negligent in his rights to her. The answer that was given to her was that she had the right to do so to even out the scales; as the husband rebelled, she also had the right to rebel.

4. *Tatfeef* in the workplace

- If an employee shows excellence (*ihsaan*) in their work by doing overtime or similar out of their own goodwill and their employer pays them well, this isn't considered *tatfeef*. However, if the workload is more than the employee can handle and they aren't being paid enough, this can be *tatfeef* on the employers' part.

- If an employee is being paid well but falls short in their obligations, this is *tatfeef* as they are being paid more than they deserve for the amount of work that they are doing.

We should aim to respond to any evil or short-change that we experience with justice at the bare minimum, we do not go beyond justice, but the best response would be to respond with excellence (*ihsaan*). It is better for us to forgive their *tatfeef* and not have a like-for-like attitude. Although almost every relationship has some imbalance to it with one party doing more, we should ensure that the gap does not become so big that injustice or unfairness begins to take place.

A famous incident that took place in the Caliphate of Umar bin al-Khattab, may Allah be pleased with him, showcases *tatfeef* very well: A man once came to Umar bin al-Khattab complaining of his son's disobedience to him. Umar then called the son and asked him about the negligence of his father's rights, to which the son said, "Oh *Ameer al-Mu'mineen*! Doesn't a child have rights over his father?" Umar replied, "Certainly." The son then asked, "What are they Ameer al-Mu'mineen?" Umar replied, "That he should choose a good mother, give him a good name, and teach him the Qur'an." The son then said, "Oh Ameer al-Mu'mineen! My father did none of these. My mother was a magian (fire worshipper), he gave me the name of Jul'a (meaning beetle) and he did not teach me a single word of the Qur'an."

Umar then turned to the father and said, "You have come to me to complain about the disobedience of your son, yet you have failed in your duty to him before he failed in his duty to you. You have done wrong to him before he wronged you."

Whilst parents are capable of doing *tatfeef* to their children, it is more common that a child shows ingratitude towards their parents. As they grow older and more independent, they begin to short-change their parents.

Imam al-Ghazali mentioned that the believer (*mu'min*) has the characteristic of doing things to completion. A *mu'min* fulfils the rights of others and doesn't slack in their responsibilities; sloppiness or leaving things incomplete is to shortchange (*tatfeef*). However, being detail-oriented and wanting to do something to the best of our ability is the opposite of *tatfeef*. Modern versions of *tatfeef* could be demanding full payment but not doing the job properly or fixing the scales in the gold market, a practice that still exists.

5. *Tatfeef* in brotherhood

> ● Muhammad bin Sireen said, "It is injustice to your brother that you mention the worst of what you know about him, but you don't mention his good qualities."

- Imam Shafi said, "I swear that if I did good ninety-nine times out of one-hundred, and I made one mistake, they would count that one against me." Ignoring the good and waiting for someone to make a mistake to call them out is *tatfeef* towards your brother.

6. *Tatfeef* of the scholars

- Some people treat scholars as though they can do no wrong, whilst others wait for them to make the slightest mistake in order to point it out.

- Ibn Qayyim said about his teacher Ibn Taymiyyah, "All of the small mistakes of Ibn Taymiyyah don't matter because the Prophet Muhammad ﷺ said that a large body of water never becomes impure." What is meant here is that all the good that he had done outweighed the small mistakes and so his goodness was not affected by them. This is how we should also treat our scholars as they spend their lives doing and spreading good, we should not allow small mistakes to pollute the good (*khayr*).

When looking at the world today, we can see that there is an unfortunate global culture of *tatfeef*. It has become normalised in society due to people being selfish and greedy; and we can find that whenever there is more greed, there is also more *tatfeef*. We live in a time where people are self-oriented, we worry about ourselves and become narcissistic, paving the way for destructive behaviour.

Selflessness is becoming rare in our time, as believers it is important that we promote this characteristic in ourselves and in society. If everything becomes just about ourselves then our indulgences start to take precedence over the rights that other have upon us. It does not mean we should accept oppression or abuse, rather it means that we put others before ourselves as Allah says in *Surah al-Hashr* 59:9: *"And they would give preference over themselves even if they were in need."* We should not give our rights preference and instead make them secondary to the rights that others have upon us. However, once we start thinking about ourselves only, the gaps in society such as wealth, health and quality of life begin to widen. Rich people get richer, whilst the poor get poorer and this is a major injustice.

Many people base their relationships upon how much they must give and how much they can get in return. When it comes to the point that they have to give more to a person than they are receiving, then that person does not hold any importance anymore; they are only interested in that person whilst there is benefit for them, and this is *tatfeef*. It is important to remember that it is not limited to finance, *tatfeef* can also be spiritual and emotional.

We should remind ourselves that Allah says at the end of the passage, *"Do they not think that they will be resurrected, on a tremendous Day?"* (*Surah al-Mutaffifeen* 83:4-5)

Allah wants us to remember that we will be resurrected on a Mighty Day and He will be the judge, He will compensate those who were short-changed and fulfil the rights due to those people. Allah will not forfeit those rights as those rights are not His; Allah can forgive the sins and shortcomings that involve us and Him but when it comes to the rights of others, He will not forgive on their behalf as He has allowed them to forgive or have their rights fulfilled. In other words, the only right that Allah will not forfeit on the Day of Judgement is the right that was not His.

I would like to end the chapter with a Hadith in which the Prophet Muhammad ﷺ said that a person will fall short of one good deed of what is required for them to enter Paradise (*Jannah*), and he will ask people for help but not one person will offer one of their good deeds. People will be saying *"Nafsi, nafsi!"* on the Day of Judgement, meaning they will only be worried about themselves.

This example makes it clearer to understand that if we do or give just a little bit more than what is required in this world (*dunya*), we won't end up in the position that is illustrated in this Hadith. We should do the opposite of tatfeef, by taking less and giving more in order to ensure that we will not be held accountable for short-changing anyone on the Day of Judgement.

May Allah protect us from doing *tatfeef* with Him, our family, our friends, our community, our employers, and employees. Amin.

12

WHOEVER DECEIVES IS NOT FROM US

Abu Hurairah (ra) said, The Messenger of Allah ﷺ happened to pass by a heap of corn. He thrust his hand in it and his fingers felt wetness. He said to the owner of that heap of corn, "What is this?" He replied: "O Messenger of Allah! These have been drenched by rainfall." He remarked, "Why did you not place it on top so that the people might see it? Whoever deceives is not of us."

THE THEME OF this chapter is similar to the previous chapter, as it involves our interactions with other people. The Hadith is narrated by Abu Hurairah, may Allah be pleased with him:

The Messenger of Allah ﷺ happened to pass by a heap of corn. He put his hand in it and his fingers felt wetness. He said to the owner of that heap of corn, "What is this?" The owner replied, "Oh Messenger of Allah! These have been drenched by rainfall." The Prophet remarked,

"Why did you not place it on top so that the people might see it? Whoever deceives is not from us."[60]

In another version of this Hadith, the Prophet Muhammad ﷺ said, "Whoever deceives is not from me (not from the *ummah* of Rasool-Allah ﷺ). This does not mean that they are not Muslim, but it means that they are not behaving as the followers of the Prophet ﷺ should behave.

There is a profound meaning in the ending of this statement of the Prophet ﷺ in this Hadith; how can we claim to be committed to the Prophet Muhammad ﷺ and the followers of the Prophet Muhammad ﷺ (his *ummah*) if we deceive or cheat the very same people? We do not have true allegiance to the *ummah* if we are deceiving them to gain benefit for ourselves.

Another Hadith that I would like to mention is again narrated by Abu Hurairah: The Messenger of Allah ﷺ told us that once there was a man who used to sell wine. He would dilute it with water, thereby cheating people. He was selling his wine on a ship journey that he was on with a group of people. One day a monkey got hold of all the money he had made and came on top of the ship's deck. He then proceeded to throw one coin onto the ship's deck and one into the sea until he reduced his money to half.[61] The monkey in this account was being used by Allah to purify this man's wealth because he had been cheating people.

There are many different stories that enable us to understand the seriousness of deceiving. One such story is narrated by at-Tabaraani who said that Jareer bin Abdullah al-Bajali, may Allah be pleased with him, asked his freed slave to buy a horse for him. So, the slave bought him a horse for three hundred dirhams, and he brought the horse and its owner to Jareer so that he could pay him. Jareer said to the owner of the horse, "Your horse is worth more than three hundred dirhams. Will you sell it for four hundred dirhams?" He said, "Yes, oh Abu Abdullah." Then he said, "Your horse is worth more than four hundred dirhams. Will you sell it for five hundred dirhams?" He kept increasing it by one hundred each time, with the owner agreeing and Jareer saying that his horse is worth more than that, until he reached eight hundred dirhams and then bought it at that price. Jareer then said concerning this matter, "I gave my oath of allegiance (*bay'ah*) to the Messenger of Allah ﷺ that I would be sincere towards every Muslim."

Jareer, may Allah be pleased with him, did not have to keep increasing the price of the horse, but his piety, sincerity and fear of cheating someone made him increase the price. It would have remained a *halal* transaction if Jareer bought the horse for three hundred dirhams, or even if he bargained over the price to lower it slightly but the fact that he paid five hundred dirhams more shows how seriously he took this matter.

It is also befitting here to share three incidents involving Imam Abu Hanifa, may Allah be pleased with him, as we can gain a lot from him. He was not only the founder of one of the four major schools of law (*fiqh*), he was also known as one of the most wealthy and honest merchants in the marketplaces of Madinah.

1. Abu Hanifa once had a woman come to him and try to sell him something. He asked her how much it was for, and she said one hundred dirhams. He disagreed and said it is worth more, to which she said two hundred, and this carried on until Abu Hanifa called a man and asked him how much he thought it was worth and he said five hundred. Abu Hanifa then bought the item for five hundred dirhams.

2. Abu Hanifa stayed in business even after he became a scholar, and he had a partner named Hafs bin Abdul Rahman. On one occasion, Abu Hanifa saw that they had a garment with a defect in it so he told Hafs to ensure that he showed this defect to any potential customer before selling it. Hafs had forgotten to do this and had sold the garment to a customer without showing the defect. When Abu Hanifa returned, he saw that the garment had been sold and asked Hafs if he had told the customer about the defect, to which Hafs replied that he forgot. Abu Hanifa then asked how much he had sold it for, and then gave the entire day's profit to charity and broke his partnership with Hafs. After this he told his son to go and search for the customer so that they could inform him of the defect.

3. Once Abu Hanifa asked his son Hammad to take an item off the shelf for a customer, as he was taking it off the shelf he sent *salawat* (salAllahu alayhi wasallam) upon the Prophet

but did so in a way that made it seem as though he was praising the item in front of the customer. Abu Hanifa heard this and said, "Indeed upon him (Muhammad ﷺ) is peace and blessings but you have praised the garment, so I am not selling it." By praising the garment, Hammad had increased the value of it and Abu Hanifa did not want to take advantage of the customer who may have been led to believe that the garment was something special.

These examples illustrate just how high Abu Hanifa had set standards for himself. He did not want to risk committing the slightest bit of injustice, and we should seek inspiration from this. Ibn Hajar said that it is injustice to hide a defect in an item and then to sell it at a price that the customer would not have paid had they been aware of the defect. Selling items by hiding defects becomes a form of deception.

Furthermore, the Prophet Muhammad ﷺ mentioned in a Hadith that "Every traitor will have a banner on the Day of Resurrection, and it will read: This is the person who betrayed so-and-so."[62] Betrayal is a form of deception and it is something that we must avoid as it could cost us our place in Paradise, as the Prophet ﷺ mentioned in another Hadith narrated in Bukhari, "God said: There are three whom I will oppose on the Day of Resurrection; a man who gave his word and then betrayed it, a man who sold a free man into slavery and kept the money, and a man who hired someone, benefited from his labour, then did not pay his wages." When we learn of this Hadith, it becomes paramount that we do not commit any of these injustices, even in the slightest, otherwise we risk having Allah oppose us on the Day of Reckoning.

Ibn Hajar also said that the worst type of deception is that which is done with regards to religion. It may not seem like a big thing, but even saying "Wallahi" about something that is not true is a form of religious deception. Imam al-Qurtubi wrote about the people who would try to appear religious in the marketplace so that others would want to do business with them, when in reality, they were not religious. In modern times where there is an increase in online shopping, sellers can easily cheat customers by putting on false appearances and boosting their ratings with fake reviews; so not only do they deceive by selling their products with false claims, they also put on a fake appearance and make themselves out to be trustworthy and successful.

Another powerful Hadith narrated by Abu Hurairah, may Allah be pleased with him, says: "The Messenger of Allah ﷺ said, 'Towards the end of time there will come men who will swindle with religion for materialistic ends, deceiving the people in soft skins of sheep, their tongues are sweeter than sugar but their hearts are the hearts of wolves. Allah (Mighty and Sublime is He) says, 'Is it Me you try to delude or is it against Me whom you conspire? I swear to send upon these people a trial (*fitnah*) that leaves them utterly devoid of reason.'"[63]

This Hadith explains that people will use otherwise religious actions or deeds for the purpose of gaining materialistic things; rather than seeking the Hereafter, they will seek the life of this world (*dunya*) and cheat people in the name of religion.

Zahr al-Shahree wrote a book called *Al-Ghish* in which he discussed many different manifestations of deception (*ghish*), some of which we will go through to understand the context with more detail:

1. **Deception in business transactions**

   - Traders selling fruit or vegetables may deceive customers by putting leaves or paper at the bottom of the basket to make it seem fuller than it is, or they may put the best quality produce at the top to make the customer believe that all the produce is of the same quality as they see on the top.

   - Merchants mixing food oil with perfume to increase the quantity and then pouring it into perfume bottles to sell.

   - Some sellers buy a product (by weight) in light packaging and then replace the packaging with something much thicker and heavier to increase its weight. They then sell the product at an increased price due to the weight of the contents and the wrapper. Also, things like replacing the tag with another tag or replacing the packaging with more expensive looking packaging to create a false appearance of the product and make it seem like something that it is not.

   - Someone selling clothes may do some light mending on clothes that were otherwise flawed due to being worn before or becoming old. They then sell the clothes by disguising the flaw and not informing the customer that the garment has been mended; thus, selling it as if it were brand new.

- Some shopkeepers light their store with certain colours or levels of brightness in order to make their products look better than they are, such as making rough products look smoother and ugly products look attractive.

- Some goldsmiths mix gold with copper or other metals, and then sell the product as though it is pure gold.

- Some sellers take a refurbished product and sell it as if it is brand new. (This is extremely easy to do in modern times with online shopping; sellers can buy something second-hand or refurbished and market it as brand new without customers ever knowing).

- Some traders turn back the odometer on a car to fool the buyer into believing that the car has done less mileage than it has. They may also repaint or disguise certain areas of the car, and not inform buyers of any previous accidents or damage to the car.

- Some people will praise a product excessively and falsely swear by Allah that it is better than it really is and will fabricate reasons as to why they are selling it or why the customer should purchase it.

- Some sellers will do superficial bidding on a product to create an artificial inflation on the price of the product; the seller could have a friend in the shop with them and have the friend act as though they are a customer, when a real customer walks in, they begin bidding on the same product to force the customer to purchase it.

- Butchers inflate the animal carcass or have the animal drink lots of water before being slaughtered to give a false impression that the animal has lots of meat on it, and then sell it at a much higher price than it is worth.

The Prophet Muhammad ﷺ forbade all such practices, as deception can eventually become a habit. Giving false impressions of something is deception, whether it is about ourselves as sellers or the product that we are selling. Once a person learns how to deceive, they will find new ways to cheat people in other aspects of life in addition to business.

2. Deception in marriage

- Concealing a sickness or fault (such as physical) when meeting a potential spouse. This does not, however, include spiritual issues that occurred in the past, as we are not obliged to share past mistakes or sins after repenting for them and changing our ways.

- Concealing financial troubles such as debt or lack of income before getting married; these issues must be disclosed openly to a potential spouse. Disguising things for the sake of swaying the person's decision towards you and gaining their commitment is deception.

- Some guardians unfortunately do not put in any effort to find out about a potential suitor for their daughters. They do not learn about his religious commitment, or his personality and thus they cheat against their own daughter.

- Some people may know that someone was abusive towards his previous wife, and not tell the next potential wife of that person, even if they come to ask about them. The Prophet ﷺ was wholly honest and advised women openly against marrying people with dangerous flaws in their character.

- It is also deception when people overly praise a potential suitor in front of the family whose daughter he wishes to marry. Scholars have said that praising someone in a way that is not befitting to them (i.e. describing the person as someone who prays five times a day and is righteous when in fact he is not) is deception, and also dangerous as it is a sacred bond that is being put at risk. An example of this can be found in the story of Bilal bin Rabah, may Allah be pleased with him. A man who claimed to be the brother of Bilal, through ties of migration, wished to marry an Arab woman, and the family of the bride said, "If you bring Bilal with you, we will approve the marriage." Bilal then went with him and said, "I am Bilal bin Rabah and this is my brother, we were slaves and Allah has freed us. My brother has shortcomings, so if you want to approve the marriage, you may do so, and if you do not approve the marriage, you may do so." Bilal did not falsely praise his brother but told them openly about his flaws.

- Hiding other wives or getting married to a second wife secretly is deception. The Prophet Muhammad ﷺ made it clear that marriage should be publicised, or in other words, it should be announced and be made known to the community. This is to honour the rights of the wives and to ensure that there is no room for secrecy, hence there is accountability on the husband's part.

3. Deception in sincere advice (*naseeha*) or legal ruling (*fatwa*)

- The Prophet ﷺ said that anyone who gives a legal opinion (*fatwa*) in ignorance, the sin is upon them.[64] Some people do not like to admit they do not know something, they will give a misguided or misinformed opinion, and this is a form of deception.

- To give the wrong advice intentionally to a person is also a form of deception.

- Narrated by Abu Hurairah, the Prophet ﷺ said: "If anyone is given a legal decision ignorantly, the sin rests on the one who gave it." Sulayman al-Mahri added in his version:

"If anyone advises his brother knowing that guidance lies in another direction, he has deceived him."

- One example of deception through advice is of Maymoon bin Mihran who said that he saw a woman whom he wanted to marry and so he asked a friend for advice regarding her. The friend replied to Maymoon saying that she was not suitable because he had seen her kiss a man. Maymoon took this advice but later found out that his friend had married the same woman. He went to ask his friend why he had married the woman even though he saw her kiss a man, and his friend told him that the man she kissed was her father. Although he did tell the truth about the woman kissing a man, his intention was to deceive Maymoon, and so he had withheld the rest of the truth and misguided Maymoon.

- Misguiding someone to do something that is detrimental to them because you do not want them to interfere with your own success.

The Prophet Muhammad ﷺ said, "If any ruler with the authority to govern Muslims dies while he is deceiving them, Allah will forbid Paradise for him."[65] Although this Hadith is referring to those in governance or leadership positions, we should think about it on a personal level and consider our relationship with those whom we have some level of authority over.

4. Cheating on job applications

- Exaggerating your virtues when applying for a position is permissible as long as the exaggeration is within acceptable boundaries. For example, if you sincerely consider yourself to be a responsible person or a good leader, it is permissible to slightly exaggerate in your description about yourself as long as you are not being deceptive. It becomes impermissible when you step out of the boundaries by lying or being deceptive regarding your education, qualifications or characteristics.

- Grey areas such as this are governed by piety. For example, when Yusuf, may the blessings of Allah be upon him, put himself forward for the post of minister in the government of the Pharaoh, he praised his own skillsets and knowledge in a way that was acceptable and did not exaggerate or falsify his skills.

- Claiming that you are a patient or calm person whilst you very well know that you are impatient is an outright lie. Doing so in order to try and get a job is deceptive and can cause issues if you are offered the job and are put in a position in which you are required to show patience.

Scholars have mentioned that there are three major problems that come with deception:

1. We are not paying attention to the One who is watching us. We believe that we have successfully deceived people, but we fail to remember that Allah cannot be deceived. This attitude shows a lack of God-consciousness and a significant weakness of faith as we feel that we will not be held accountable in this world.

2. We harm people by selling them a defective product or we deceive them with a false appearance.

3. We suffocate honesty through our deceptive ways, making it impossible for people doing business honestly to make a living. This creates a culture of cheating with more people becoming involved in deception because everyone else is doing it and it has become the norm in society.

We must keep in mind the Hadiths of the Prophet ﷺ to help us stay away from doing anything that involves cheating or deception or things that might make us from those who are not righteous. Last but not least it is important to note that these rules apply to all people, Muslim and non-Muslim alike. It is unacceptable to short-change, cheat or deceive anyone.

May Allah protect us from portraying ourselves as that which is not true, cheating or deceiving with appearances or short-changing anyone. May Allah also forgive us for our shortcomings and guide us towards the best practices for ourselves and our communities. Amin.

13

CORRUPT LAWYERS AND UNSERVED JUSTICE

Abu Umamah narrated that the Messenger of Allah ﷺ said, "Al-Haya' and Al-'Iy are two branches of faith, and Al-Badha and Al-Bayan are two branches of Hypocrisy."

BEFORE GOING ON to share this chapter's Hadith, I would like to give an introduction into this chapter's topic. In the previous chapter, we looked at deception and it is worth noting that some people are better at deception than others. It is a similar scenario when two people argue their case, and the one who is wrong does a better job of arguing their case and takes what is not rightfully theirs. Or, there may be a public dispute and one person makes an incorrect statement or gives a false impression, which leads to the grief of another person who has thus been wronged.

In Sahih Muslim, there is a chapter that talks about judging in accordance with the appearance. This essentially means that whoever is making the judgement will inevitably make a judgement based on what is apparent to them, however some people will do a better job of arguing their proofs. One such Hadith is narrated by Umm Salama, the wife of the Messenger of Allah ﷺ, who said: "The Prophet ﷺ said, 'You bring to me your disputes, and some of you might be better at arguing your case than others, so I give judgement on their behalf according to what I hear from them. Bear in mind, in my judgement, if I slice off anything for him from the right of his brother, he should not accept that, for I sliced off for him a portion from Hell.'"[66]

What we learn from this is whoever deceives a judge or the public, when a judgement is being made, they are taking a portion of Hellfire. If you find yourself in a favourable position, do not take anything extra that is not rightfully yours.

There is also another powerful story about the Prophet ﷺ and the inhabitants of Madinah. Two men came to the Messenger of Allah ﷺ with a dispute regarding old inheritance that had not been resolved for a long time. Neither of the men had any solid proof and so the Prophet ﷺ said to them, "Both of you have brought forward your cases, and one of you might do a better job of arguing your side but don't do it because that would be your portion of Hellfire." After the Prophet ﷺ had said these words to the men, they both started to weep out of fear and asked the other to take it all because they realised that anything from this world is not worth the punishment of the Hereafter. Whilst they were willing to give up their right out of fear of a greater punishment, the Prophet ﷺ told a third person to go and divide the land evenly as best they can, and then cast lots to see who will take which piece of land. And then he turned to both men again and said, "Each of you should forgive the other for any discrepancy that you see," and they both agreed to this resolution.

Therefore, we have been taught through the actions of the Prophet Muhammad ﷺ that sometimes we may argue our case better and hence justice will not be served in this world, but justice will most definitely be served in the Hereafter in order to right the wrongs or shortcomings that were committed in this world.

Things were very different at that time, people were usually their own lawyers as they presented and argued their own case. It was not like the way the system works today, with a rich person being able to hire a good lawyer and a poor person getting assigned a lawyer, thus putting them in an unfavourable position from the very onset. People are cheated to the point that it is not even worth seeking justice, because the person that they are seeking justice from can influence the judge. And it is this very thing that the Prophet Muhammad ﷺ prohibited because it is inherently unfair.

Another beautiful story that I would like to share with you is from the time that Ali bin Abi Talib, may Allah be pleased with him, was the Caliph. During the Battle of Siffin, the shield of Ali was stolen, and later when he was walking in Iraq, he saw a Christian citizen that had his shield. Ali approached the man and said that it was his shield that the man was holding, which the man denied. Ali, being the head of state, could have threatened the man with punishment, but he said, "Let's take this case to a judge." They went to Shuraih bin Harith who had not been able to meet the Messenger of Allah ﷺ himself but was still highly regarded by the Companions due to his ability to judge fairly (Umar bin Khattab called Shuraih to judge on a particular matter and Shuraih had judged against Umar, to which Umar patted him on the back and said that this is why he liked Shuraih – because he was not swayed by power, nor was he intimidated by influence).

Ali and the Christian man both went to Shuraih, Ali said that the Christian had taken his shield. Shuraih then asked Ali, "What proof do you have that it is your shield?" Ali replied, "I will call my servant and my son Hassan, they will both testify that it is my shield." Shuraih said that this was not acceptable because the servant may be afraid of Ali and falsely testify that the shield is Ali's, whilst Hassan was his son and he would be in favour of his father. Ali said, "*Subhan'Allah*, you would reject the testimony of one whom the Prophet ﷺ guaranteed Paradise?" Shuraih said "Oh leader of the believers, he is your son, it is a conflict of interest, I cannot accept these testimonies." Ali laughed and said, "Shuraih is right." After this, he told the Christian man that he could go, the man was taken aback by this behaviour, saying, "This type of behaviour could only be inspired and taught by a prophet of God," and then followed this by declaring his faith (*shahadah*) and giving Ali back his shield. The man told Ali that he saw the shield fall as he was leaving Siffin and he took it, but he had never seen this type of justice before. Ali, may Allah be pleased with him, then gave the shield to this man as a gift because he had just accepted Islam.

These are just a few examples of the type of justice that the Prophet Muhammad ﷺ inspired, and they set the tone for the Hadith that we will now look at. It is narrated by Abu Umamah, who said: The Messenger of Allah ﷺ said, "Modesty or shyness (*al-hayaa*) and guilelessness (*al-'Iy*) are two branches of faith (*iman*), while vulgarity (*al-badha*) and eloquence (*al-bayaan*) are two branches of hypocrisy."[67]

Al-'ly is a difficult word to translate into english, but it generally means to be simple in speech, straightforward, not being able to play with their words. Whilst it is usually used in a derogatory sense, in this Hadith the Prophet Muhammad ﷺ is praising this attribute because simplicity in language involves honesty, and being a bad liar is one the of the best blessings we can have from Allah as it is better that we are caught in this world with our lie than for us to suffer because of it in the Hereafter.

In comparison to this, the Prophet ﷺ said that eloquence is from a branch of hypocrisy; being eloquent in speech can enable a person to take advantage of others and deceive. However, being eloquent is not always linked to hypocrisy – the Prophet Muhammad ﷺ is referred to as *Mubeen*, the one who speaks with clarity and eloquence. However, we have seen throughout history and in modern times that politicians especially can use eloquent speech to deceive people and take advantage of the masses. Eloquence can be a gift or a curse depending on how it is used, and the Messenger of Allah ﷺ also said, "Some eloquent speech is as effective as magic."[68]

The Hadith also mentions that vulgarity, is a branch of hypocrisy. The Prophet Muhammad ﷺ said in another Hadith that, "A true believer is not involved in taunting, or frequently cursing (others), indecency or abuse." Some people may resort to using taunts or vulgar language when arguing out of anger or because they think it will validate their points, however, as believers we must never become vulgar in our speech or actions. Vulgarity or indecency is the opposite of modesty, just as speaking simplistically is the opposite of eloquent speech; the Messenger of Allah ﷺ has used counterweights of each characteristic to make it clear what is and is not acceptable in Islam.

Ibn Taymiyyah wrote, "*Hayaa* (modesty) is derived from *hayaah* (life), because the person with a living heart is alive, and his modesty prevents him from indecency – for the heart's life is its immunity against the indecencies that corrupt the heart." Indecency can be extremely dangerous in that it can lead people to lying, deception and corruption. Similarly, a person may be able to argue their side of a case eloquently, and win, but it will become a punishment for them in the end because knowing they can use the power of deception tempts us to use it over and over again.

Hakeem bin Hizam, may Allah be pleased with him, narrated: The Messenger of Allah ﷺ said, "Both the buyer and the seller retain the option (to abort the sale) until or unless they separate. If both are truthful and making things clear, their sale is blessed for them. If they conceal defects or lie, the blessing of their sale is eliminated."[69] A person might be able to falsely represent a product very well, thus deceiving the seller and eliminating any goodness (*barakah*) from that transaction.

An example of this can be found during the lifetime of the Prophet Muhammad ﷺ. An *Ansari* man named Basheer bin Ubayriq had stolen a shield from another Muslim. He had concealed it in a sack of flour and the flour began to leak from the sack, making a trail to his house. Once Basheer had realised this, he feared that he would be caught and threw the shield into the house of a Jewish man named Zayd bin as-Sameen, in order to have him wrongly accused of theft. Banu Ubayriq came to the Prophet Muhammad ﷺ after this had occurred seeking the defence of Basheer whilst blaming Zayd for stealing the shield.

As the Prophet ﷺ was assessing the situation, he saw that on one side there was a Muslim man (who later turned out to be a hypocrite), and on the other side there was a Jewish man who appeared to have stolen the shield because it was found in his home. The Messenger of Allah ﷺ was on the verge of having Zayd punished when Allah revealed the following in *Surah an-Nisaa* 4:105-112:

"Indeed, We have revealed to you (Oh Muhammad), the Book in truth so you may judge between the people by that which Allah has shown you. And do not be for the deceitful an advocate. And seek forgiveness of Allah. Indeed, Allah is ever Forgiving and Merciful. And do not argue on behalf of those who deceive themselves. Indeed, Allah loves not one who is habitually a sinful deceiver. They conceal (their evil intentions and deeds) from the people, but they cannot conceal them from Allah, and He is with them when they spend the night in such as He does not accept of speech. And ever is Allah, of what they do, encompassing. Here you are – those who argue on their behalf in this worldly life – but who will argue with Allah for them on the Day of Resurrection, or who will then be their representative? And whoever does a wrong or wrongs himself but then seeks forgiveness of Allah will find Allah Forgiving and Merciful. And whoever commits a sin only earns it against himself, and Allah is ever Knowing and Wise. But whoever commits and offence or a sin and then blames it on an innocent (person) has taken upon himself a slander and manifest sin."

Allah revealed these verses in defence of the innocent Jewish man in order to warn the Prophet ﷺ about the eloquent hypocrite Basheer, and to not be swayed by his deception. Whilst in this case justice was served right away, sometimes in this world justice is not served straight away, it may be delayed by Allah as the Prophet Muhammad ﷺ said that a person who gets away with such deception will have it as a testimony against him on the Day of Judgement.

Shyness for the sake of Allah will keep us away from cheating others and deceiving them by misusing the gift of eloquence from Allah. Eloquence can be used for beautiful things, such as spreading the word of God or for the worst things such as lying and deceiving others for your own benefit. Some people use eloquence to advocate for negative causes, for example tobacco lobbyists, or those who work for pharmaceutical and insurance companies or media pundits are predominantly corrupt advocates. Even the sugar industry has some level of corruption in it as they deceitfully hide some of the truth; the Harvard Business Journal uncovered in 2015 that the sugar industry funds research into the dangers of fat in order to divert attention from sugar itself.

An interesting account that illustrates the importance of hearing both sides of a story is from the time of Qadhi al-Iyyad who was a great judge. He was once approached by two women who were crying, and he began to listen to their complaint. Once they had told the judge their complaint, he asked to hear the other side of the story in order to be just in his decision. A man who was present at that point asked Al-Iyyad, "Don't you see these women crying in front of you? Why don't you judge in their favour?" The judge replied saying that Allah has mentioned in the Qur'an about the brothers of Yusuf going back to their father Yaqub crying about their brother Yusuf, even though they had left him for the worst. Crying alone is not proof that someone is truthful, and that he could not make a judgement without hearing both sides.

Enticing sympathy through acts such as crying can sway a person in their favour even when they are in the wrong. Being led by emotions in making judgements would lead to wrong decisions and Allah explains this beautifully in the Qur'an, in *Surah al-Ma'idah* 5:8: *"And do not let the hatred of a people prevent you from being just. Be just; that is nearer to righteousness."*

A beautiful saying of Imam Shawkani is, "If the person being testified against is rich, he should not be favoured because of his richness – in order to benefit from him or avoid his harm – and hence not testified against. And if he is poor, he should not be favoured because of his poverty – out of mercy and compassion for him – and hence not testified against." Judging should be done fairly without favouring a person due to their financial or social status.

Currently in America we see an increase in police brutality, and people who have witnessed it first-hand are unwilling to speak up or to be on a jury because they do not want the police to cause issues for them. They choose not to testify because people in a position of power or influence cause fear in their hearts, and this is unjust. It is equally unjust if we wrongly favour someone due to compassion for their poverty or lack of wealth, thus causing unfair judgement to someone who may be wealthier but truthful.

We also must ensure that we never knowingly misrepresent a situation, use our eloquence or status or position to wrong someone. False testimony is a major sin in Islam, and we must be careful not to say anything that could cause an unfair judgement for someone. Defending a guilty party can sway the judgement and result in injustice, and today when lawyers are paid vast amounts, it is easy to fall into the trap of lying or misrepresenting something for the sake of money. People are disproportionately targeted and made to suffer at the hands of this unjust and cruel system.

Short-changing others requires the ability to deceive, meaning that if two people are arguing about a certain matter and one is better at arguing their point even when they are in the wrong, they are in fact cheating or deceiving with their eloquence. If a judge favours the eloquent person, knowing that they are getting more than they deserve, then they are on the path to receive a portion of the Hellfire. A person may be able to hire a better lawyer in order to increase their chances of winning a case in this world, but in the Hereafter that same person will have nobody but themselves to stand in front of Allah in the court of justice.

Our God-consciousness (*taqwa*) must govern us, and we must not allow ourselves to take more than we deserve if we ever find ourselves in the position that a judgement is giving us more than our fair share. Justice must be applied to everyone equally; being in a favourable position due to wealth or power should not be used to a wrong advantage.

May Allah allow us to be just in our judgements and protect us from taking more than what is rightfully ours. Amin.

14

ELITIST PRIVILEGE

Narrated by Aisha (ra): A woman of Quraysh, from Banu Makhzum, was caught stealing, and she was brought to the Prophet. They said: 'Who will speak to him concerning her?' They said: 'Usamah bin Zaid.' So Usamah went to the Prophet and spoke to him. But he rebuked Usamah, and said, 'Nations who came before you were destroyed because if a rich person stole, they would let him go. But if a poor person stole, they would cut off his hand. By the One in whose hand is the soul of Muhammad, if Fatima bint Muhammad were to steal, I would cut off her hand.'

THE TOPIC OF this chapter is again very much in line with the previous two chapters. The Prophet Muhammad ﷺ sought to do away with this concept of elitist privilege due to its unfairness and injustice in society. Privilege is natural and comes in many forms: by virtue of race or tribe, by virtue of gender, by virtue of finances or even by virtue of geography. When we find ourselves in a place of privilege, we must recognise it and then use that privilege to help those that are not in the same position as ourselves. This is the lesson we learn from the life (*Sunnah*) of the Prophet Muhammad ﷺ.

The Hadith that we will look at in this chapter is narrated by Aisha, may Allah be pleased with her, who said: A woman of *Quraish*, from Banu Makhzoom, was caught stealing and she was brought to the Prophet ﷺ. They said, "Who will speak to him concerning her?" They said, "Usamah bin Zaid." So Usamah went to the Prophet Muhammad ﷺ and spoke to him, but he rebuked Usamah and said, "Nations who came before you were destroyed because if a rich person stole, they would let him go. But if a poor person stole, they would cut off his hand. By the One in whose hand is the soul of Muhammad, if Fatima bint Muhammad were to steal, I would cut off her hand."[70]

What is important to note in this Hadith, is that this incident occurred towards the end of the Prophet's life – after the conquest of Makkah, when he was the sole authority in both Madinah and Makkah. Aisha specifically mentioned the tribe that the woman belonged to. The tribe of Banu Makhzoom was also the tribe of Abu Jahl; one of the most elite and powerful tribes in Makkah. Banu Makhzoom was also a competing tribe with the tribe of the Prophet Muhammad ﷺ, which was what made Abu Jahl take it to heart and make it his mission to not allow the spread of Islam or even allow the claim to Prophethood to be heard because it would result in the tribe of Muhammad outdoing Banu Makhzoom. The people of Banu Makhzoom were highly privileged and were not used to being held accountable in any way, and so Aisha makes it a point to mention that this woman belonged to this particular tribe.

We also find in various other narrations that this woman was a habitual thief and now, on this occasion, she had finally been caught red-handed. After she had been caught, the people came together and asked who would intercede on her behalf in front of the Messenger of Allah ﷺ, to which they decided it would be Usamah bin Zaid (who was the son of Zaid bin Harith, the freed slave and adopted son of the Prophet ﷺ).

Usamah was very beloved to the Prophet Muhammad ﷺ; he was also a very wise young man, so much so that he was entrusted with the position of commander of the Muslim army at the young age of seventeen. When Usamah went to the Prophet ﷺ to speak about the thieving woman, the Prophet ﷺ said to him, "Do you think that your intercession on behalf of someone who is royal will cause me to disobey Allah?" After this the Messenger of Allah ﷺ stood up and gave a sermon to the people, telling them about previous nations who were destroyed because they used to punish the weak and forgive the wealthy.

The Prophet ﷺ also then went on to say something very profound and powerful, he swore by Allah that if his own daughter Fatima were to steal, he would cut off her hand as punishment. This was to ensure that the people of Makkah understood that he did not accept the status quo and he wanted to get rid of the unfairness that it brought. He wanted the people of Makkah to realise that this was not the same situation as when he had returned at the conquest of Makkah; then, he had made concessions and he did not punish people for what they had done to him in the past. An example of this was as he was entering Makkah, the Prophet ﷺ said, "Whoever enters into the house of Abu Sufyan is safe." Abu Sufyan was the person who spent two decades fighting against Muhammad ﷺ but he chose to forgive him and made his house a place of sanctuary in order to maintain Abu Sufyan's place in society. However, this incident now was not just a matter of someone doing something to the Prophet ﷺ – it was a matter of fixing the wrong in society.

Though this particular narration of the Hadith does not mention the name of the woman, her name was also Fatima (her full name being Fatima bint al-Aswad al-Makhzumiya). This makes the statement of the Prophet more profound in the sense that he was essentially saying that he would punish his own daughter Fatima just as he would punish the thief Fatima bint al-Aswad. This was to show that there would be no more privilege in their society, whether it be because of tribe or anything else. The Messenger of Allah ﷺ wanted to show them that his decision were not based on vengeance for what Abu Jahl did in the past, such as boycotting the tribe of Banu Hashim and making them suffer for three years.

When looking into the history of Fatima bint al-Aswad, we find that she was a frequent thief; she used to borrow things from people and not return them when they asked by denying that she ever took them. She also used to steal from the caravans that came from Madinah to Makkah, including some items that even belonged to the Prophet Muhammad ﷺ himself. However, at this point he chose not to mention that he was a victim of her thefts too.

The same rules must be applied to everyone because it was due to this very reason of injustice due to privilege, that previous nations were destroyed. Allah says in the Qur'an, *"We punished them when they became oppressors,"* and this was what the Prophet ﷺ wanted to avoid. Islam brought justice, and privileges would no longer be a means to avoid justice. Prophet Isa, may the blessings of Allah be upon him, was unhappy with the people of his time as they would only punish the weak and excuse the elite. By letting the elite get away because of their privileges, they would be overlooking their flaws, no matter how bad they were. This meant the weaker people in society would suffer the harshest punishments, and the scholars would give the excuse that they are applying the law of God, although they knew that they were being unjust.

The Bible also mentions this complaint of Isa in Matthew 23:23: "Woe to you, scribes and Pharisees, hypocrites! You practice your religion very well, but you have neglected the weightier matters of the law; justice, and mercy and faith." The Prophet Isa came to bring back the spirit of the law and rectify the misuse of the law at the hands of the Pharisees.

One of the wisdoms of this Hadith is that the Prophet Muhammad ﷺ responded by mentioning someone even more beloved to him than Usamah – his daughter Fatima – and that even she was not exempt from punishment if she committed wrong. The people sent Usamah because they knew he held a special place with the Messenger of Allah ﷺ, and thus they assumed that this relationship would help keep Fatima bint al-Aswad away from any punishment and soften the Prophet's stance. However, the Prophet's ﷺ statement of his own daughter not being exempt from punishment was said in her presence to drive home the point that even members of the ruling class, such as Banu Makhzoom and Banu Hashim, would be subject to the law and the new standards that Islam brought.

When we look into the different standards that Islam introduced into society, we come across examples showing the fairness and mercy of Islam. One such example is of when Umar bin Khattab was Caliph and the people were suffering from a great famine. This resulted in an increase in people stealing because they were desperate and hungry. Umar came to realise this and he suspended the penalty for stealing, not that it made stealing acceptable but that the circumstances had changed; people were not stealing out of monetary greed, but hunger. He lifted the punishment (*hadd*) for the sake of the poor as he said that there cannot be punishment for theft when the people are hungry. The change in thinking that Islam introduced was that it is not the rich and powerful whose needs come first but those of the poor and needy.

This is also a principle that many of the scholars of Islamic law mentioned in the objectives of law (*maqasid al-shari'a*); if you are not providing people with the means with which they can survive and succeed or be happy, then you also cannot punish them when they resort to impermissible means to try and survive or to attain happiness. Opening the ways of good is far more important than preventing the ways of bad; providing the means for people to be able to live comfortably and happily should be the first priority, rather than condemning the bad. For example, the focus would not be on punishing adultery (*zina*) if we have made it too difficult for people to get married. We must consider whether we are providing them with the avenues to marriage and that if the circumstances are compelling them to act in such a way.

The Messenger of Allah ﷺ applied these standards to himself, so how can we not admire him for beginning with himself and showing us the way. One such Hadith relates an incident after the Battle of Badr, when the Muslims found Suhayl bin Amr – a chief of the *Quraysh* who was very vocal against Islam – among the prisoners of war. Umar bin Khattab was extremely happy that Suhayl was a prisoner and wanted to take revenge by pulling out his teeth, so that he would never again preach against the Messenger of Allah ﷺ. However, the Prophet Muhammad ﷺ refused to give Umar permission to do this and said, "I will not mutilate him, lest Allah mutilate me – even though I am a prophet."[71]

Suhayl later on accepted Islam and became one of the best spokespeople for the religion (*deen*); the Prophet ﷺ did not allow for him to be punished as he understood that Allah would do the same to him, regardless of him being a prophet. He was teaching Umar that he could not afford himself such behaviour and hence Umar should not afford himself such behaviour either. He would not allow torture even if it were the worst enemy of Islam.

Another story involving Umar when he was Caliph, is of his son Abdur Rahman who was once caught drunk in Egypt, and the governor of Egypt at the time was Amr bin al-As. Amr did not want to embarrass Umar by punishing his son in public and so symbolically punished Abdur Rahman in the privacy of his home. When Umar bin Khattab came to know of this, he asked that his son be sent back to Madinah in order to be publicly punished. Amr thought that he had done well and that this would be a favour to Umar, but Umar had his son publicly flogged as he had the responsibility of carrying out justice, even if it involved punishing his own son. He wanted people to know that his son was not going to get special treatment; he would be dealt with in the same way as everybody else.

Similarly, on another occasion Umar bin Khattab punished both Amr and his son when his son hit a Christian man after a horse race. Umar told the Christian man to hit Amr's son in the same way that he had been hit, and also told him to place the stick on Amr's head as a symbolic punishment because it was due to Amr's position that his son believed that he could get away with injustice.

We see that the Prophet ﷺ showed on numerous occasions that there was no privilege for the elites in society when it came to bringing people to justice, including himself and his family. A well-known example of this is when the Prophet ﷺ poked a young man with his stick in the Battle of Badr because he was laughing too much, but then the young man said that the Prophet ﷺ had hurt him and the Prophet ﷺ told him to take his revenge by poking him back. The Messenger of Allah ﷺ did not take advantage of his position, but he made it a point to say that even he did not hold any privilege.

We see the same approach again when we look at the first sermon given by Abu Bakr, may Allah be pleased with him, as he took up the role of Caliph and he said, "The weak one amongst you will be considered amongst the strong (elite) in my eyes until I get his right back Insha'Allah. And the strong ones (elite) are weak in my eyes until I am able to take rights back from them Insha'Allah." This was his way of declaring that the rich will not be treated any differently to the poor; the strong and weak will both be dealt with justice.

However, it is unfortunate that Muslim countries in current times are not following this principle strictly, with the elite receiving lesser punishments than those who are not privileged. The punishments are being unfairly applied in these countries, with people who are less fortunate receiving the harshest punishments, for example immigrant workers in certain middle eastern countries will readily be punished whilst locals will be given a lot of leeway. The purpose of the law is to promote equality, but if it is not being applied fairly then it is not serving its purpose.

A powerful quote by Noam Chomsky that fits in very well here is: "For the powerful, crimes are those that others commit." The powerful are able to get away with committing sins and crimes, whilst the weaker in society are caught and unfairly dealt with.

Before I conclude this chapter, I want to share a Hadith with a significant message; it is narrated by Abu Masud, may Allah be pleased with him: "The example of the one who supports his people when they are wrong (one who enables oppression), is like a dead camel that falls into a well and is pulled out by its tail."[72]

There are two lessons or messages that we can take from this Hadith:

1. The one who supports the elite in their wrongdoing is the dead camel. It is an extremely powerful parable which the Prophet Muhammad ﷺ used to explain that the person will be held accountable by Allah; it will be Allah who pulls them out of the well and returns them to Him to answer for their actions.

2. The corpse of the dead camel will poison the entire well, stripping it of its benefits, as the water will no longer be drinkable. This in other words means that the person's support for oppression will poison their entire community, resulting in everyone suffering.

    When we think about what the word *shar'iah* means, the linguistic meaning of it is water; it is guidance. However, if the law is not applied with equity across society then it is as if privilege has poisoned the well. Everyone will have to suffer the consequences if one person enables someone else to take advantage of their privilege and oppress others.

In many societies, people use their connections to bypass many things and to get away with almost anything. When we take part in something like this, then we are also guilty because we are enabling this system of privilege and oppression to carry on. Instead, we should always fight for the law to be applied equally to everybody. The law should not target some people disproportionately.

May Allah enable us to be amongst those that help the least privileged in society and protect us from taking advantage of our own privileges and harming others. Amin.

15

BUILDING A COALITION OF JUSTICE: THE FIQH OF HILF AL-FADOOL

Certainly, I had witnessed a pact of justice in the house of Abdullah ibn Jud'an that was more beloved to me than a herd of red camels. If I were called to it now in the time of Islam, I would answer it.

DURING THE TIME of the Prophet Muhammad ﷺ, a man from the tribe of Zubaid came to do business in Makkah. Another man from the *Quraysh* asked for his merchandise and told him that he would give the payment the following day. The businessman was in no doubt that he would receive his payment as non-Makkan people respected and trusted the *Quraysh*. However, when he went to collect his payment the following day, the *Qurayshi* man denied any knowledge of the transaction and refused to pay.

The businessman became extremely upset and worried at this situation and went to complain to the leaders in Makkah of the *Qurayshi* man who had taken his merchandise without paying. The leaders ignored the man and dismissed his complaints, which resulted in the businessman taking his shirt off as a sign of desperation and going to stand at the door of the Ka'aba. He then began to loudly recite verses of poetry which addressed the people of Makkah as a nation of dignity and honour and asked how theft and oppression could occur in this city.

Embarrassed by this situation, the *Qurayshi* leaders called a meeting to resolve the situation, among the attendees were the Prophet Muhammad ﷺ and Abu Bakr, may Allah have mercy on him. At the meeting, they came to an agreement that they would stand with the oppressed regardless of what tribe they belonged to. Five tribes agreed to this pact, they were Banu Hashim, Banu Muttalib, Banu Zuhrah, Banu Asad and Bany Taym. The tribe of Banu Umayyah abstained from this pact; in fact they were one of the most hostile towards the Prophet ﷺ when he began sharing his message and for the most part they did not accept Islam either.

The pact of Hilf al-Fadool was also named Hilf al-Mutayibeen, or the Pledge of the Perfumed; they dipped their hands in henna and made imprints on the Ka'aba as an oath that they will stand together in support of those who are oppressed. Anyone who was wronged would have their right upheld collectively by all five tribes. This was a significant shift in their attitude as before this pledge was made, the tribes of Arabia were known to go to war with each other for the pettiest of reasons and these wars or enmities would last for generations on end.

The Hadith regarding this is related in Sunan al-Bayhaqi al-Kubra, in which the Prophet Muhammad ﷺ said: "Certainly, I had witnessed a pact of justice in the house of Abdullah bin Jud'an that was more beloved to me than a herd of red camels. If I were asked to attend such a meeting now, I would answer it."

The Prophet ﷺ here was saying that if a similar pact were to be called, he would be the first to join it. And another noteworthy point he mentioned is that such a pact is more beloved to him than red camels – the most prized assets of the Arabs. The Messenger of Allah ﷺ also mentioned that he would continue to uphold Hilf al-Mutayibeen, indicating that it was still in place when he said the above Hadith. Although many of the participants of the agreement did not become Muslim, the Messenger of Allah was still upholding the pledge, even if they rejected him as a prophet; what mattered here was that they maintained the principles that were agreed upon at the time of the meeting.

Furthermore, according to the majority of scholars, this statement of the Prophet ﷺ took place after the conquest of Makkah. The Prophet ﷺ was now in a far more powerful position, he and his followers were no longer being persecuted, but the Muslims were confused regarding what should be upheld and what should not, and so the Prophet ﷺ clarified these things for the Muslim community. Whether it was regarding theology, such as the rituals of Hajj, because Hajj was also performed in the days of ignorance, or regarding societal contracts such as interest (*riba*), which the Prophet Muhammad ﷺ condemned and abolished in his farewell sermon in Makkah. The fact that this statement was made at the height of his power makes it all the more compelling, as it is easier to call upon such agreements when you are in a position of weakness or oppressed, but he made a point of upholding the pact to ensure that everyone, whether Muslim or not, understood that oppressors will be held accountable.

There are several lessons that we can learn from this pact, or Hilf al-Fadool:

1. The pact gave Muslims a precedent for maintaining the moral responsibility of protecting the weak. This could come in the form of speaking up for them, criticising those in power or powerful positions and establishing groups that lobby for social rights.

2. The Prophet ﷺ also acknowledged that Muslims could work with non-Muslims and create such coalitions as it was for the benefit of the wider community and to help the weak and oppressed. He recognised that even though there may be other issues present in society that we may not agree with as Muslims, if people are willing to come together and fight or work together for a noble cause, then Muslims should be the first to join in such efforts. Pacts such as the Hilf al-Fadool are specific to the goal mentioned, economic oppression in this case, and are not a general alliance which could be taken as an endorsement for other actions that are not acceptable in Islam.

3. The pact also teaches Muslims to embrace anything that is for the betterment of humanity, in this life or the next. There is a wonderful verse in the Qur'an in which Allah says, *"And cooperate with one another in righteousness and piety"* (*Surah al-Ma'idah* 5:2) Many scholars have commented on this verse saying that righteousness (*al-Birr*) refers to well-being in this world, and piety (*taqwa*) refers to wellbeing in the Hereafter. We either come together for the well-being of people in this world, or we come together for the well-being of people in the Hereafter through *taqwa*.

Muslims must look at everything in the light of achieving *al-Birr wa Taqwa*, sometimes there is a seemingly just cause but it has been hijacked by a malicious agenda so Muslims need to assess the pros and cons of realising that goal as it has to be in the light of gaining righteousness and piety, as Allah has clearly told us to work with one another for the betterment of everyone.

4. The pact is not limited to a time when the Muslims are in a state of minority or a position of weakness, but also when they are in a position of power. In fact, they should be initiated when Muslims are in a state of power to ensure that all Muslims and non-Muslims understand the importance of upholding the rights of any people that are oppressed.

5. The scholars have said that such a pact is not restricted to a mixed community of non-Muslims and Muslims; a pact of this nature can also be initiated amongst a community of Muslims only, in order to resolve a disagreement among themselves or to uphold rights amongst themselves. An example of this could be that the mosques come together and decide that certain principles are to be upheld, they make a pact for the well-being of the wider community, then if that agreement is violated they can collectively hold to account the one who violates it.

6. The scholars have commented on the following statement of the Prophet Muhammad ﷺ, "Are you supported or given victory by Allah except by how you treat your poor?"[73] saying that the Prophet ﷺ was explaining that blessings (*barakah*) comes to a society when they uphold the rights of the weakest people.

    Oppression ruins a society by depriving it of blessings, and the lack of accountability leads to everyone having to suffer. However, when they formed the pact of Hilf al-Fadool in Makkah, it led to a boom in their economy; people from other tribes and countries were less hesitant to do business in Makkah as they knew that their rights would be upheld. They would not be wronged. And it was this sense of justice that brought many blessings into their transactions and economy. When people come together to protect the rights of everyone, Allah opens doors for that society and sends many blessings irrespective of whether they are Muslim or non-Muslim.

7. The Prophet Muhammad ﷺ confirmed the importance of this pact by saying that he would oblige if he were to be called to any similar agreements. A powerful incident that demonstrated the pact in action took place around seventy years after the passing of the Messenger of Allah ﷺ, the Emir of Madinah, Uthman bin Abi Sufyan, wronged a man and refused to return his money. Upon witnessing this, Hussain bin Ali, may Allah be pleased with him, said "I swear by Allah if you do not give him back his money, then I will invoke Hilf al-Fadool." Abdullah bin Zubair and Muhammad bin Talha also said the same. Hussain was a descendent of Banu Hashim, Abdullah was a descendent of Banu Asad, and Muhammad was from Banu Zuhrah – all three tribes were part of the pact at the time of the Prophet Muhammad ﷺ. The invoking of Hilf al-Fadool by these men made Uthman bin Abi Sufyan give the man back his money.

The Prophet ﷺ was never comfortable with the practices of the *Quraysh*, even before he was given prophethood. He was always eager to improve the conditions of that society in whatever way he could, and as Muslims we should take heed from this. It is very easy to become overwhelmed by injustice in society, but a good starting point is to bring people together and work together to defeat oppression and maintain justice.

May Allah use us and allow us to establish justice in both our Muslim and wider communities. Amin.

16

A SHOW OF STRENGTH

Ibn 'Umar Narrated that the Messenger of Allah ﷺ said: "O Allah! Honour Islam through the most dear of these two men to You: Through Abu Jahl or through 'Umar bin al-Khattab."

IN THIS CHAPTER we will build off the previous chapter and focus on the seeking and showing of strength. Showing strength when you are in a place of vulnerability – especially as a community – is a methodology in Islam.

There is a very famous Hadith in which the Prophet Muhammad ﷺ said: "The strong believer is more beloved than the weak believer."[74] It shows that strength is preferred and the Companions were fine examples of this. Ammar bin Yasir, may Allah be pleased with him watched both of his parents being killed in front of his very eyes, yet he rose above this and remained highly motivated. Despite the persecution and hardships that Ammar and other Companions faced, they became more determined than ever.

In another Hadith, the Prophet ﷺ said, "The upper hand (giving hand) is better than the lower hand (receiving hand),"[75] meaning that there is financial strength, physical strength, emotional strength and strength through influence. Influencing others through your deeds or words for the benefit of Islam shows strength; Najashi the ruler of Abyssinia was one of these people. He brought a lot of good to Islam with his influence and strength, and when he died the Prophet Muhammad ﷺ offered a funeral prayer for him even though he had never met Najashi. Similarly, a more recent example is the passing away of the boxer Muhammad Ali. He spread the message of Islam whenever and wherever he could, including during interviews. He was extremely influential, so much so that one sentence from Muhammad Ali was more effective than a thousand *imams*, and so many scholars had said that there should be absentee funeral prayers (*salat al-gha'ib*) offered for Muhammad Ali all over the world.

The Hadith that I have chosen to convey this topic of strength is well-known, the Prophet ﷺ had made a supplication which had significant implications for the Muslims: "Oh Allah, give victory to Islam through one of the two Umars."[76]

It also has another narration with slightly different wording, "Oh Allah, give victory to Islam through the Umar that is more beloved to You."

The Messenger of Allah ﷺ made this supplication (*du'a*) regarding Umar bin al-Khattab and Abu Jahl, whose name was Umar bin Hisham. The Muslims at this time were oppressed and in a vulnerable position, whilst the two Umars were the most hostile towards them, and the Prophet Muhammad ﷺ asked Allah to guide the Umar that was more beloved to Him to Islam. Abu Lahab was also hostile towards Muslims and he was also a lot closer to the Prophet Muhammad ﷺ in relation, but the Prophet ﷺ had seen that both Umar bin al-Khattab and Abu Jahl had particular qualities in them that could be used for the sake of Islam.

Beginning with Abu Jahl, or Umar bin Hisham, he was the maternal uncle of Umar bin al-Khattab and was of a similar age to the Prophet Muhammad ﷺ. He belonged to the tribe of Banu Makhzoom, which competed with the tribe of the Prophet ﷺ, Banu Hashim. The Messenger of Allah ﷺ wanted someone like Abu Jahl, who was in a powerful position, to accept Islam, so that he could dispel the myth that Islam was only for certain people or tribes and instead unite people. Before he earned the nickname of Abu Jahl, he was called Abu Hakim, or the father of wisdom as he was a learned man, however the Prophet ﷺ later said that it was a sin to refer to him as Abu Hakim because there was no wisdom in the way that he reacted to the message of Islam.

Abu Jahl was also a man of great physical strength and tall demeanour which played a part in his extreme pride. During the Battle of Badr, Abdullah bin Mas'ud quite literally had to climb onto Abu Jahl to kill him because of his size. Being a person of great influence, physically and mentally, he was also the greatest threat which has earned him the title of being the pharaoh of this *ummah*. He tortured and murdered the first Muslims; he imposed the harsh boycott on Banu Hashim and Banu Muttalib and he was the one who plotted the assassination of the Prophet Muhammad ﷺ. He had qualities that could have been used for the sake of Islam and Allah, and the Prophet ﷺ asked Allah to guide Abu Jahl if he was beloved to Him; this attitude of the Prophet Muhammad ﷺ shows us how pure his heart was, he did not let the hatred that was being directed at him from Abu Jahl stop him from making supplication (*du'a*) for his guidance.

Umar bin al-Khattab was very similar to Umar bin Hisham in terms of being wise, learned and physically very strong. He was younger than both the Prophet ﷺ and Abu Jahl, but because of his strong skillset, he ascended the ranks very quickly. He was a person that everybody feared; nobody dared to stand up to Umar bin al-Khattab. His personality was somewhat raw compared to that of Abu Jahl as he was young blood, but people kept within their limits when dealing with Umar.

The day that Umar became Muslim, his Islam was strength, honour and dignity. Abdullah bin Mas'ud said that Islam became victorious the day that Umar declared his testimony of faith (*shahadah*). The Muslims who were previously hiding out of fear of persecution, were now able to walk out in the open in Makkah and declare their faith. When he accepted Islam, he marched outside into the streets of Makkah and asked the Muslims to follow him to proclaim their faith. He also went to the house of Abu Jahl to inform him that he had become Muslim.

Abdullah bin Mas'ud also described the strength of Umar, when shortly after becoming Muslim he went outside, and many non-Muslims tried to attack him. Umar fought them off with ease, with the remaining few running away out of fear. The rest of the Muslims knew that they were now safe with Umar; they could hide behind him knowing that he would protect them. However, his strength was also paired with humility. He would humble himself in front of other Companions such as Bilal about whom he said, "This is our master who was freed by our master Abu Bakr." He would humble himself in front of Abdullah bin Mas'ud by physically getting down on his knees in order to see eye to eye with Abdullah, so as not to have Abdullah bin Mas'ud looking up at him to speak. His humility tamed his strength, and so he only exerted his strength for good.

When the Prophet Muhammad ﷺ made this *du'a* to Allah to bring one of the Umars to Islam, he knew that the strength and qualities they possessed would do amazing things for the spread of Islam. When his supplication was accepted and Umar bin al-Khattab became Muslim, Umar's motto was to be fearless about declaring faith. He asked why they were hiding when they were on the truth – they should never feel weak, no matter what the circumstances. He had a great sense of pride before he accepted Islam and that remained even after he accepted Islam. He did not shy away from acting upon Islam in public because he knew he was upon the truth (*haq*).

Umar, may Allah be pleased with him, made a very powerful supplication in which he asked, "Oh Allah, I complain to you of the incompetence of the trustworthy people and their weakness." He wanted to show Islam in every context and did not want to appear weak at any point; the Prophet Muhammad ﷺ saw his strengths and saw great good with Umar coming to Islam.

Showing strength for the sake of Islam is good and appreciated, one such example of this is during the Battle of Uhud when Abu Dajana put on his red bandana and was strutting and taunting the other army, the Companions*h* thought it was boastful and not acceptable. However, the Prophet Muhammad ﷺ said that Allah hates this kind of behaviour except in these circumstances. It is only in such circumstances that Allah approves of boasting and taunting, as it shows the enemy your strength and your fearlessness.

Allah also says in *Surah al-Anfal* 8:60: "*Strike fear by showing strength*," which in other words means to show the enemy your power in the context of battle, to intimidate them and show them that you are neither weak nor afraid of them. Some of the Companions (*sahabah*) would stay up at night asking Allah to grant them victory, they would wear their best clothes and stand with pride, completely unafraid and that was something that Allah praised.

One such incident that showcases the courage of the Muslims was in the Battle against the Persians. The Persians would bring elephants to trample the opposing army, and whilst the Muslims were trying to figure out a plan, a Companion named al-Qaqa came up with the idea to make their own elephants. He used his wit and intelligence to put a structure on top of the camels to make them look much bigger than they were, which in turn scared the elephants of the Persians as they had never seen such huge beasts before. This was an extremely clever move which made the Muslim army look more powerful than the Persian army with its elephants.

This example shows that even if we as Muslims are in a disadvantaged position, we need to make an appearance of strength, and it is a methodology that works. However, we must be careful and govern this strength with strength against ourselves so that we don't become unjust; and this was the beauty of Umar bin al-Khattab, his strength did not lead him to arrogance but instead it led him to humility.

Imam Maalik spoke about clothes of power or clothes that were distinguishing, and Imam Maalik himself used to wear the best clothes. Imam Abu Hanifa also used to wear the best clothes and also bought the best clothing for his students. When Imam Maalik was asked about the type of clothing that he wore, he said that it was important for scholars to be respected and so wearing distinguishing clothing would enable them to receive that respect. Wearing such clothing however does not justify extravagance, nor does it mean that the wearers of such clothing can be arrogant. Umar bin al-Khattab, during his reign as Caliph, raised the salaries of the government workers and scholars so that they could be self-sufficient and independent. It was to protect them from being vulnerable to bribery and for them to be able to show a sense of dignity.

When scholars become beggars, it leads to other extremes. When their salaries are low, they can be bribed or forced into a position of compromise and it is for this reason that the Prophet Muhammad ﷺ wanted people to display honour and to be self-sufficient without touching on to extravagance.

Abdullah bin Mubarak was a great scholar and was also extremely wealthy because of his work as a merchant alongside his scholarly work.

He shared his wealth and provided enough money to other great scholars such as Sufyan at-Thawri so that they would not have to worry about money. Abdullah bin Mubarak also went on to say that if it was not for these scholars, he would not work anymore.

Umar bin Abdul Aziz on the other hand, during his Caliphate, wanted to strip the mosques of all the ornaments but some scholars told him that it is important that they remain on par with churches and other places of worship. It does not need to be extravagant, but it needs to look respectable and it needs to show strength and dignity. This is why Muslims took their architecture seriously over the course of history; they became pioneers of certain styles and they understood the reasoning behind having the mosques looking attractive and respectable.

The idea of displaying strength holds high importance in Islam; the Prophet Muhammad ﷺ himself would have the best swords from Rome and Persia. He would equip himself with the best that he could have.

Whilst strength, power and prestige can be harmful when used for the wrong thing, Muslims should also not purposely put themselves in a position of vulnerability or weakness. Going back to the boxer Muhammad Ali and the great legacy he left, he took a strong anti-war stance and refused to go to war in Vietnam by fearlessly saying that the very people who are asking him to go to war, are his enemies when he wants freedom. He showed strength even at a time when he was vulnerable, and this is what we as Muslims should endeavour to be like.

May Allah enable us to display strength for the sake of those that are more vulnerable than ourselves and seek the means of strength that will allow us to be in a position of influence so we can benefit the wider community. Amin.

17

FINDING AND CHANNELLING YOUR RIGHTEOUS ANGER

A'isha, the wife of Allah's Apostle ﷺ said that whenever he had to choose between two things he adopted the easier one, provided it was no sin, but if it was any sin he was the one who was the farthest from it of the people; and Allah's Messenger ﷺ never took revenge from anyone because of his personal grievance, unless what Allah, the Exalted and Glorious, had made inviolable had been violated.

IN THIS CHAPTER we will look at the concept of righteous anger. The Hadith that conveys this concept is narrated by Aisha, may Allah be pleased with her: "Whenever the Prophet ﷺ had to choose between two things, he adopted the easier one, provided it was not a sin, but if it was any sin, he was the one who was the farthest from it of the people. And Allah's Messenger ﷺ never took revenge from anyone because of his personal grievance, unless what Allah, the Exalted and Glorious, had made inviolable was violated."[77]

The Hadith describes the balance in the character of the Prophet Muhammad ﷺ, with the first part making it clear that whenever he was presented with two options, he did not choose the more difficult one to show more piety, but he chose the easier option so long as it was not sinful. But if it was sinful, then he would be the farthest from it. However, the main point here is that he never enjoyed or wanted to make things difficult for himself or for others.

The second part of the Hadith explains that he never took revenge for personal reasons, but he became angry if the law of Allah had been violated. He was not a vengeful person, he was not someone who demonstrated perpetual anger, but if what Allah made inviolable was violated, he did not hold back his anger.

Before we go into more detail, I would like to mention a Hadith that supplements the above Hadith very well. It is reported by Abu Hurairah, may Allah be pleased with him: "The Prophet ﷺ said, 'Verily, Allah the Exalted has protective honour (*gheerah*) and becomes angry, and His Anger is provoked when a person does what Allah has declared unlawful.'"[78]

If a believer violates something that Allah has commanded them not to violate, it beckons the anger of Allah. And it was for this very same reason that the Prophet ﷺ was angered; it was a sense of protective and righteous anger.

Imam Bayhaqi, may Allah have mercy upon him, commented on the Hadith narrated by Aisha saying, "If we were to say all anger is bad, that leaves no room for *gheerah* and zeal." It was never over petty matters or because the Prophet ﷺ was offended, it was regarding serious matters regarding the Laws of Allah. His anger during these times showed his *gheerah*, about which he also commented on himself in the following Hadith: "Do you marvel at the *gheerah* of Sa'd? I have greater *gheerah* than him, and Allah has greater *gheerah* than me. And it was from His *gheerah* that He forbid indecency."

Imam Nawawi, may Allah have mercy upon him, also said that part of the human condition is that we have this feeling of protective honour (*gheerah*) because the word comes from the phrase meaning a change of heart. It is part of our humanity that Allah gave us these emotions, however it is our duty to channel them properly. One of the most frequent supplications of the Prophet ﷺ was, "Oh turner of hearts! Make my heart firm on your path." The heart can change, our emotions can vary, and it is only human that we have these emotions. However, it is important to keep in mind that the emotions and qualities that Allah has given us, must be channelled and expressed appropriately.

Imam Ghazali, may Allah be please with him, said that when referring to the believers, Allah did not say those who do not have anger, but rather He said those who swallow their anger. The emotion is natural and is meant to be present, but it is how we channel it, and turn it into righteous anger that is a quality of the believers. The Messenger of Allah ﷺ praised the person who has righteous anger as it is showing anger towards something that is worth getting angry over with a sense of protective honour, and he also said the person who does not have any sense of righteous anger is disgraceful. Anger in itself is not something to be praised as there is a famous Hadith in which the Prophet ﷺ was asked for advice from a man and he repeated the answer of "do not become angry" three times.[79] But showing righteous anger is a quality that is appreciated and loved.

When we think or ask about where to begin with righteous anger, the scholars have answered this and said that it begins with ourselves. Righteous anger at oneself is a sign of spirituality and humbleness. The Messenger of Allah ﷺ also said regarding this, "If you are pleased by your good deed and bothered by your bad deed, then you are a believer."[80]

Umar bin al-Khattab, may Allah be pleased with him, would not get angry at anyone else as much as he did with himself. He admonished himself if he felt he had wronged someone; he would not wait for someone else to tell him that he had done wrong. If we possess this quality, we will be able to increase our humility, whereas if we only focus on admonishing others, we become arrogant, which is hated. By starting with ourselves and taking ourselves to task, we are able to show a sense of righteous anger.

It was also Umar bin al-Khattab who said that we must hold ourselves accountable before we are held accountable. We must ask ourselves are we as angry with ourselves as we are with everybody else regarding a sinful act? Being quick to admonish or become angry at other people for their actions whilst not paying attention to ourselves is hypocrisy.

When looking at the concept of righteous anger, it is a quality that the Prophet Muhammad ﷺ and other messengers had, and it is something that Allah also has. Righteous anger, or *gheerah* is to be angry out of a sense of protection, and there are two determining factors with regards to it:

1. Ask yourself why you are angry.
2. How are you displaying this anger.

Both of these factors are indicative of one another, for example if you violate the boundaries of Allah, you cannot claim that you are angry for the sake of Allah. The way in which anger manifests itself is an indication of where it is truly coming from, whether it is for the sake of Allah or for the self (*nafs*).

Cursing people or using foul language to admonish them and claiming that this is for the sake of Allah is wrong and it is not righteous anger. The Prophet ﷺ made it very clear that the believer is not someone who curses or abuses people with their tongue. Being abusive is from the nafs and is egotistical with no benefit for people or Islam, and it is a way in which the devil (*shaytan*) tricks us. We might be arguing the correct point, but the way that we argue may show that we are not arguing for the right reason, and so we must step back and review and renew our intention.

The Messenger of Allah ﷺ described the hypocrites as people who would transgress limits and be unjust when arguing. He also said that the signs of a hypocrite are that when they speak, they lie, when they make a promise, they break it and when they are given a trust, they betray that trust. The Prophet described the unhealthy qualities of a hypocrite and if we show any of these characteristics, we cannot say it is for or from Allah – even when we are angry for something that seems valid.

How we display our anger often relates to why we are angry, and the best person to look to as an example of this is the Prophet Muhammad ﷺ. Aisha, may Allah be pleased with her, had seen the Prophet ﷺ in all of his emotions and she described him as having excellence in all of them. She had seen the raw moments of the Messenger, in which he displayed his different emotions, and she describes him to be the most balanced and beautiful person.

One such example is in a Hadith narrated by Ibn Abi Mulaika in which Aisha said: "The Jews came to the Prophet ﷺ and said to him, 'As-Samu Alaika, May death be upon you,' and the Prophet ﷺ replied back with 'And upon you.'" I said to them, 'Death be upon you, and may Allah curse you and shower His wrath upon you!' but the Messenger of

Allah ﷺ said, 'Be gentle and calm oh Aisha! Be gentle and beware of being harsh and saying evil things.' I said, 'Didn't you hear what they said?' He said, 'Didn't you hear what I replied to them? I have returned their statement to them and my invocation against them will be accepted but theirs against me will not be accepted.'"[81]

Another example is narrated by Anas: While the Prophet ﷺ was in the house of Aisha, one of the mothers of the believers sent a meal in a dish. Aisha struck the hand of the servant, causing the dish to fall and break. The Prophet ﷺ gathered the broken pieces of the dish and then started collecting on them the food which had been in the dish and said, "Your mother (my wife) felt jealous." Then he detained the servant until a sound dish was brought from Aisha, he gave the sound dish to the wife whose dish had been broken and kept the broken one at Aisha's house.[82]

There was however one occasion when the Prophet ﷺ did truly get angry, and that was when Aisha made comments in relation to Khadijah, may Allah be pleased with her, saying that she had been replaced and that he should stop mentioning her so often. It was the angriest she had ever witnessed the Messenger of Allah ﷺ. His face turned red with anger and he said to Aisha that Allah did not give him anyone better than Khadijah as she believed in him when others disbelieved, she spent on him when others deprived him and Allah blessed him with her children whilst having no children from any other of his wives. It is important to note here that although he praised Khadijah he did not insult Aisha, but he was angry on behalf of Allah and on behalf of Khadijah.[83]

When comparing the two incidents, the Prophet ﷺ could have become extremely angry and yelled at Aisha for embarrassing him in front of the other Companion, but instead he realised that she felt jealous and acted in a way that was not the best and simply asked for the dish to be replaced. When there are people around, that is the point at which your ego can get the better of you, however the Prophet ﷺ did not say anything that would embarrass her further. Whilst, when it was just the two of them and Aisha spoke about Khadijah in a way that was not befitting, he became angry as it was an injustice to Khadijah.

A similar occurrence happened when Abu Bakr and Umar got into an argument, and Abu Bakr went to the Masjid where the Prophet Muhammad ﷺ noticed that Abu Bakr seemed upset and worried. Abu Bakr told the Prophet ﷺ that he and Umar had had an argument and

Umar was now upset with Abu Bakr and was not willing to accept his apology. He was not complaining about Umar, but rather sharing his worry with the Messenger of Allah ﷺ. Umar also went looking for Abu Bakr to clear and forget the matter, and he found him with the Prophet ﷺ who looked at Umar with an expression of extreme upset and anger. Abu Bakr saw the expression on the Prophet's face and exclaimed, "Ya Rasoolullah! I was the one who transgressed, and Umar didn't forgive me, I was worried. It was me not him."

The Prophet ﷺ looked at Umar and said, "When I began calling people to Allah, all of you gave me a hard time except for Abu Bakr. So will you leave my Companion alone?" The Messenger of Allah ﷺ stood up for Abu Bakr in front of Umar; Umar was second only to Abu Bakr from the Companions. The Prophet ﷺ knew when and how to show this type of anger; he knew how to deal with every situation accordingly.

Another Hadith which shows the righteous anger of the Prophet ﷺ is reported by Jabir: Mu'adh bin Jabal al-Ansari led his companions in the night prayer and prolonged it for them. A man from amongst us, after separating himself from the congregation, said his own prayer. Mu'adh was informed of this and he called the man a hypocrite. When the man heard of this, he went to the Messenger of Allah ﷺ to inform him of what Mu'adh said, and upon this the Messenger of Allah ﷺ said to him, "Mu'adh, are you going to be a tribulation for the people?"

And yet again on another occasion, the Prophet ﷺ saw a woman from the opposing side who had died in the battlefield and he expressed his anger over her death. He did not approve of women being killed and he made it known through his anger.

When looking at the many examples of the Prophet's character, we can see that he was composed even in his anger. His anger was calculated, he knew what he was saying and he did not do or say anything that could harm another person, and this was due to the fact that his anger was always channelled in the right way and he was angry in a manner that would befit being angry for the sake of Allah. The Messenger of Allah ﷺ never had to be asked to calm down as he never let his anger take control of his words and actions, whereas we may need a third person to come in and try to diffuse the situation because we have no control over our anger.

Righteous anger is something that has been seen in all of the Messengers of Allah. For example, when Musa, may the blessings of Allah be upon him, returned from the mountain after receiving revelations from Allah, he found the people worshipping a golden calf. He became extremely angry, not for himself, but for Allah. They had been saved from the Pharaoh and were rescued by Allah, but they turned back to polytheism whilst Musa had been away for a short time, thus making him angry.

Isa, may the blessings of Allah be upon him, also showed controlled, righteous anger towards the priests and scholars of Bani Israel when pointing out that they were disguising injustice with religious language. He said to them that they had put the material world on top of their heads and the Hereafter under their feet, and whatever they say may be a cure but their actions were nothing but disease. He used very strong words towards them because his anger was justified.

An incident that is narrated in Sahih Muslim shows the righteous anger of the Companions, although it may not have been entirely correct, it was still praiseworthy. Bilal, Salman and Suhayb were walking past Abu Sufyan – before he had accepted Islam – and said that the swords of Allah did not reach the neck of the enemy of Allah (meaning to say, Abu Sufyan was lucky that they did not kill him). Abu Bakr witnessed this, and he was afraid that such comments would disturb the treaty of Hudaibiyyah, and so he admonished the other three Companions. He was angry for the right reasons as he believed it would disturb the peace that the treaty had brought. Abu Bakr then went to the Prophet ﷺ to inform him of this matter, to which the Messenger of Allah ﷺ said to Abu Bakr that he may have made the three Companions angry by admonishing them, and if he made them angry then he may have made Allah angry too. The Messenger of Allah ﷺ did not say to Abu Bakr that he was wrong, but he warned him that speaking to three of the best Companions in such a way may have made them and Allah angry. Abu Bakr then rushed back to the three and asked for their forgiveness, to which they said do not worry. Bilal, Salman and Suhayb's anger was also praiseworthy as they did not transgress their limits. They did not abuse Abu Sufyan verbally or physically but showed him the honour of Islam.

Following are a few points that can help in finding and channelling our righteous anger:

1. We must remember the supplication of the Prophet ﷺ in which he said, "Oh Allah, I ask for the ability to speak a word of truth when I am pleased and when I am angry." No matter

what our state of emotion is, we should focus on speaking the truth. If we are angry, we must be angry for the right reasons, our intentions should be righteous, thus enabling our anger to manifest itself in a way that is pleasing to Allah.

2. Another Hadith to remember is of the Prophet Muhammad ﷺ saying, "Let not one of you make a judgement between two people when he is in a state of anger."[84] We should not make decisions or do things in a state of anger, as it could ultimately lead to the wrong decision.

3. One of the Companions who came in the Year of the Delegation said, "There is no good in forbearance and patience if there are no controls or checks that would stop a person from being taken advantage of." In other words, this was to say that there is no good being a forgiving and gentle person if it involves naivete. The Prophet Muhammad ﷺ was an extremely gentle person but he also showed diligence and intelligence in the way that he handled matters, knowing when to be angry and for what reasons.

May Allah guide us and help us to control our anger and be angry only for the right reasons. May Allah give us a sense of protective honour for His *deen* and allow us to do that which pleases Him. Amin.

18

THE RIGHTS OF THE NEIGHBOUR

It is reported on the authority of Abu Hurairah that the Messenger of Allah ﷺ said: ...He who believes in Allah and the Last Day should treat his neighbour with kindness...

IN THIS CHAPTER we will look into a topic that is very different from the previous chapters, again it is something that is usually only discussed in a shallow manner. The topic of the rights of neighbours is not discussed in depth enough, and there is very little practical advice on applying it in our modern lives – especially when considering it in the context of justice.

There are several narrations conveying this message, which I will share before we move onto looking at them in more detail:

Abu Hurairah, may Allah be pleased with him, reported that the Messenger of Allah ﷺ said: "He who believes in Allah and the Last Day should treat his neighbour with kindness."[85]

Anas, may Allah be pleased with him, narrated that the Prophet Muhammad ﷺ said: "Whoever believes in Allah and the Last Day, let him honour his neighbour."[86]

In other narration the Prophet ﷺ said, "He does not truly believe until he loves for his brother, or neighbour, what he loves for himself."[87]

In another narration, the Prophet ﷺ said, "By Allah, he does not believe – thrice – the one whose neighbour is not secure from his harm."[88]

In this last narration, the Prophet ﷺ repeated his words three times to capture the attention of his Companions, to make them curious and to make them understand the gravity of his statement. They asked the Messenger of Allah ﷺ who he was referring to, and he said the one whose neighbour is not secure from his harm. In another version of this Hadith, the Prophet ﷺ said that he will not enter Paradise whose neighbour does not feel secure from his harm. We learn the severity of harming our neighbour from this Hadith and that it can cost us our place in Paradise.

The term 'not feel secure' does not mean that we pose an imminent danger to our neighbour, but it means that our bad attitude or character causes our neighbour to feel uneasy around us. This Hadith does not apply to neighbours who are islamophobes or similar, as they may cause you to fear your own safety.

Dr Hatem commented on this Hadith saying that part of our neighbour's right is that we reduce noise pollution for their comfort, and that we mow our own lawn so their property value does not depreciate due to an untidy neighbourhood.

The first thing we take from these Hadiths is that we cannot show injustice to our neighbour. We must fulfil their rights and ensure that we do not do anything that can cause them to feel discomfort. The second lesson we can take from them is to think about the Day of Judgement and the people that we will have to face. We usually only think about enemies or people who oppressed us, and we forget about our neighbours. However, in an authentic Hadith from the Prophet Muhammad ﷺ, he said that the first two people who will be judged on the Day of Judgement for disputing will be two neighbours. Allah will ask us if we fulfilled the rights of our neighbours.

The Messenger of Allah ﷺ always treated his neighbours with the best of manners and excellence. He overcame evil with love, mercy and compassion; he visited them when they were sick and gave in charity to them. In a Hadith narrated in Bukhari and Muslim, the Prophet ﷺ said that Jibreel (Gabriel) would come to him and keep telling him to take care of his neighbour until he thought that Jibreel would ask him to give a portion of his inheritance to his neighbour. What this shows is that neighbours are like family and they have rights upon us.

There is a narration from Jabbar, may Allah be pleased with him, and although it is weak it is a wonderful supplementary evidence regarding the rights of the neighbour. He narrates that the Prophet ﷺ found out about the sickness of his neighbour on a routine visit; he did not go for the first time after hearing that he was ill, but he visited on a regular basis. The neighbours were Jewish, and the boy was on his deathbed. The Prophet ﷺ sat next to him and told him to say the declaration of faith at which the boy looked up at his father, and his father told him to listen to the Prophet ﷺ as he was a good man. The Messenger of Allah ﷺ made it a routine to visit his neighbours and check that they were doing okay.

The rights of the neighbour do not just stop at us visiting them; in an authentic Hadith reported by Samura bin Jundab, the Prophet Muuhammad ﷺ said: "The neighbour of a home has greater right to the home of his neighbour, or the property, when it is being sold."[89]

What we learn from this Hadith is that before we sell our home, we should ask our neighbour if he wants to purchase it as he may have a use for it, such as extending his own home. Doing so, will be an act of kindness and giving our neighbour his due right.

A wonderful example from more recent times was shared by Dr Muhammad Ismail al-Muqaddam, where he mentioned that a fellow Muslim brother kept collecting newspapers that were thrown into his neighbour's front garden whilst the neighbour was away on a trip. When the neighbour returned, the Muslim man went over to his neighbour's house to hand him a box filled with the newspapers that he had collected. The neighbour was taken aback and asked why he did so, to which the Muslim man replied that he wanted to make sure his home looked occupied whilst he was away to keep it safe and that Islam teaches us to look after our neighbours. The neighbour was so amazed with this gesture and teaching of Islam that he later became a Muslim.

This is the beauty of Islam. It places these duties and expectations upon us before we are asked by people, or before people even think about asking us. Another example is of a Muslim sister I know from New Orleans who accepted Islam around the age of sixty-five, and every time she went out to mow her lawn, she would also mow her neighbour's lawn. She was not asked to, she was not expected to, but she did so because of the teachings of our beloved Prophet Muhammad ﷺ. There are so many things that the Prophet ﷺ has told us to do that we do not even consider or think about. We have become too isolated in our homes and lives that we do not give a second thought to the rights of our neighbours.

Another important point that the Messenger of Allah ﷺ made was that we should not belittle even the smallest deeds or gifts. One such Hadith was reported by Abu Hurairah in which the Prophet Muhammad ﷺ said: "Oh Muslim women! No one of you should consider insignificant (a gift) to give her neighbour even if it is a gift of the trotters of a sheep."[90]

Aisha, may Allah be pleased with her, also narrated that she asked the Prophet ﷺ who she should send her gifts to as she had two neighbours, to which the Prophet ﷺ replied, "The one whose door is nearer to you."[91] The neighbour that is closer to us has more rights, and we should keep this in mind so as not to do injustice.

In a Hadith reported by Abu Dhar, the Prophet Muhammad told him, "Oh Abu Dhar! Whenever you prepare a broth, put plenty of water in it, and frequent your neighbours with it."[92] This was to say to make enough for him and his family, but also extra to give to his neighbours out of kindness and courtesy. However, sometimes courtesy to our neighbours may be limited to tolerating them and their annoyances. We should not refuse a neighbour from fixing something in their wall, however annoying it may be to hear the constant knocking. Abu Hurairah narrated that the Prophet ﷺ said, "None of you should prevent his neighbour from fixing a wooden peg in his wall." And when Abu Hurairah saw people doing so, he said to them, "Why do I see you refusing this nowadays? By Allah, I will certainly continue proclaiming it."[93]

Another Hadith narrated by Abu Dhar cements this notion of tolerating our neighbours, "Of those who Allah loves, a man who has a bad neighbour but he bears with it with patience until they die or Allah settles the matter for them." Showing patience is better for us and our neighbours; if we were to become angry with them it could further ruin the neighbourly relationship and make matters more difficult in this life and on the Day of Judgement.

The Messenger of Allah ﷺ also mentioned a very simple but powerful point, "He is not a believer who eats his fill while his neighbour beside him goes hungry."[94] It is worth noting that none of the Hadiths mention whether the neighbour was Muslim or not, rather there is no distinguishing factor and all neighbours must be treated with kindness and compassion even if they are non-Muslim. The Companions internalised these concepts and would ensure that their neighbours, Muslim or not, were given their due rights.

One Hadith that I would like to mention here provides a real insight into how we treat our neighbours and the effects it will have in the Hereafter. It is reported by Abu Hurairah: "A man asked, 'Oh Messenger of Allah! There is a woman who prays, gives charity and fasts a great deal, but she harms her neighbours with her speech (by insulting them.' He said, 'She is (bound to be) in the Hellfire.' The man said, 'Oh Messenger of Allah! There is another woman who is well-known for how little she fasts and prays, but she gives charity from the dried yoghurt she makes, and she does not harm her neighbours.' He said, 'She is (bound to be) in Paradise.'"[95]

Ibn Abdil Barr commented on this Hadith saying that someone will be standing on the Day of Judgement with many good deeds, but because they were abusive to people either through their words or actions, their good deeds will go to the people that they hurt or abused. And after all their good deeds have been taken by those that they hurt, they will say that they have nothing left, after which Allah will tell the people to give that person their sins. This is an extremely profound message in that we could have an entire mountain's worth of good deeds that we did with sincerity, but because of our abusive nature towards our neighbours and other people, our good deeds will be given away to pay off our moral debts. When considering this in light of our neighbours, it is compounded because a neighbour will have double right over us (we cannot be abusive towards anyone under any circumstances, and the fact that they are our neighbours gives them further rights).

When Ibn Mas'ud asked about the worst major sins, the Prophet Muhammad ﷺ told him adultery (*zina*) with your neighbour's spouse is of the worst. Adultery in and of itself is a major sin, but when it is committed with the neighbour's spouse, the enormity of the sin is incomprehensible.

There is also a Hadith in which the Prophet Muhammad ﷺ mentions the three worst types of people, and one of them is "... a bad neighbour who, if he sees something good, he conceals it, and if he sees something bad, he broadcasts it."[96] Making it known to everyone that your neighbour did a sin or some evil, rather than sharing their goodness makes you from the worst of people. Imam Abu Hanifa had a neighbour with whom he shared a wall, and this young neighbour of his used to become drunk every single night, singing and making lots of noise saying "They've forgotten about me." Abu Hanifa tolerated this every night and did not broadcast his neighbour's actions to anyone; in fact, one night, Abu Hanifa woke up from his sleep and realised that he could not hear his neighbour; he was either sober or not at home. Abu Hanifa then went to check on his neighbour and found that he had been arrested because he was drowning in debt and owed money to many people. Abu Hanifa then asked where he was being held and went to find out how much debt he owed; it was a very large amount of twenty-seven thousand dinars. The Imam being a wealthy man himself, paid off the young man's debt. The young man came out of prison and saw Abu Hanifa and asked him why he had paid off his debt and Abu Hanifa put his hand on his shoulder and said, "Did we forget about you? I missed hearing you at night." He lightened up the mood and took the young man home, who later went on to become one of Imam Abu Hanifa's best students.

We must also aim to be the best to our neighbours, so much so that they would cry over our departure (that could mean because we are moving to a new house, or because of death). Abdullah bin Mubarak had a Jewish neighbour who kept getting asked by Abdullah's students to sell his house to them so that they could live next door to their teacher. The Jewish neighbour doubled the price of his house and when asked why he said one part of the price is the value of the house, and the second part is due to having a neighbour as good as Abdullah bin Mubarak.

When thinking about situations applicable to today, one example is of car parking spaces in mosques. If you park your car in more than one space, you are taking up your neighbour's space. It is a tangible form of abuse; you are hurting your neighbour by taking up their space and making parking difficult for them. Another example is of weddings and the fact that some people elongate their wedding parties and they carry on for several days, which results in inconveniencing their neighbours with noise and troublesome car parking.

We should also try to be the first to greet our neighbour, rather than wait for them to initiate the greeting. The Messenger of Allah taught us to be the first to greet our neighbours, the first to visit them, the first to check up on them – we must strive to be the best we can. We should be willing to help our neighbours in their time of need, no matter how big or small the need may be. Simple things such as lending a lawnmower or making some extra food to share with them is a way of showing excellence towards our neighbours.

May Allah allow us to fulfil the rights of our neighbours, our families, our communities, and above all the rights of Allah. Amin.

19

THE DEFINITION, CATEGORISATION AND PROHIBITION OF TORTURE IN ISLAM

It has been narrated that Hisham bin Hakim bin Hizam (May Allah be pleased with him) happened to pass by some (non-Arab) farmers of Syria who had been made to stand in the sun, and olive oil was poured on their heads. He said: "What is the matter?" He was told that they had been detained for the non-payment of Jizyah. (Another narration says that they were being tortured for not having paid Al-Kharaj). Thereupon Hisham said: "I bear testimony to the fact that I heard the Messenger of Allah ﷺ saying, 'Allah will torment those who torment people in the world.'" Then he proceeded towards their Amir and reported this Hadith to him. The Amir then issued orders for their release.

WE WILL LOOK at a very complex topic in this chapter, and that is the topic of torture. There are sub-topics within this topic but it all falls under the umbrella of social justice. The word for torture in the Arabic language is *ta'theeb*, but it also means punishment, depending on the context that it is used in.

The Hadith that we will look at first gives a clear indication of the gravity of this subject and we see how it is applied by Hisham bin Hakeem:

It has been narrated that Hisham bin Hakeem bin Hizam happened to pass by some farmers in Syria who had been made to stand in the sun, and olive oil was poured on their heads. He said, "What is the matter?" He was told that they had been detained for the non-payment of taxes. Hisham then said, "I bear testimony to the fact that I heard the Messenger of Allah ﷺ saying, 'Allah will torment those who torment people in the world.'" Then he proceeded towards their leader and reported this Hadith to him. The leader then issued orders for their release.[97]

The Hadith does not refer to whether the people being tortured are Muslim or non-Muslim, but it is the prohibition of tormenting or torturing in general. It also does not matter whether a person is in a position of authority or not; the fact that they tortured other people will result in Allah doing the same to them.

Another powerful Hadith by the Prophet ﷺ is, "Do not punish (torture) with the punishment of God."[98] This Hadith is in particular referring to the punishment of fire, as it is the punishment that will be used by Allah for those that disobeyed and disbelieved. This narration also brings us back to the Hadith *Qudsi* that I mentioned in the very first chapter: Abu Dharr reported that the Prophet Muhammad ﷺ said, "Allah Almighty said: Oh my servants, I have forbidden oppression for Myself and I have forbidden oppression amongst you, so do not oppress one another."[99]

Allah has forbidden oppression on Himself and on us, so how can we torture others? We have no right to oppress or to torture others, doing so is putting ourselves in the position of Allah which is a grave sin. The Prophet ﷺ could have simply said do not punish with fire, but he used the words "do not punish with the punishment of God," because only Allah reserves the right to punish people with fire, and He will only punish those who are deserving of it as He is the Most Just.

However, throughout history people have unjustly punished people by burning them at the stake or throwing them into fires. The people of Ukdhood, as mentioned in the Qur'an, were thrown into a ditch of fire for believing in the Oneness of Allah. Similarly, and unfortunately, today we can see our fellow Rohingya Muslims being punished for their belief. Furthermore, the Prophet Ibrahim, may the blessings of Allah be upon him, was thrown into the fire, but Allah saved him. Ibn al-Qayyim commented on this and made a very profound statement saying, "The fire was the punishment that was used against Ibrahim, and not by the followers of Ibrahim." Nobody who claims to believe in the message brought by Ibrahim can resort to torturing people in the manner that they attempted to torture Ibrahim.

There are many general Hadiths that teach us that the way in which we deal with others, will be the way in which Allah will deal with us. One such example of a Hadith is when the Messenger of Allah ﷺ said, "Allah is merciful only to those of His slaves who are merciful to others."[100] We are being given both positive and negative reinforcements through this Hadith; if we treat others with mercy, we will be treated with mercy by Allah, but if we do not treat others with mercy, we will also not be treated with mercy by Allah.

The subject of torture in Islam is not limited to humans but spans further afield and an interesting point to note is that the vast majority of Hadith relating to torture are in reference to animals. A very prominent Hadith about torturing animals is the one about the woman and the cat. It is narrated by Abdullah bin Umar who said: "Allah's Messenger ﷺ said, 'A woman was tortured and put in Hell because of a cat which she had kept locked until it died of hunger.'"[101] She had caged the cat, so it was unable to fend for itself, whilst she also did not provide any food or water to the cat. The woman behaved unjustly, and torturing the cat resulted in her entering the Hellfire.

There are many such Hadith regarding torturing animals. The Prophet ﷺ spoke about those who brand their animals, thus causing them pain as torturing them. The Prophet ﷺ also spoke about overburdening camels and other animals such as donkeys as they will testify to Allah on the Day of Judgement that they were overburdened. The fact that there are numerous such Hadith makes it clear that if torturing animals is forbidden, there is no question that torturing humans is also forbidden.

The Prophet Muhammad ﷺ also forbade torturing prisoners; it did not matter how evil the prisoner was, Muslims were not to torture prisoners. In fact, prisoners of war were treated in ways that they had never seen before, such as being asked to teach those who could not read or write. We can see many examples of prisoners being tortured in the world we live in today, in prisons such as Guantanamo Bay. There are also discussions on torture techniques such as waterboarding that take place in many prisons around the world. Torturing of prisoners is not something that has been wiped out over the centuries, unfortunately it still exists today with countries that claim to be democratic and law-abiding being involved in these practices.

One Hadith in particular is in reference to Thumama who was the chief of Banu Hanifa, he was one of the greatest enemies of the Prophet Muhammad ﷺ, and he used to target and harm Muslims. Abu Hurairah narrates: "The Messenger of Allah sent some horsemen to Najd and they brought a man of Banu Hanifa called Thumama bin Uthal who was the chief of the people of al-Yamamah and bound him to one of the pillars of the mosque. The Messenger of Allah came out to him and said, 'What are you expecting Thumama?' He replied, 'I expect good, Muhammad. If you kill me, you will kill one whose blood will be avenged. If you show favour, you will show it to one who is grateful and if you want property and ask, you will be given as much of it as you wish.' The Messenger of Allah left him until the following day and asked him, 'What are you expecting Thumama?' He repeated the same words in reply. The Messenger of Allah left him until the following day, and he mentioned the same words. The Messenger of Allah then said, 'Set Thumama free.' Thumama then went off to some palm trees near the mosque and took a bath there. He entered the mosque and said, 'I testify that there is no god but Allah and I testify that Muhammad is His servant and His messenger.'"[102]

Scholars have said that this Hadith shows that the Prophet Muhammad ﷺ refused to treat Thumama the way in which he and his tribe would treat Muslims, which was the way of torture. The Prophet ﷺ did not allow the practices of Banu Hanifa to become part of practice in his life (*Sunnah*). After witnessing the beautiful character of the Muslims and the Prophet Muhammad ﷺ, his heart inclined towards Islam. After he accepted Islam, he asked the Prophet ﷺ how to perform *umrah* as he wanted to make the pilgrimage. He was a powerful and well-respected man in Makkah, and he was the first man who was able to perform *umrah* while the rest of the Muslims were boycotted and stopped from performing pilgrimages. After performing the *umrah*, he placed Makkah under economic boycott because of the way they were treating the Prophet ﷺ and the Muslims.

Allah also talks about the people who give food, in spite of their love for it in *Surah al-Insan* 76:8: "And they give food, in spite of their love for it, to the needy, the orphan and the captive." The verse speaks about how we should spend on prisoners and provide food for them because in the days of ignorance, prisoners would be let out for an hour or two during the day to beg for food as they would not feed the prisoners themselves. Islam teaches us to provide prisoners with dignity at the very least; they should not be made to beg for food or any simple rights.

Ibn Abbas, may Allah be pleased with him, who was the cousin of the Prophet Muhammad ﷺ said, "In those days their prisoners were *mushrikeen* (idol worshippers); on the day of Badr, the Messenger of Allah ﷺ commanded them to be kind to their prisoners, so the Muslim soldiers used to put the prisoners before themselves when it came to food." The Muslims would feed the prisoners before they would feed themselves and their families. Another commentator of the Qur'an named Mujahid said, "They would give food to these prisoners even though they themselves desired it and loved it."

What we learn from this is that the prohibition of torture went beyond the physical aspects, it included the prohibition of depriving people of sleep, or food and drink, or clothes, or their dignity. In one Hadith it was said that the Prophet Muhammad ﷺ was pacing and had tears in his eyes after the Battle of Badr. When the Companions asked why he was pacing and upset, he said, "I could hear Abbas (his uncle) moaning because of the chains", meaning that the chains were causing him discomfort. One of the Companions then went to loosen the chains for Abbas. The Prophet ﷺ told his Companions that he was pleased with them, but they would need to do the same for all the other prisoners too in order to be equal. They made sure that they did not keep their prisoners or captives in a condition that could be considered torturous; their goal was not to cause them pain.

We also find that the Prophet ﷺ spoke about forced confessions and said, "Allah has pardoned people for what they do out of mistake, forgetfulness, or under duress."[103] The way in which this relates to torture is that you do not have to insist upon things that will result in you getting tortured or further tortured. The most famous example is of Ammar bin Yasir, when he and his parents were being tortured by Abu Jahl and forced to curse the Prophet ﷺ. His parents did not curse the Prophet ﷺ and were martyred for that, but Ammar cursed the Prophet ﷺ and felt extremely guilty about this, he told the Prophet ﷺ that he only spoke with his tongue, not his heart. The Messenger of Allah ﷺ then told him that if they torture him again, he can curse again; Ammar was told not to put himself in a situation where he would be tortured. The early Muslims especially were given this exception because of the harsh persecution they faced on a regular basis; they were allowed to say things that they did not mean to escape torture at the hands of the non-Muslims.

Another form of torture is investigative, which is mentioned in an authentic narration during the time of Nu'man bin Bashir – one of the youngest Companions of the Prophet ﷺ. Azhar bin Abdullah al-Harari said: "Some goods of the people of Kila were stolen. They accused some weavers of theft and went to Nu'man bin Bashir, the Companion of the Prophet ﷺ. He confined them for some days and then set them free. They came to Nu'man and said, 'You have set them free without beating and investigation.' Nu'man said, 'What do you want? You want me to beat them. If your goods are found with them, then it is alright. Otherwise, I shall take from your back as I have taken from their backs (retaliation).' They asked, 'Is this your decision?' He replied, 'This is the decision of Allah and His Apostle ﷺ.'

Nu'man kept the group of accused men for a few days and asked them if they stole and a simple search of their belongings was done; there was nothing intrusive or harsh. And when he let them go after not finding anything, the accusers wanted him to do more, they wanted a thorough and harsh investigation involving beating, to which he said that if the weavers are still found to be innocent after a beating, then the accusers will need to have the same beating.

This is a powerful narration because it truly highlights the prohibition in Islam of investigative torture. The early scholars completely prohibited any form of investigative torture, regardless of who the person was. However, later scholars in the eleventh and twelfth centuries discussed this matter and started to allow some exceptions in regard to showing some physical force in the process of investigation, but only with those who had a known history of criminal activity. The later scholars did this in response to the European Criminal Procedure which was similar to half proof; it was becoming the norm of the world and the scholars understood that they had to deal with the changing circumstances and definitions of torture. Islam had set boundaries, but there was room for discussion within the grey areas, but they worked within the limits set by Allah and His Messenger ﷺ.

The United Nations defines torture to be "any act by which severe pain or suffering, whether physical or mental, is intentionally inflicted on a person for such purposes as obtaining from him or a third person information or a confession, punishing him for an act he or a third person has committed or is suspected of having committed, or intimidating or coercing him or a third person, or for any reason based on discrimination of any kind."

Whilst the United Nations has limited this to humans, Islam's definition of torture goes further than humans and includes animals. Torturing animals is included within the same prohibition; they are also created by Allah and we have no right to oppress them or torture them. The Prophet Muhammad ﷺ mentioned to us that the first proceedings on the Day of Judgement would be between the animals and that Allah will do justice between them. So, what then of a human who had more power than someone else and abused or oppressed them, or abused an animal?

May Allah protect us from oppressing or wronging other people and animals in any capacity. Amin.

20

PROPHETIC GUIDANCE ON WORK CONDITIONS AND EMPLOYEE TREATMENT

It was narrated from 'Abdullah bin 'Umar that the Messenger of Allah ﷺ said: "Give the worker his wages before his sweat dries."

IN THIS CHAPTER we will look into the relationship between an employer and an employee, the main focus being the rights of the employee. In the next chapter we will focus more on the rights of the employer. Two of the Hadith that I will be sharing are narrated by the same Companion, and it is interesting to note that particular subjects are narrated by specific Companions of the Prophet ﷺ. You can tie the personalities of these Companions to the subject matters if there is a consistency in the Hadiths being narrated.

The first Hadith is narrated by Abdullah bin Umar, may Allah be pleased with him: The Messenger of Allah ﷺ said, "Give the worker his wages before his sweat dries."[104]

This Hadith is very well-known but rarely spoken about in a modern application. The command that the Prophet ﷺ gives is a metaphor; as soon as the work is completed, they should be paid. It is a form of excellence (*ihsaan*) to pay someone before they finish the job and it becomes a form of injustice if you do not pay them after they have completed the work. It has been said that, "It is impermissible to delay and postpone payment when someone is able to pay their labourer."

When we try to apply this Hadith in a modern setting, for example in a corporate setting, it is easy to see that nobody will be sweating whilst sitting down in an office chair. However, they should still be paid on time, as soon as they have completed their work, and it is even better to pay them before they finish their job. In another Hadith related in Bukhari, the Prophet Muhammad ﷺ said, "The withholding of a payment by a person who is wealthy is a form of oppression."

Whilst in certain circumstances it may be that a person is not able to give the full payment in one instalment, they can work out a deal with their employee, making it lawful. However, these Hadith are focused on employers withholding payments unjustly and as a form of greed.

In a Hadith related in Abu Dawud, the Prophet Muhammad ﷺ said, "The one who delays in payment even though he is able to pay, there are two things that become lawful. One is his reputation, and second is punishment." It does not count as backbiting to talk about a person who wrongs their employees because it is a means of warning others. However, what we say should be kept limited to only that which will protect others from falling victim to their injustice. Just as it becomes permissible to speak of such a person's reputation, punishment also becomes permissible for them. Scholars have said that the type of punishment that is permissible is that they can be detained; this was revolutionary in the sense that selective justice was common at that time, with poorer people being punished whilst the wealthy were let go.

There is a chapter in Sahih Bukhari which is dedicated to the sin of the one who fails to pay their employees, and a Hadith within it is reported by Abu Hurairah: The Prophet ﷺ said, "Allah has said 'I will be an opponent to three types of people on the Day of Judgement. The first one is someone who makes a covenant in My name but proves to be treacherous. The second, who sells a free man and keeps their price. The third is someone who employs a labourer and takes their labour but doesn't pay them.'" This Hadith illustrates the gravity of the sin of not paying an employee or labourer on time. Becoming lazy in paying an employee will result in Allah opposing us on the Day of Judgement, and if Allah Himself has said that He will be an opponent to such a person, what chance do we have of entering Paradise? We do not know the needs of the worker; they may be too shy to tell us that they need to make a payment for something else or they may worry that if they ask us directly for their rightful payment, we may not employ them again. We cannot assume that their silence is approval of our delay in payment and must strive to at least give their payment on time if we cannot show excellence by paying them beforehand.

Another Hadith from Abu Saeed al-Khudri narrates that the Prophet Muhammad ﷺ said, "Whoever employs someone to work for him he must specify the wages in advance."[105] It is prohibited to discuss wages once the work has begun; even if we enter a simple verbal contract with someone, we must specify the payment beforehand. There should be no room for disappointment or argument when entering into a contract and the employee should be given their full right. We will be wronging the person if we do not specify their wages in advance; if they start doing the job and we decide what to pay them in the midst of it, it could very well be that the payment is not enough, but they do not have the heart to stop doing the job as they have already started, or their financial circumstances are so bad that they accept it.

We cannot make assumptions on what will be an acceptable wage; whether we know the person or not, whether the person is Muslim or not.

The Prophet Muhammad ﷺ taught us that this act of courtesy goes beyond the Muslim community; we are not allowed to take advantage of non-Muslims. He taught us that the ethics of labour go beyond payment, and he spoke first and foremost about the *muaith*. A *muaith* is someone who has a covenant – they were protected people who were non-Muslims that lived in Muslim lands. In a Hadith narrated by Abdullah bin Amar, the Messenger of Allah said: "Whoever wrongs a *muaith*, infringes on his rights, burdens him with more than he can bear, or takes something of his against his will, I will prosecute him on the Day of Judgement."[106]

This is an extremely powerful statement from the Prophet ﷺ as he will be standing against someone from his own followers (*ummah*) because they wronged or harmed a non-Muslim. The Hadith also involves the concept of labour as the Prophet ﷺ mentions burdening them, and burdening someone with more than they can handle is prohibited.

Compassion is a big part of Islam and we are taught neither to take advantage of people, nor withhold their rights, but instead to aim to deal with people with excellence (*ihsaan*). The concept of pension for elderly people was first introduced within the Islamic system by Umar bin al-Khattab, may Allah be pleased with him. He said, "What kind of a people let a man go helpless in his old age after getting service from him in his youth?"

In another Hadith the Messenger of Allah ﷺ said, "Your servants are your brothers. Allah has placed them under your hand. He who has someone under their hand should feed them with the same food he eats, clothe them with the same clothes he wears, and not burden them beyond their capacity. And if you do, you need to help them."[107] The Prophet ﷺ did not leave out servants as recipients of just treatment; he made it clear that we cannot burden them with something that they cannot handle, and if we do give them something that is difficult, then we must ensure that we assist them in the task.

Labour ethics go beyond payment, they also include the way that we speak to them, the way we deal with them and the way we respect them. Many of the scholars mentioned a specific Hadith when talking about the workplace, or the relationship between an employer and employee. This Hadith is narrated by Anas bin Malik who said: "I served the Prophet ﷺ for ten years. Never did he say uff to me. Nor did he criticise something I did. He never said why did you do that or ask why didn't you do that."[108] What we learn here is that the Prophet ﷺ never showed any sign of frustration or annoyance towards Anas, nor was he critical of how Anas did things. If the Prophet ﷺ wanted things done a certain way, he had a way of conveying that message without degrading Anas who had started serving the Prophet ﷺ when he was a child. If the Prophet ﷺ treated a child with such dignity, we must ask ourselves what this means when it comes to an adult employee?

The Hadith teaches us not to be overly critical with employees. We must be lenient and patient; we must aim to get our wants or needs across in a dignified manner. It also brings about the realisation that often a person who is in a position of power in the workplace, will come home and speak to their spouse in the same way as they do with their employees. When we are constantly in a position of power, we can very well start seeing ourselves as superior to others and thus it becomes a problem of pride.

In one Hadith the Prophet ﷺ said: "A person cannot have pride if they do these three things: a person eats with their servant (or employees), a person who rides a donkey through the marketplace (not a camel or a horse, but a modest transport), and a person who ties their own sheep and milks their own sheep."[109] The Messenger of Allah ﷺ used to sit with Anas bin Malik on the floor to eat; he led by example and showed us how we should humble ourselves. We may not be in a society where we use horses and camels to travel on a daily basis but humbling ourselves by walking or using public transport rather than taking our nice cars, helps to save ourselves from pride. We need to go out of our way to remove arrogance and pride from ourselves. If we start viewing ourselves as inherently superior because others are inferior in terms of a contract, then we risk treating them in an unjust way and destroying ourselves in the process. It paves the way to developing pride which can be dangerous for us on a spiritual basis.

The Prophet Muhammad ﷺ taught us that we should show appreciation for those that work for us. He showed appreciation for the woman who used to clean the mosque even after she had passed away. Another example is of Rabiah ibn Kab al-Aslami who used to serve the Prophet Muhammad ﷺ and the Prophet ﷺ said to him "Ask me for anything that you want," and Rabiah said he wanted the companionship of the Prophet ﷺ in Paradise. He obviously felt appreciated after years of service to the Messenger of Allah, which is why he could not think of anything else to ask for.

Allah also says in *Surah ash-Shu'ara* 26:183: *"And do not deprive people of their due and do not commit abuse on earth, spreading corruption."* It is an extremely powerful verse and the scholars have said that there is a correlation between a person who withholds wages and a person who spreads corruption; rarely can we find a person that withholds wages that is not guilty of spreading corruption. If a person does not show dignity to those that work for them, or does not give them their due, it is highly likely their arrogance will also play a part in spreading corruption in other ways.

Lastly, the Hadith that I would like to end this chapter with is another beautiful Hadith. As mentioned before, this Hadith is also narrated by Abdullah bin Umar: "There were three men that came from a previous nation, they went into a cave and a boulder blocked the entrance of that cave. They advised each other to make a supplication with a good deed that they have done for Allah's sake in the hope that the boulder would move. The first two men made supplications (*du'a*) and the boulder moved, but not enough for them to be able to leave the cave. The third man made *du'a* and said, 'Oh Allah, I employed many labourers and I gave each one of them their wages on time. But there was a man who I did not get to pay because he disappeared, so I invested those wages for him. From that small investment, Allah blessed me with all sorts of property (land, livestock etc). When the man returned, he said 'Oh Abdullah, pay me what you owe me.' And I said, 'You see all this, this is all yours.' He said, 'Are you making fun of me?' And I said, 'I invested it for you, so take it. It is all yours.' Oh Allah if I did that only seeking your pleasure then remove this difficulty for us.' And because of that, the boulder moved and cleared the way."[110]

It is a wonderful example of a man fulfilling his trust and returning it with excellence (*ihsaan*). He took the wages of the person that had worked for him and invested it so that it would continue to increase and then returned it to him when he came to collect his wages. Although it was only the original wage that was owed to him, the employer acted with pure sincerity and gave the man everything that had come about because of that small investment. The employer could have simply given him his original wages and benefited from the property, but he was conscious of Allah and did a great act of excellence.

May Allah make us just in all our affairs, and may Allah protect us from oppressing others or being oppressed. Amin.

21

THE CHARACTERISTICS OF A PIOUS EMPLOYEE

Buraidah narrated that the Prophet ﷺ said: When we appoint someone to an administrative post and provide him with an allowance, anything he takes beyond that is unfaithful dealing.

IN THE PREVIOUS CHAPTER we looked at some of the rights of the employee, with the main one being that they should be paid their wages as soon as they have completed their work. Or to reach the level of excellence (*ihsaan*), they should be paid before they have completed the work (unless there is an obvious risk that they will not complete it and take advantage of an early payment). The Prophet Muhammad ﷺ placed far more weight of responsibility on those people that are in a position of power, however, because the life example of Prophet Muhammad (*Sunnah*) is a comprehensive model for social justice, there is responsibility upon each and every person. For example, we may come across a Hadith that talks about the violations of the government and warns those in a position of power, but we can also find a Hadith that will tell us how to be a better citizen. Similarly, we will find Hadith that cover both sides of the employer and employee relationship.

Before going on to study the Hadith regarding the characteristics of a pious employee, I would like to mention that we will most definitely find differences in the contracts that existed at the time of the Prophet ﷺ and the ones that exist today; we must essentially extract the values from the lessons given. It is difficult to go into the specifics because the way that contacts functioned were different in Makkah than in Madinah (one society focused on trade whilst the other focused on agriculture), so there will be clear differences between then and now.

One of the biggest values that we can extract is the value on trust, or *amanah*. The concept of trust in Islam is very encompassing in the sense that it is not just limited to representing a trust that you have been given, but it includes a conversation that you have, it includes friendship and leadership. It is through our values and ethics that Islam has spread and can continue to spread across the world. Indonesia has the world's largest Muslim population, but Islam reached there through traders and Muslim merchants who arrived in the 14th Century. It was due to the values and ethics that the Muslims showed that they won the hearts and minds of the locals and Islam was able to spread.

It is also helpful to note that there were very few employer-employee relationships during the time of the Prophet Muhammad ﷺ, especially within the Islamic models of finance. It was however common to have an agent that acted on your behalf; they would be a temporary employee that was hired to provide a service for you. The employer-employee relationship as we see and understand today was virtually unfound in the Prophet's ﷺ society.

The first Hadith that we will look at is narrated by Buraidah: "The Prophet ﷺ said, 'When we appoint someone to an administrative post and provide him with an allowance, anything he takes beyond that is unfaithful dealing.'"[111]

What this means is that if someone is hired and they are given the rightful amount which they are owed, there is no transgression from the side of the one who is hiring or commissioning this work. However, if the hired individual takes more than their right, then it is a form of treachery regarding finances, or embezzlement (*ghulool*). Allah also mentions this in the Qur'an in *Surah al-Imran* 3:161: *"It is not befitting to any prophet that he would act unfaithfully (in regard to war booty), and whoever betrays (takes unlawfully), will come with what he took on the Day of Resurrection."* The spoils of war were entrusted with certain individuals before distribution to the people, and Allah is saying that it is unlawful to put some aside or take a bribe.

Abdullah bin Umar narrated that: "The Prophet ﷺ said, 'Salah will not be accepted without purification, nor charity from *ghulool*.'"[112] In the context of this Hadith, the word *ghulool* is referring to a person taking more than he was due; anything beyond what the person was owed becomes unlawful, or *ghulool*. Just like an employer can hold power over an employee to take less sometimes an employee can put pressure on his employer to be given more than his right, and this is also condemned.

There is a chapter in Sahih Bukhari titled, "*The chapter of gifts to those who have been appointed to do work.*" A Hadith within it is narrated on the authority of Abu Humaid as-Sa'idi who said: The Messenger of Allah ﷺ appointed a man from the Asad tribe, who was called Ibn Lutbiyya, in charge of collecting zakah (authorised him to receive zakah from the people on behalf of the state), When he returned with the collections, he said, 'This is for you and this is mine as it was presented to me as a gift. The Messenger of Allah ﷺ stood on the pulpit and praised God. Then he said, 'What about a state official whom I give an assignment to and who comes and says, this is for you and this has been presented to me as a gift? Why didn't he remain in the house of his father or the house of his mother so that he could observe whether gifts were presented to him or not. By the Being in Whose Hand is the life of Muhammad, any of you will not take anything from it but will bring it on the Day of Judgement, carrying on his neck a camel that will be growling, or a cow that will be bellowing or an ewe that will be bleating.' Then he raised his hands so that we could see the whiteness of his armpits. Then he said twice, 'Oh God, I have conveyed Your Commandments.'

The Prophet ﷺ in this Hadith is saying that the man should recognise that the gifts which were given to him were not because somebody genuinely wanted to gift him with something, but because they were trying to get him to compromise the integrity of his position. And the mention of the animals is that whoever takes something unlawfully will have an extra burden around their neck when they come to be judged on the Day of Judgement.

Imam al-Bughawi commented on this Hadith saying that it indicates that gifts accepted by employees, governors, and judges are unlawful earnings. Such gifts are given to sway a verdict in their favour, and this has been forbidden by the Prophet Muhammad ﷺ. This Hadith applies, by analogy, to all forms of favouritism and bribery.

When Umar bin al-Khattab sent Muslims to Persia to engage in the Battle of Qadisiyya and the conquest of the palace of Kisra took place, hordes of treasure were brought back to Madinah as spoils of war, but not one thing was missing from the booty; none of the Companions were tempted to steal or keep even the smallest thing for themselves. Ibn Jareer at-Tabari said, "When the sword of Kisra was brought forward with the rest of the treasures, Umar said, 'A people who deliver this are certainly people of profound integrity.' Then he was told by Ali, 'You restrained your hand (from the Muslim's wealth) so your subjects restrained themselves.'"

Ali said to Umar that it was due to his own integrity that everyone else followed suit. Scholars also commented on this incident and said that this culture of integrity transfers to all of our dealings and interactions. However, once somebody starts to take unlawful earnings, it becomes a culture of treachery rather than a culture of trust. Umar was able to establish this sense of trust throughout society, with nobody feeling tempted to take something unlawfully.

There is also a Hadith regarding the Companion named Urwa; someone we seldom hear about. Hakeem bin Hizam, may Allah be pleased with him, reported that the Prophet ﷺ sent Urwa to buy a sheep with one dinar. Urwa bargained and managed to buy two sheep with one dinar, and then sold one of the sheep to earn one dinar and returned to the Messenger of Allah ﷺ with one sheep and one dinar. The Messenger of Allah ﷺ said, "Sacrifice the sheep and give the dinar in charity."[113] In another narration the Prophet ﷺ supplicated for Urwa to be blessed in his trade, and he became someone that would be able to profit from dust if he were to purchase it.[114]

Scholars who commented on this Hadith have mentioned that one of the lessons we learn from this incident is that the Prophet ﷺ may have felt like the extra dinar was doubtful and so it was best to give it away in charity (*sadaqah*). Therefore, when we think about transactions or professions in this day and age, where there can be some form of doubt in the flow of income in almost everything, there is a need to regularly give charity in order to purify the income.

Imam al-Shawkani commented on the Hadith saying that as the animal was referred to as *udhiyah* (not permitted to be sold on), Urwa essentially made a mistake by buying an extra sheep and selling it, and so the Prophet ﷺ asked him to sacrifice the sheep that he had brought as a means of expiation. Another point he made was that the dinar was supposed to be given as a means of nearness to Allah by buying the sheep, so the Prophet ﷺ asked Urwa to give that dinar in charity and keep that contract with Allah.

When looking into the topic of doubtful income, there are two types:

1. Income that was seized and taken unlawfully. This category is prohibited (*haram*) in its entirety and should be returned; it cannot be given away in charity (*sadaqah*).

2. Income that is doubtful based on the nature of the action. This category can be given in charity as a means of purifying your wealth; however, whether you are rewarded or not is Allah's decision.

When we intend to give in charity, the Prophet Muhammad ﷺ has forbidden us to change our mind once we have committed to giving a certain amount in charity. We should maintain that trust with Allah and not go back on our word.

There are also several other examples from the life of the Prophet Muhammad (*Sirah*) that serve as lessons regarding this topic:

1. Abdullah bin Mas'ud, may Allah be pleased with him, was one of the earliest Companions to accept Islam; he was also very young, around thirteen years old. He was a shepherd for Uqba bin Abi Mu'it – one of the staunchest enemies of the Prophet Muhammad ﷺ. One day whilst he was doing his work as a shepherd, the Prophet Muhammad ﷺ and Abu Bakr were passing by him, and at this point neither knew who the other person was. The Prophet ﷺ asked him, "Would you mind giving us some milk from one of these goats?" Abdullah replied, "I cannot as I have been entrusted with these goats, they do not belong to me." The Prophet ﷺ then asked, "Do you have a goat that has no milk in it?" Abdullah then brought over the goat that did not produce any milk,

and the Prophet ﷺ recited Bismillah and started milking the goat. The goat began producing plentiful milk and all three of them drank from it, and after they had their fill, the goat returned to not producing any milk again. Abdullah bin Mas'ud was shocked at what was happening and said to the Prophet ﷺ "Oh my uncle, teach me the words you said," as he heard the Messenger of Allah ﷺ recite Bismillah and thought that he could also do the same if he knew the words. The Prophet Muhammad ﷺ then smiled at Abdullah and said, "You are a learned and trustworthy young man." Abdullah bin Mas'ud later went to find the Prophet ﷺ and accepted Islam.

Despite being a young boy who had not yet accepted Islam, he fulfilled his trust and remained a loyal and pious employee for an evil man.

2. Abdullah bin Umar noticed that a shepherd was fasting on a very hot day. Abdullah bin Umar asked the man, "Why don't you break your fast? It is hot." The shepherd replied, "I want to use whatever days I have left to fast and there is sweetness in the struggle." Abdullah bin Umar then asked the shepherd to sell him one of the sheep so they could cook it and eat from it together. The shepherd replied, "I don't own these sheep. I was entrusted with them; they belong to someone else." Abdullah bin Umar continued to test the man and said, "Why don't you tell the owner that one of them got eaten by a wolf or it got lost?" The man replied, "What am I supposed to say to Allah?" Abdullah bin Umar was highly impressed with the trustworthiness of the shepherd, and so he bought his freedom and asked Allah to free him from the Hellfire on the Day of Judgement. He also bought the entire flock of sheep and gifted it to the shepherd as a reward for his piety.

3. The Messenger of Allah ﷺ started to work as a broker at the age of eighteen for his uncle Abu Talib. He would earn commission on connecting buyers and sellers and transferring the goods. The Prophet ﷺ had not had a big job until he was

hired by Khadijah, may Allah be pleased with her, to take her caravan to Syria. Her caravan was bigger than everybody else's from Makkah. Khadijah used to be cheated by her employees all the time, but because Allah had blessed her with so much wealth, she was able to carry on. The Prophet ﷺ had been recommended to Khadijah by her sister, and upon hearing about his trustworthiness, she hired him. The reputation of the Prophet ﷺ was highly commendable, and due to his noble character, she decided that she would pay him twice the amount that she paid her previous employees. The Messenger of Allah ﷺ took this trust and earned her twice the profit. This shows that if the employer shows excellence towards you, you as the employee should return the *ihsaan*. The Prophet ﷺ felt that he should go above and beyond her expectation of him because he had been given that trust (*amanah*) by Khadijah, and she was already willing to pay him more than she had paid anyone else.

One of the early books of jurisprudence (*fiqh*) talks about the worker being a trustee (*ameen*), an employee (*ajeer*), a representative (*wakeel*) and a partner (*shareek*). We can extract all of these aspects from this contract between Khadijah and the Prophet Muhammad ﷺ; the Prophet ﷺ was an *ameen* in the sense that he was given the assets by Khadijah to sell and the money that was earned from the assets was in his possession until he returned. He was an *ajeer* in the sense that his time was valued, and he was serving Khadijah as an employee. He was a *wakeel* in the sense that he represented Khadijah in the marketplace when he was buying and selling, and he was a *shareek* in the sense that he was a partner in the profits.

We should derive lessons from these examples and ask ourselves how well do we represent our employers? How well do we handle a trust that has been given to us? These are all values that play a vital role in us becoming pious employees.

May Allah make us a people of trust; whether we are in a position of power or vulnerability. May Allah allow us to always place the fear of Him above all things, and to be conscious of Him at all times. Amin.

GREED – THE ROOT OF ALL SOCIAL INJUSTICE

Jabir b. Abdullah (ra) reported that Allah's Messenger ﷺ said: Be on your guard against committing oppression, for oppression is a darkness on the Day of Resurrection, and be on your guard against stinginess for stinginess destroyed those who were before you, as it incited them to shed blood and make lawful what was unlawful for them.

IN THIS CHAPTER we will move towards a more spiritual dimension of justice and injustice. The Hadith that we will be looking at speaks about the foundation of justice and how greed causes a deep void in our chests.

The Hadith is narrated by Jabir: "The Prophet Muhammad ﷺ said, 'Beware of injustice because it will result in darkness upon darkness upon darkness on the Day of Judgement. And beware of greed (*shuh*) because greed is what destroyed those before you. It drove them to spill each other's blood.'"[115] Greed was the reason that nations were destroyed, and it was greed that led those people to kill each other and violate each other's sanctities.

Another Hadith of the Prophet ﷺ was said during one of his sermons: "Beware of greed. It destroyed those that came before you. First it caused them to spill each other's blood, and then it caused them to break off family relationships. And oppression is darkness upon darkness on the Day of Judgement."

Lastly, there is a Hadith which connects the two Hadith above together and is narrated in multiple books: "Had the son of Adam been given a valley of gold, then he would try to use that valley of gold to attain another valley of gold. And if he was given a second valley of gold, then he would use those two to attain a third valley of gold. Nothing would fill the mouths of the sons of Adam except for dirt."[116] What he meant here was that nothing would stop a person from pursuing more except for death (his mouth being full of dirt).

When looking at greed from the perspective of social injustice, the Prophet ﷺ told us that greed is the starting point and it manifests itself in every aspect of our lives. Greed causes us to wrong the people that are most precious to us; it causes us to disregard another person to the point that we may even take that person's life. Greed, when it remains unchecked, destroys our relationships, our communities, and leads to the unlawful killing of others and destroys us spiritually.

The Prophet Muhammad ﷺ also said in regards to this hated trait, "By Allah, it is not poverty that I fear for you, but I fear that this world will be opened up with its wealth for you as it was opened to those before you; and you vie with one another over it as they did and eventually it will ruin you as it ruined them."[117] Greed puts us in a situation where we try to attain as much wealth and power as possible, which then makes us look at everyone and everything as either something that can help attain that wealth, or as a hindrance for us attaining it. Greed stops us from seeing people as people; we lose empathy and consciousness all in this lust for wealth, for which Allah has said, *"You have been destroyed by quantity."* (102:1) The destruction is not just limited to us, but it extends to our families and communities; greed is the greatest enemy of social justice.

The Prophet Adam, may the blessings of Allah be upon him, wanted one more tree, even though he had access to every other tree, which is what caused him to slip in Paradise. Adam's son wanted that one more thing that his brother had and he did not. Iblis wanted that one rank above man. When we look at the first parties in the story of human creation, we see that it is greed that manifested itself in some form; it leads to envy, hatred, rivalries and pride. A point that must be clarified here is that while it was desire that caused Prophet Adam and his son to sin, in the case of iblis is was his pride that caused his ongoing doom.

When the Prophet Muhammad ﷺ spoke about greed (*shuh*) he said: "The dust in the cause of Allah (battle) will not be combined with the fire of Hell. Faith and greed can never be combined in the same part of man."[118]

The second part of this Hadith is essentially saying that greed expels faith (*iman*) out of the heart. Whilst greed makes one see every person as expendable in the pursuit of wanting more, faith involves the constant renewal of wanting Allah's pleasure. *Iman* is at risk of diminishing without this renewal and greed overtakes the heart, resulting in the love and pursuit for Allah to vanish. We should not allow greed to overtake faith, but rather faith should overtake greed. We should realise that we should not be attached to this worldly life in the first place; this pursuit of the world at the expense of our relationship with Allah, can be tamed through *iman*.

The resources of this world are finite, there is a limit and we cannot have it all, this often results in people taking something from someone else. Those who already have wealth are more likely to become greedy, they become afflicted with greed (*shuh*) and want more. The richest Companion of the Prophet Muhammad ﷺ, Abdul Rahman bin Awf, had so much wealth that when he would enter the city of Madinah, there were so many camels that came with him that the people would think it was an opposing army. Yet, it is known that he made an entire circumambulation (*tawaf*) around the Ka'aba whilst supplicating to Allah and saying, "Oh Allah protect me from the greed within me." He knew the dangers of greed; he knew that his wealth could deceive him into pursuing more of it and in turn lead him away from Allah.

Those who are corrupt and as a result of that corruption are filthy rich, will use anything and everything to grow their wealth. Even whilst owning ten billion in currency, and not knowing what to do with it, they will be willing to kill people to gain another ten billion. Countries – let alone individual people - are drowned in debts, different crises are created globally, all in the name of pursuing more. Greed leads to destruction and affects so many innocent people.

The Prophet ﷺ said that greed afflicts those who have more than those who do not have, and in essence, it is the mercy of Allah that He does not allow some of us to become rich. He protects us from ourselves because He knows us better than we know ourselves. He knows that we could fall into the trap of greed if we were given wealth. The Messenger of Allah ﷺ also said that the greatest trial or fitnah of this *ummah* is money, and when we look at corporate crimes, we find that they are driven by the greed and the want of more money.

Moving on slightly, we will now look at the difference between stinginess (*bukhal*) and greed (*shuh*). On many occasions whilst reading the translations of the Arabic texts, we can see *shuh* translated as stinginess as both words can be used interchangeably. However, many scholars have said that if we look closely at the Arabic language, there is a distinction between the two words. Ibn Qayyim said regarding this that *shuh* is the extreme keenness of something and becoming restlessly impatient to attain it. *Bukhal*, or stinginess on the other hand is protectiveness of something after having attained it. He also said that greed precedes stinginess, but if we have a lot and we find it easy to let it go or part with it, then it shows that we have conquered greed. By overcoming our stinginess, we have defied our greed and are not intoxicated by power or wealth. The Prophet Muhammad ﷺ described the person who is constantly in a state of giving as someone who gives with their right hand in such a way that their left hand does not even know, this indicates the quality of a person who has overcome their greed and hence is not miserly in spending their wealth.

A well-known incident during the life of the Prophet Muhammad ﷺ shows us this aspect of giving freely. It is narrated by Abu Hurairah, may Allah be pleased with him, who said: "A man came to the Prophet ﷺ and was clearly in need. The Prophet ﷺ sent a message to the homes of his wives and they said that they don't have anything to feed the man with except water. The Messenger of Allah ﷺ then asked the people, 'Who is going to take this man and entertain him as his guest?' One of the people of Madinah said that he will take him, and so he went home and told his wife to generously entertain the guest of Allah's Messenger ﷺ. She said that they have nothing to eat except for some food for the children. The man said, 'Prepare the meal, light your lamp and keep stirring the pots until the children fall asleep. When the man sits down, turn off the lamp and put the food in front of him. Put plates in front of all three of us, but only put food on his plate so he will think that we are eating too.' After the Fajr prayer in the morning, the Prophet Muhammad ﷺ said to the *Ansari* man, 'Allah laughed at one of your actions and revealed the verse in *Surah al-Hashr* 59:9: *'They prefer others to themselves even if that is to their own detriment. And whoever is protected from the stinginess of his soul – it is those who will be successful.'*"

This verse was revealed in connection to this incident and it tells us that stinginess is the fruit of greed, whilst charity is the fruit of selflessness. People who prefer others over themselves, even if it means less for them, are truly successful in this world and the next.

Furthermore, Allah says in *Surah al-'Adiyat* 100:6: "*Indeed mankind, to his Lord, is ungrateful.*" He says that He is a witness to this lack of gratitude as our pursuit of this world, or wealth becomes violent and intense. Our greed and pursuit of wealth becomes so severe that we do not let anything, or anyone get in the way. We do not stop until we are in the grave; we may collect all the wealth in the world and pile it on top of our grave, but in the end, we will become part of the dirt.

The Messenger of Allah ﷺ also said, "The worst two qualities a man can have are an alarming level of greed, and unrestrained cowardice."[119] There is wisdom behind this saying of his as there is a relationship between these two qualities. Both of these qualities result in us going into self-preservation; when we are called to give for the sake of Allah, we become stingy and when we are called to an occasion of courage, we become cowards. When we are overcome by greed, we lose all sense of integrity as greed does away with principles. The lack of principles affects the way that we deal with everyone, including our families and ourselves, and it is down to us to conquer greed within ourselves.

May Allah make us from those who are selfless, and never allow us to pursue this world to the extent that it disconnects us from Him, our families and the people around us, or from the potential good that He has put within us. May Allah allow us to be people of charity, generosity and people who long for Him and not for this material world. Amin.

23

WHY IS USURY (*RIBA*) PROHIBITED?

Sulaiman b. 'Amr narrated on the authority of his father: I heard the Messenger of Allah ﷺ say in the Farewell Pilgrimage: Lo, all claims to usury of the preIslamic period have been abolished. You shall have your capital sums, deal not unjustly and you shall not be dealt with unjustly.

IN THE PREVIOUS CHAPTER, we looked into the topic of greed and when we begin to peel back the layers of social injustice, we find that the majority of social injustice is in some way connected to greed. Social injustice draws from the fountain of greed, and we were able to touch on the spiritual elements of it in the previous chapter. Now, however, we can move on to the outwardly aspects of greed, and one of its greatest manifestations is usury or interest *(riba)*.

The Hadith that I have chosen to begin with is narrated by Sulaiman bin Amr, on the authority of his father: "I heard the Messenger of Allah ﷺ say in the Farewell Pilgrimage, 'Verily, all claims to usury of the pre-Islamic period have been abolished. You shall have your capital sums, deal not unjustly and you shall not be dealt with unjustly.'"[120] The farewell sermon of the Prophet ﷺ contained the many ethical guidelines that are required for a community to function properly, with the first and foremost being the abolishment of racism and other forms of social injustice. The abolishment of usury brought a great change into how finances would work within the Muslim community and holds great relevance to our lives today for several reasons such as:

1. It is difficult for people to understand why there is such a strict prohibition on usury when the society we live in functions on interest. For many Muslims the prohibition of interest (*riba*) seems to be harmful rather than beneficial as they believe the prohibition is exclusive to Muslims, whilst in other societies it is completely normal.

2. The prohibition of usury is meant to free and liberate, but unfortunately many people feel that it is restrictive and that it is holding them back. They feel as though the prohibition stops them from achieving their full potential as a business or as an individual.

3. Questions that keeps arising are why is Islam so strict about usury? Why is there strictness on the person who gives interest? It is understandable why the one who takes usury would be prohibited, but why are there harsh rulings for the person who needs to take out a loan?

4. We are reactive and not proactive in trying to understand the prohibition of usury (*riba*) as being something that brings about good in society and a creates a healthier financial system.

During the farewell sermon of the Prophet Muhammad ﷺ, he made it a point to mention that the first case of usury that he was abolishing was the usury of his family – his uncle al-Abbas. This was the opposite of the elite putting down the poor; he was starting with his family to show that there were no exceptions. His uncle Abbas had many interest-bearing transactions, he could have said that people should pay the interest that has been agreed to and then adhere to the abolishment, but instead he abolished it right there and then. The only thing that remained was the capital sum.

When we look into the topic of usury and interest, we must first understand the connection between them and greed. Living within our means is a major part of our religion. And during a time when people are easily able to purchase through credit and get pulled into contracts – which can cause large amounts of debt – people also increase in their greed and want for more. The average American has around five-thousand dollars-worth of debt, because they are reaching for and buying beyond their means.

Allah mentions in the Qur'an in *Surah al-Hashr* 59:7: *"So that it will not become a perpetual distribution (solely) among the rich from among you."* What is meant here is that money is not meant to belong to a few elite individuals whilst everyone else suffers, rather money should be distributed amongst the poor in society too. The Messenger of Allah ﷺ outlawed profiting from loans by saying, "Profit is dependent upon liability (the possibility of loss)."[121] Islam prohibits the concept of making money off of our money, as this allows the rich to get richer whilst the poor get poorer and become buried in their debts.

Another interesting point is that after Allah mentions usury in the Qur'an, He also says that He does not burden a soul beyond what it can bear. This statement has different connotations such as:

- Allah does not burden us in our religious obligations with more than we can bear. Islam has made our obligations reasonable and achievable within our capacity, and if for any reason we cannot fulfil an obligation, there is a relaxation of it to cater to our abilities.

- We incur burdens upon ourselves by feeling compelled to become involved in interest-based transactions.

When it comes to understanding the sin of usury, it is the most underestimated of the seven major sins. The Prophet Muhammad ﷺ said regarding this sin, "A dirham which a man consumes as usury (*riba*) knowingly is worse before Allah than thirty-six acts of adultery (*zina*)."[122] And he also said, "There are seventy-two types of *riba*, the least of which is like a man committing incest with his mother."[123] These two statements of the Prophet show the gravity of this sin of engaging in usury; it is worse than committing adultery multiple times and is even likened to committing incest. Yet, usury and interest has become normalised in society and is not seen in the same light as the other major sins such as adultery and murder. We must stop and ask ourselves why *riba* is worse than *zina*.

Al-Baghawi said, "On a societal level, when an economy becomes richer because of usury (*riba*), the rich commit more shamelessness (*fahisha*) and the poor indulge in their sorrow and fall into the same sins." The rich indulge in these sins because they can easily access such things, whilst the poor become depressed and find cheaper alternatives of the same. The inequality that usury (*riba*) causes forces people into these directions; usury causes much more harm to society than other sins. By involving yourself in usury, you contribute to a system that impoverishes and continues to lead people towards wrong.

In the last verses of Surah al-Baqarah, Allah mentions a verse of charity, followed by a verse regarding *riba*, and then another verse regarding charity and so on. Allah draws a contrast here between people who spend in charity and their reward and people who are involved in usury and deplete others through the practice of usury and their punishment. Societally, if people distribute charity the way that they are meant to, people will not feel the need to take out loans with interest. If society functions properly, those who can afford would be taking care of the education or food or other such necessities of those who are less able to afford them. The system should be built in such a way that those who can afford to, should take care of those who are in less favourable positions, removing the need for them to involve themselves in interest-based loans or contracts.

On an individual level, people who see money as burden give from it in charity on a regular basis; they want to rid themselves of the money and give it to those who need it. Those who act so, have passed the test that Allah has given them. Wealth is a huge test; those who become greedy and want more cause problems within society, whilst those who feel a sense of debt to Allah will spend day and night, both publicly and privately. Allah also mentioned in *Surah al-Baqarah* 2:275: *"Those who consume riba will not stand on the Day of Resurrection except like the standing of a person beaten by Shaytan leading him to insanity."* Ibn Abbas, may Allah be pleased with him, said regarding this that on the Day of Judgement, the one who deals in usury will be in such a state that he will be beaten to the point of insanity, and then he will be told to take his weapons and prepare for a war with Allah and the Prophet Muhammad ﷺ. Not even the disbeliever will be able to stand in this state.

Allah has forbidden usury and has encouraged the act of charity for people; societies can survive without *riba* but cannot survive with it. The global economy collapses repeatedly because it is based on a system of interest, and that system is doomed to fail. It is a system that leads to poverty, inequality and great economic disparity – all of which Islam came to rid society of.

In regards to loans, Islam does not view them as business transactions but charity. The concept of a loan in Islam is to lend money as a means of charity if you cannot give it away. Abdullah bin Umar, may Allah be pleased with him, said that there are three types of loans:

1. There is a loan which you lend because you desire the pleasure of Allah and so you gain the pleasure of Allah.

2. There is a loan which you lend desiring the pleasure of your companion. People may not have liked you previously but because you lent them money, they will gain respect for you.

3. The third type of loan is a loan in which you take what is impure by that which is pure, meaning that it is usury (*riba*). Benefiting financially from the money that you lend to someone else is the third type of loan, one which is prohibited in Islam.

There was an incident involving Imam Abu Hanifa in which he had lent a man some money, but the man had not paid him back for some time. One day Abu Hanifa was taking a break whilst travelling and sat underneath the shade of the man's tree (the tree was on the other side of the wall, but its shade was on the outside). All of a sudden, Abu Hanifa realised that this tree belonged to the man that he had lent money to and began to fear that sitting in the shade of his tree may be interest.

Islam, however, is not unique in its prohibition of usury – all the Abrahamic faiths have prohibited it. In Judaism, it says in Leviticus and

Exodus, *"If you lend money to any of my people, even to the poor, you shall not be to him as a creditor, neither shall you lay upon him interest. And if your brother is poor and his means fail him, take no interest of him but fear your Lord that your brother may live with you."* In the book of Deuteronomy, it says that interest can be put upon foreigners but not amongst the community of Israelites. The Talmud says, *"It is not only the creditor who takes interest and violates the prohibition, but also the debtor who agrees to pay interest, the guarantor who guarantees the debt that bears interest, the witnesses who attest the creation of an interest-bearing debt, and even the scribe who writes out the agreement."* Whilst the prohibition was similar to that in Islam, it was limited to the community of Israelites.

Thomas Aquinas, a Christian, on the other hand had said very famously, *"To take usury for money lent is unjust in itself, because this is to sell what does not exist, and this evidently leads to inequality which is contrary to justice."* Interest was prohibited in the Catholic Church until the year 1832; they finally gave in to the pressure from the Protestants after their Protestant Reformation in the seventeenth century, which reinterpreted the rulings and verses of usury and allowed people to deal in it.

Old philosophers such as Aristotle who did not even belong to the Abrahamic faiths viewed interest to be a lowly transaction. Making money from money, or breeding money using any method that one can think of was seen as unnatural and wrong. Usury has been looked down upon because it essentially creates economic slavery. People become buried in debt, and the rich use this to further impoverish the poor and fill their own pockets.

Linguistically, the word *riba* means increase, which is also the same as the word *zakah*. However, the difference here is that *zakah* is an increase with purification whilst *riba* has no benefit and has been made prohibited (*haram*). In an authentic Hadith narrated by Ibn Mas'ud, the Prophet Muhammad ﷺ said: "There is no-one who deals in usury a great deal (to increase his wealth) but he will end up with little (his wealth will be decreased)." Allah will cause the wealth of the person who deals with *interest* to deplete, even though that person is trying to increase his wealth by taking interest.

The Messenger of Allah ﷺ also knew that usury would spread because all major sins spread. In another Hadith narrated by Abu Hurairah, the Prophet Muhammad ﷺ said: "There will come a time when there will be no-one left who does not consume interest, and whoever does not consume it will nevertheless be affected by it."[124] Even if we do not deal with interest first-hand, we may still be engaged in it without knowing and without wanting to. Things such as bank accounts or credit cards could mean that we are in engaged in interest in some capacity.

The Prophet Muhammad ﷺ also said, "Allah curses the one who consumes *riba*, the one who gives it, the one who witnesses over it and the one who writes down the transaction; they are all equal in sin."[125] This Hadith is similar to the quote I mentioned earlier from the Talmud, and bears the same message that no matter how small the capacity in which a person is involved in a transaction involving interest, he will be equal in sin to the one who consumes interest. Thus, when we look at the long-term, we must realise that we are not to become mere products of our society and simply look to survive, we must better our society. Our society should collectively thrive; we should not look for excuses to make interest acceptable. In the 1990's, people kept pushing scholars that lived in other countries to pass a ruling (*fatwa*) to allow buying a house on a conventional mortgage. Yes, it is a necessity to have a house to live in, but no collective effort was made to create real Islamic alternatives, resulting in the passing of such fatwas. As Muslims, we are not tasked with finding a way out just for ourselves, but we should try and create alternatives that are Islamically acceptable. Insistence can open doors; the more Muslims demand halal alternatives, the more providers will be forced to comply and supply these alternatives. By not giving in, we can help establish solutions for the entire Muslim community and allow these model solutions to become successful and grow to such an extent that they become a realistic replacement and easily accessible.

The former president of Nigeria made a profound statement in which he commented on their debt crisis and said that they had borrowed five billion dollars, they had paid around sixteen billion dollars, yet they were still being told that they owed twenty-eight billion dollars. He said that the worst thing in the world was compound interest; the injustice of the foreign creditors meant that the debt on Nigeria was not ending. Such greed and selfishness are not acceptable in Islam; it goes against the empathy that Islam entails. Interest creates money that is not there and sinks nations into poverty and adverse circumstances; it creates economic systems that are always meant to fail, and only the richest are able to recover.

A powerful and horrifying Hadith that depicts the severity of usury is from when the Prophet Muhammad ﷺ witnessed Hellfire and said:

"We proceeded until we came upon a river which was red like blood. In this river was someone swimming, and at the shore was a man who had collected many stones. The swimmer would swim to the shore, where the man would hurl a stone into his mouth which would send him back to the middle of the river, and he would swim back, only for the same to happen again and again. I asked who are these two? They said to me 'Move on, move on.'"[126]

The person who was swimming in the river and was being fed stones, was the consumer of interest. Every time he tried to come out, he was driven back into the river of blood with the stones, just as he did with the people who borrowed from him – they thought they would be free from their debts, but he increased them in it with interest. Scholars have also mentioned that the red represents the gold or wealth that he drowned himself in. The consumer of interest believed that he was smart by cornering or forcing people into debt and taking advantage of their needs, but he will show up on the Day of Judgement stumbling like a madman.

In a world where it is extremely difficult to see justice, hearing about it is reassuring; knowing that Allah will provide justice in the end. May Allah protect us from becoming involved in interest in any capacity, and may He allow us to purify ourselves from it but to also purify our financial systems from it. May Allah never allow us to be in a vulnerable situation where we feel forced to succumb to it. Amin.

24

INSURANCE COMPANIES AND VULNERABLE CITIZENS: THE CONCEPT OF GHARAR (UNCERTAINTY) IN ISLAM

Abu Hurairah (Allah be pleased with him) reported that Allah's Messenger ﷺ forbade a transaction determined by throwing stones, and the type which involves some uncertainty.

SIMILAR TO THE previous chapter, the subject of this chapter also deals with finance. However, the focus is on how injustices take place within or due to financial transactions. I want to begin by introducing the concept of *gharar* in Islam. *Gharar* means uncertainty, and most often it falls into the discussion of insurance.

As mentioned previously, Islam has a strong stance against usury, as usury and interest become a tool for the rich to exploit the vulnerable in society. Loans, or lending in Islam is not done for the sake of business but for charity, for the benefit of people. The goal in Islam is to end the exploitation of the weak in society and to end the concept of wealth maximisation (making money off of money). Taking advantage of people due to their vulnerability is completely contradictory to Islamic ethics and law.

The Messenger of Allah ﷺ forbade transactions that involved uncertainty, as mentioned in a Hadith reported by Abu Hurairah: "The Prophet Muhammad ﷺ forbade a transaction determined by throwing stones, and the type which involves some uncertainty."[127]

The use of the word *gharar* in the Arabic version of this Hadith means deceptive uncertainty, or an unacceptable level of ambiguity. After the prohibition of usury (*riba*), the prohibition of deceptive uncertainty (*gharar*) is the most important Islamic safeguard against injustice in commercial transactions. The prohibition of *gharar* is to minimise deception and deceit and to remove any ambiguity that may increase the likelihood of disputes, in order to prevent and protect people from being cheated.

The literal translation of *gharar* is danger. It means exposure to destruction, excessive risks, deception and uncertainty. In financial terms it refers to fraud through uncertainty and both the buyer and the seller can be a party to it; it is prohibited for the buyer to enter into a transaction that they are not entirely certain of. Ibn Taymiyyah, may Allah be pleased with him, explained deceptive uncertainly (*gharar*) as when a person does not know what is in store for them at the end of the trade, it resembles gambling as it involves entering into a contract of excessive risk. It is a combination of risk taking and devouring of the property of one party by the other. It raises the question that since every business transaction carries risk how is this applicable? Islam stipulates liability of loss on both parties in order for it to be a valid transaction, therefore risk is always present but Islam requires that both parties share that risk equally. There has to be as much clarity and definition as possible in the terms of the transaction and the burden of risk should not be on one party alone.

When considering what could be termed as deceptive uncertainty (*gharar*) in regards to a business transaction, it could be that there is uncertainty in the actual value of the subject matter. There could also be uncertainty regarding the time of payment e.g. deferred payment, or the quality or quantity of something. The Messenger of Allah ﷺ prohibited the purchase of fruits before they had become ripe, and he also prohibited the advance payment for fish as you need to see what is caught in the net before you can purchase it. There could also be uncertainty on the existence of something such as an unborn animal, as there is no guarantee that the pregnancy will follow through, or if the baby animal will be delivered alive. There are specific Hadith detailing these prohibitions because like every society, the Arabs also had very unique schemes which led to the distribution of wealth in a way that was not equitable.

Uncertainty in ownership, availability and deliverabilty are an issue in modern times, almost everything today depends on selling something we do not fully possess; especially those that sell things in large quantities. Technically speaking, you cannot sell something that you do not own; that is impermissible (*haram*). The scholars however, have spoken about whether the prohibition is in regards to the actual possession of that item or if there is uncertainty in whether you will be able to deliver. There is a difference between the two and ibn Qayyim has said that if there is no uncertainty in the ability to deliver then there is no prohibition. However, if you buy something from someone thinking that they own it or are able to deliver it, but in reality, they are not, there is an element of deception and that brings about the prohibition.

There is *gharar* that is acceptable and *gharar* that is unacceptable. We cannot sell someone a mobile phone without telling them the model – this is unacceptable. We must be as specific as possible when selling someone something. However, when purchasing a phone from a shop, it may be that the particular piece you buy had been damaged in transit, that is an acceptable level of uncertainty and is in fact unavoidable; it is the intentional deception that is being prohibited. There are three rules to *gharar*:

1. The uncertainty must be significant for it to be impermissible. Ibn Qayyim said that if the uncertainty is slight, or it cannot be avoided, then it does not affect the validity of the contract.

2. The uncertainty must exist in that which is contracted itself. If there is uncertainty about an added benefit or bonus, then it does not affect the validity. For example, we can buy a tree, but fruits may or may not grow on it; meaning that there is some uncertainty (*gharar*), but the sale of the tree is not prohibited.

3. The contract must not be warranted by a need. Ibn Taymiyyah, may Allah be pleased with him, said that the harm in uncertainty (*gharar*) is less than interest and usury (*riba*), and so it can be accepted in cases of need. In America, health insurance is permissible because people cannot afford to become ill without insurance. In other countries such as the UK, car insurance is permissible because people will be going against the law if they drive without insurance.

This brings us back to the wider topic of societal justice and how insurance impacts upon it keeping in mind that the goal of Islam is to end exploitation. Islam had some of the most innovative models in this regard dating back to the Prophet Muhammad ﷺ; pooling resources and mutual co-operation are part of Islam. One particular Hadith narrated by Abu Musa al-Ashari says that the Prophet Muhammad ﷺ said: "When the Ashari tribe are on an expedition and they run out of food supplies, or food becomes scarce for their families in Madinah, they put everything together into one lot and then they divide it equally amongst themselves." The Prophet ﷺ also said, "They are from me and I am from them."[128]

The Messenger of Allah ﷺ praised their idea of pooling resources in order to take care of everyone, or maintaining a pool of resources so that if anyone from the tribe would find themselves in a difficult situation, then they could help that person. Cooperative insurance is permitted and praised in Islam. We can find examples of this such as when the Muslims began to travel by sea and had a type of ship insurance; they pooled together their money before embarking on their journeys so that if one person's ship became damaged, there was enough money to repair it.

When it comes to natural disasters or unforeseen circumstances, the treasury would be used. The concept of government social security existed in early Islam; it became the responsibility of the government to look after its citizens in times of need. There is no profit that is made from such insurance, as the sole purpose of it is to unite and benefit the community. Insurance is permissible if the insurer provides profit shares instead of fixed amounts. There should be mutual participation in the insurance for it to be permissible and beneficial.

If we look at how insurance companies function today with the aim of understanding how the system is inherently unjust, less than three percent of that which is collectively given to insurance companies goes back to those who are paying. Insurance companies profit from people's vulnerabilities, whilst there are lobby groups who ensure that these models stay in place. The competitive nature of the industry ensures that they use ways to raise premiums and force people into paying higher premiums yet return only a small proportion of that money. The excess money is *riba*, as well as there being *gharar* because of the uncertainty of what is going to happen, with it being highly likely that most of the money will not return to the policy holders. The money circulates amongst the companies and their directors, with the rich getting richer by taking advantage of people's vulnerability.

In order for one person to experience financial benefit, another person has to go through financial loss, and this is achieved through the selling of ambiguity. Insurance today can be seen at the same level, or worse, than gambling. At least in gambling there is the chance that you will get more but with insurance the most you will get is a replacement. Furthermore, it creates an atmosphere of deception with the main aim of insurance companies being not to pay the policy holders back.

Insurance companies scrutinise the claims and the conditions to a very high extent and on many occasions deny help or benefits to those that deserve it. So many people pay in so much money to these insurance policies, get buried under debt, but are denied legitimate compensation for things that were meant to be guaranteed. Then there are also people who cheat insurance companies by falsifying their claims and receiving pay-outs that are not rightfully theirs. There is cheating and lying from both sides, and neither is justified.

A major flaw with insurance companies and their policies is that they create major social injustices. A lot of games are played by people to ensure that they do not get the worse end of the deal. It becomes important for us as Muslims to realise that the issue becomes more than just what is allowed or prohibited on an individual level to what is creating injustice and hardship in society as a whole. Islam offers a real alternative with cooperative insurance, with people coming together to take care of each other. Such insurance schemes can be implemented on a wide community level, or between a group of families, or even by a small group of friends. Due to the fact that there is no exploitation of people and no profit to be made, this Islamic model of insurance is a worthy solution. Islam encourages that the consequences of hardship be shared amongst the community. Countries like Kuwait and Malaysia are trying to come up with Islamic finance or insurance models whereby the amount that is left at the end of the year is given back to the policy holders; there is no profit in the system and hence the incentive for explitation is vastly reduced.

Western insurance models feature fixed payments for uncertain returns, it is the uncertainty that is the issue; Islam aims to eliminate that uncertainty. Mutual insurance is the closest form to the Islamic model; it may not be perfect, but they are very different to the stock insurance companies and are closer to what Islam permits. Their aim is more closely aligned with the intention to take care of people.

Warranties are yet another topic that we must look into because of their frequency in today's society. It is highly likely that a product that we purchase will come with a warranty and scholars have said that warranties are permissible because *gharar* is their secondary quality. The first quality of a warranty is that the company or seller guarantees the functionality of the product by either fixing any issue with it or replacing it. However, the point that makes warranties impermissible is that we must not purchase a warranty from a third party as third-party warranty providers are not the sellers of the product.

Takaful (mutual agreement and co-operation) in many Islamic countries is replicating commercial insurance and the nature of it but repackaging it to fool people into thinking that it is acceptable, yet it is a multi-billion-dollar industry. It is unfortunate that these insurance companies in Islamic countries are keeping the essence of commercial insurance and profiting from it, whilst the needy suffer losses. A wonderful quote by Joe Bradford regarding this in *Fatwah and its Role in Regulatory Capture* is, "What is needed is not more Islamisation, but better use of Islamic law to create equitable, just and fair markets for all stakeholders." It should not end at shifting things around or repackaging them to make them look permissible at face-value, but the focus should be on fulfilling the ethical values that Islam has taught from the very beginning. The focus should be to protect the vulnerable in our communities as opposed to exploiting them as is done by commercial models nowadays.

May Allah protect us from committing or falling into contracts that have deceptive uncertainty (*gharar*), and may He help us to help those in need in our communities. May Allah allow us to create true Islamic alternatives which will be of benefit to everyone. Amin.

25

JUSTICE BETWEEN PARENTS AND CHILDREN

Abu Hurairah reported Allah's Messenger ﷺ as saying: A son does not repay what he owes his father unless he buys him (the father) in case he is a slave and then emancipates him.

IN THIS CHAPTER we will move on to discuss the family realm of social justice. As a general rule, Allah and the Prophet Muhammad ﷺ have assigned clear authority in regards to rights and responsibilities in the Islamic texts, leaving no place for ambiguity in the main points. When it comes to the family sphere in particular, it is the correct balance of responsibilities that needs to be taken into considerstion in order to ensure fairness there are many things to take into consideration to ensure there is the correct balance of responsibilities. Most commonly, for example, when someone gets married how do you balance out your responsibilities as a good child with your responsibilities as a good spouse to your responsibilities as a good parent yourself. Whilst a person should always try to fulfil these relationships with excellence (*ihsaan*), sometimes the situation becomes such that it becomes difficult to navigate around the tensions.

When one person is showing *ihsaan*, it is very typical for the other person to abuse that *ihsaan* by taking advantage of it or becoming restrictive. Kindness can however be taken advantage of unintentionally, because the person does not show any sign of displeasure, thus making it easier to abuse their kindness.

The relationship between parents and children is a complicated terrain, especially when looking at it within the context of justice. We will be looking at the responsibilities and rights of both parents and children (including adult children). To begin with, I want to mention a Hadith that is reported by Abu Hurairah, may Allah be pleased with him: "The Messenger of Allah said, 'No son can repay the kindness shown by his father, unless he finds him a slave, purchases him and sets him free.'"[129]

Many scholars have said that this refers to any parent and child relationship and is not limited to a father and son relationship. The Prophet Muhammad ﷺ used this expression to convey the message that none of us could ever really repay our parents, even though it was quite possible in those days for a person to have come upon such a situation, it was quite unlikely. Furthermore, when Allah speaks about the treatment of parents in the Qur'an, He says that we should show excellence and beautiful character to our parents. Allah also uses the word 'ordained', which carries the meaning of a trust. Allah has entrusted us with good treatment of our parents. The fact that Allah has mentioned the good treatment of our parents right after the obligation of worshipping Him alone, shows the seriousness of not being respectful to our parents. Just like the right of Allah is so great that none of us can truly fulfil it; the only other right in human releationships that is so great that we will never be able to fulfil it is that of parents on the child.

A very moving and powerful incident is of when Umar bin al-Khattab, may Allah be pleased with him, met a man who was taking care of his mother who had reached the point where she was like an infant. He had to carry her, clean her and feed her just as you would a little child, and he claimed that he had fulfilled his duty; he had done what she had done for him when he was a child. Umar then said to the man, "You do all this but at the same time you are asking Allah to let her pass on soon, whilst she used to do the same for you but asked Allah to give you a long life." What this shows is that whilst on the outside it may seem like you are repaying your parents for what they have done for you, in reality this is not the case. There is a special mercy that Allah put in the heart of a parent towards their child.

This is why when ibn Umar saw a man carrying his mother on his back for hajj and he asked ibn Umar, 'Have I repaid her yet?' Ibn Umar replied not even for one of her cries in labour. It is fairly common to see a person carry one of their parents on their back when performing Hajj or *umrah*, and there is no doubt that it is a difficult task. However, we cannot repay them, and this is why Allah and His Messenger ﷺ taught us that it is not a matter of us claiming that we have repaid our parents with an equal amount of what they provided us with, whether it be in the financial sense or through service, but rather this relationship is different from every other relationship and we can never claim that we have done for them what they did for us. So, we should go above and beyond for our parents in terms of respect and good treatment towards them. This manifests itself in showing them love and respect that does not decrease over time rather we value them even more.

Zain al-Abideen, the great-grandson of the Prophet Muhammad provides a great example of excellence (*ihsaan*) towards parents. Whenever he used to eat with his mother, he would not eat until she had eaten first, because he did not want to touch any item that his mother may have wanted to eat. As children, we eat what we want with our mothers giving us what we prefer, whilst she eats whatever is left. Islam has not ruled that we should wait until our parents have eaten before we eat, however Zain al-Abideen expressed his love and showed *ihsaan* towards his mother as a way of pleasing her and Allah.

Another example is of Imam Ahmad who did not get married until his mother passed away, when he was at the age of forty. This does not in any way mean that we should all wait until our parents pass away to get married, but the circumstances of Imam Ahmad were special and unique. His mother was a single parent who struggled endlessly to take care of him, and Imam Ahmad wanted to do as much as he could for her. He could not balance or equal what his mother had done for him, but his decision to delay marriage was a means to convey his love and respect towards his mother.

Scholars have said that if our parents reach old age in our lifetime, we should see it as a blessing and not as a curse. They provide an opportunity for us to earn Paradise (*Jannah*), and we should seize the opportunity by taking care of them and their needs. We should not neglect our parents in their old age, nor should we allow ourselves to succumb to narcissism and selfishness – we should not be from those who allow our parents to suffer and die alone.

Allah has told us in the Qur'an not to show displeasure towards our parents, especially when they are older. It is during old age that it becomes more likely for them to require more time from us, due to weakness or vulnerability. Islam recognises emotional rights and we must not make our parents feel unwanted or disrespected. Whilst at times it may feel burdensome or unreasonable whilst serving them, we cannot say "uff," or show any type of displeasure towards them, instead we should speak to them with dignifying and honourable words. Raising our voices whilst speaking to them can make our parents feel weak, unknowledgeable and neglected, which is why Allah says, "And show complete powerlessness in front of them."

We should lower ourselves in humility in front of our parents, out of mercy and respect. They may be mistaken but stopping ourselves from raising our voices or becoming angry is better in the sight of Allah. The Prophet Muhammad ﷺ would show humility and mercy towards the women who nursed him; he humbled himself like a child even when he was middle-aged.

This behaviour that dignified and honoured the parents – especially the mother – was completely new to the Arab culture. The ignorant culture of the Arabs before Islam had always belittled the mother, and if the mother gave birth to a daughter, it would make things even worse for her. Islam changed all of this by honouring the mother more than the father, as it is the mother who has carried the child inside of herself for months, followed by the pain of birth and recovery, along with sleepless nights. Allah and His Messenger ﷺ fully recognise and appreciate the hardships that a mother endures.

Ibn Abbas was approached by a man who confessed an unlawful killing that he had committed; he liked a woman but she married someone else and so he killed her out of jealousy. He knew that he would have to go on trial and be punished, but he wanted to know if he had any chance of being forgiven by Allah and entering Paradise . Ibn Abbas asked the man if his mother was alive, to which he replied no, after which he was told to repent to Allah as much as he could in order to draw nearer to Allah. People asked Ibn Abbas why he had asked the man if his mother was alive, and he replied, "I do not know of any action that brings a person closer to Allah than honouring one's mother."

Whilst there is much emphasis on the importance of dealing with parents with excellence (*ihsaan*), this by no means gives parents the right to exploit or abuse their children. It is unfortunate however, that this does take place. Allah is aware of all things and is never unreasonable towards His creation, nor was the Prophet Muhammad ﷺ unreasonable in any sense as he understood the complexities of the parent and child relationship.

Furthermore, the Messenger of Allah ﷺ made it clear that we cannot obey the creation of Allah when they tell us to disobey the Creator. Yes, we must obey our parents as much as we can, but that obedience is limited in its nature – we cannot exceed the limit by going against Allah and His rulings. Obedience is always contingent upon it being reasonable. We can not place an unreasonable burden upon someone and thenmentally abuse them because they are not living up to the unrealistic expectations that we have put upon them.

Forcing a child to eat something repulsive or marrying someone they do not want to marry through guilt is strictly prohibited in Islam. A young woman came to the Prophet Muhammad ﷺ and complained that her father had forced her to marry someone without her consent, to which the Prophet Muhammad ﷺ said that she was free to go. He did not ask why she was against the marriage or any other such details because justice had to be served by ensuring that the young woman was not forced into something by her father. Such a marriage contract is not valid in Islam, due to the fact that there is no compulsion in the religion. Parents do not have the right to force anything unreasonable upon their children, however, even if they are being unreasonable it still does not warrant the child to be disrespectful towards them.

The Prophet Ibrahim, may Allah be pleased with him, was told by his father to worship other than Allah – the most unreasonable of requests that a parent can make. Yet, the Prophet Ibrahim spoke to his father with honour and dignity. He did not show any form of disrespect towards his father, even though his father went to the point of even trying to kill him.

And yet again, during the time of the Prophet Muhammad ﷺ, Sa'ad bin Abu Waqas, may Allah be pleased with him, was being emotionally blackmailed by his mother. Sa'ad had accepted Islam, but his mother wanted him to renounce the religion and starved herself to the point that they had to force her mouth open to feed her, so she would not die. It was an extremely difficult situation for Sa'ad, who was known for being a strong man, but he was reduced to tears. He stayed with his mother and begged her to eat, whilst respectfully telling her that he could not and would not abandon Islam for anything. Allah tells us that even when our parents insist that we abandon our religion, we should not obey them, but we should continue to show them kindness and respect. And the same goes for when they are forcing other unreasonable things upon us, such as disrespecting or depriving our spouse or children.

There are unfortunate situations in which children have to seek protection from their parents; no child should have to tolerate abuse from their parents, physical or mental. The child is not held accountable for leaving their parents, but they are not given the right to disrespect them even in such circumstances.

There is a famous incident which I have mentioned earlier in the book in which Umar bin al-Khattab was approached by a man complaining about his son, and the son asked Umar if children have rights over their parents, to which the answer was yes. The man did not fulfil his rights as a father towards his son, which took away his right to complain about his son. Depriving a child of their rights is a failure on the part of the parents, and there is nobody else to blame but themselves if their children do not show the best of character. Neglecting children by not giving them time, love, education or appreciation is the fault of the parent.

I would like to end this chapter by sharing a wonderful story of a sister that accepted Islam in Louisiana (USA), but unfortunately her parents kicked her out of the house because of this. She had always made her parents breakfast in the morning, and even though they were abusive towards her and had told her to leave the house, she would go back in the early hours every morning before they had woken up to prepare their breakfast and then leave. Her parents eventually accepted Islam because they saw the respect and love that she continued to show them. She showed excellence in her character and behaviour towards her parents, which led them to accepting Islam too.

The relationship between parents and children is governed and elevated by excellence (*ihsaan*). Both parties have rights upon each other, and for parents, there is no greater investment in this world than righteous children. By investing the time and effort in our children, we are investing in our Hereafter (*akhirah*). Righteous children will understand the importance of honouring their parents and will use any opportunity to earn the pleasure of Allah through their treatment of their parents.

May Allah allow us to recognise the blessing of our parents. May Allah allow us to serve our parents whilst they are amongst us, and if they have passed away may He have mercy upon them. May Allah allow us to become righteous parents to our children, and allow us to fulfil their rights properly, and protect us from becoming amongst those who wrong their children. Amin.

26

THE SIN OF FAVOURITISM: BE JUST WITH YOUR CHILDREN

It was narrated that An-Nu'man said: "My mother asked my father for a gift and he gave it to me. She said: 'I will not be contented until you ask the Messenger of Allah to bear witness.' So my father took me by the hand, as I was still a boy, and went to the Messenger of Allah. He said: 'O Messenger of Allah, the mother of this boy, the daughter of Rawahah, asked me for a gift, and she wanted me to ask you to bear witness to that.' He said: 'O Bashir, do you have any other child apart from this one?' He said: 'Yes.' He said: 'Have you given him gifts like that which you have given to this one?' He said: 'No.' He said: 'Then do not ask me to bear witness, for I will not bear witness to unfairness.'"

IN THE PREVIOUS chapter we looked at the importance of treating our parents with excellence (*ihsaan*), whilst also touching on the topic of being reasonable towards children, and not asking too much of them.

Islam is a religion of balance, and it may seem difficult to be able to strike a balance when it comes to relationships, but it is not impossible. There must be a balance when it comes to dealing with children, otherwise we fall into sin if we show favouritism towards one child and not the other. Treating children differently for whatever reason, such as comparing the first child to the second, or preferring boys over girls is unacceptable in Islam's view of the family dynamic.

I would like to begin by mentioning a Hadith that sets the tone for this topic and helps us gain an understanding of the Prophet Muhammad's ﷺ position. It is narrated by Nouman bin Bashir, who said: "My father wanted to give me a gift, but my mother stepped in and said that she would not agree to him giving me the gift unless the Prophet Muhammad ﷺ approved of it. So, my father went and said to the Prophet ﷺ, 'I was going to give my son a gift, but my wife will not allow me unless you approve of it.' The Prophet Muhammad ﷺ responded, 'Do you have any other children? Have you given your other children the like of what you are giving him?' My father said no, and the Prophet ﷺ said, 'Be mindful of your Lord and be just with your children. Do not make me a witness to you giving this gift because I do not bear witness to oppression or injustice.'"[130]

These words of the Messenger of Allah ﷺ are extremely strong in the sense that he did not want to bear witness to a father giving one of his children a gift, whilst his other children were left without. The Prophet ﷺ made it clear here that we are not to give preferential treatment to children, even when it comes to giving gifts. Each child should receive something similar; the Prophet Muhammad ﷺ did not say that it should be the exact same gift, but it should be similar in value and enjoyment or benefit that a child would gain from it.

In another Hadith, the Prophet ﷺ said three times, "Be just with your children, be just with your children, be just with your children."[131] And yet in another Hadith he said, "Be just with your children in the same way that you would want them to be just with you." This second narration sounds very similar to the well-known and often-used phrase of, 'treat others how you want to be treated,' however, it is rarely seen or used in regards to family dynamics. We do not really think about treating our family members the way in which we would like to be treated, but the Prophet Muhammad ﷺ very beautifully mentioned this to ensure that parents do not cause any injustice to their children.

In many instances, children that are abused turn out to be abusive parents, and it turns into a vicious, unjust cycle. The Messenger of Allah ﷺ wanted parents to know how important it was to set a good example for their children, by treating them fairly and not abusing them in any way.

The Hadith narrated by Nouman bin Bashir has different variations (none of which contradict each other, but rather further contexts are provided). There are practical manifestations of this Hadith which the scholars say are not limited to how gifts or financial support are distributed amongst children. The Hadith extends to how we emotionally give and even welcome our children. The teacher of Imam Bukhari, Ibrahim Naqahi said, "The Companions used to encourage justice amongst the children even in the proportion of kisses, and to not give more food to one than the other except for a valid reason." The Companions paid close attention to how they maintained their relationships with their children, because they had seen the Prophet ﷺ show love and mercy towards children. One very famous incident is of a time when the Prophet Muhammad ﷺ was playing with his grandsons Hassan and Hussain, and he was kissing them. A man witnessed this and told the Prophet ﷺ that he had ten children and had never kissed any of them, to which the Prophet ﷺ said, "What can I do if a man has no mercy in his heart?"[132] The natural feeling of love towards children was looked down upon amongst the Arabs at that time, and the Prophet Muhammad ﷺ showed them that expressing love towards children should even be done publicly.

A beautiful incident narrated by Hassan further solidifies this attitude and teaching of the Prophet Muhammad ﷺ: "When the Prophet ﷺ was speaking to his Companions, a young boy came in and walked up to his father. He stroked the head of his child and sat him down on his lap. Some time passed, and a young girl (his daughter) came to him, and the father caressed her hair and then sat her down on the ground next to him. Although the father greeted them both, he did not greet them equally. The Prophet Muhammad ﷺ noticed this whilst speaking to his Companions and said, 'Don't you have another side to give (of your lap)?' The father then sat his daughter on the other side of his lap. The Prophet Muhammad ﷺ said, 'Now you have shown justice.'"[133]

The Messenger of Allah ﷺ paid attention to something that would otherwise seem so small but he made it a point to mention straight away that children should be treated fairly.

Hassan and Hussain are both known to be beloved grandsons of the Prophet ﷺ, but he also had another grandson in the sense of Usama bin Zaid, who was the son of his adopted son Zaid bin Harith. The Messenger of Allah ﷺ treated Usama in the same way as he did his blood-related grandsons; Usama said regarding this, "When the Prophet ﷺ used to see me, he used to put me on one of his thighs and he put Hassan on his other thigh. He used to embrace us and say, 'Oh Allah, be merciful to them as I have been merciful to them.'"[134] He would not make any of the children feel less loved than the other, he recognised the importance of their emotions and would show them all equal treatment.

The scholars also commented on this and said that there might be a natural inclination or closer attachment towards one of your children, even the most righteous of people had this happen to them, but they would keep it in their heart and not let it translate into injustice between their children. Umar bin Abdul Aziz also had one son whom he loved the most out of all of his children, yet he said to his son, "Know that I love you, but it is not possible for me to prefer you over one of your brothers even with a bite of food."

Imam Ahmad, may Allah be pleased with him, discussed this topic of justice between children in his book of jurisprudence (*fiqh*). He stated that if a person has more than one daughter, and he gives one daughter a certain amount of jewellery at her wedding, then an equal amount must be given to his other daughters.

There are certain permissible exceptions when more can be given to one child over another:

- Sometimes the equations of inheritance work out in a way that some children will inherit more than others.

- When a child is unwell.

- When a child has financial difficulties.

- When one child lives further away, the parents may want to give them more gifts when they see them.

- If a child is extravagant and irresponsible, parents would give more to another child in order to teach the irresponsible one responsibility.

- If the children are at different stages of their lives; sometimes there are big age gaps between children and so the difference is acknowledged (if a parent gives their two-year-old something, they are not expected to give their twenty-year-old the same thing).

Studies have been done into the effects of favouritism and it can be understood that favouritism does nott just affect the neglected child, but it also has deep psychological ramifications on the entire household. It has implications for the parents themselves and the siblings; it effects all the children as they become older and is not just an injustice towards the child or children not receiving an equal amount of attention, emotional support or love.

Even in situations where parents do not show favouritism, jealousy can develop between the children which can in turn create harmful effects within the family. The greatest example of such a situation is of the Prophet Yaqub, may Allah be pleased with him, and his sons. Prophet Yaqub did not treat Yusuf any differently than he did his other sons; he was not unfair in his treatment nor did he outwardly show preference towards Yusuf. Although Yusuf was the best out of his children, he did not compare him to them, nor did he say to his other sons, "Why can you not be more like Yusuf?" Doing such comparisons does not inspire siblings to be like one another, rather it will make them resent not only their siblings, but their parents too.

Had Yusuf told his brothers the dream that he had, they would not have agreed to throw him in the well in the first place but would rather have killed him straight away. Yaqub had advised Yusuf not to tell his brothers his dream, otherwise they would plot against him. By heeding his father's advice, Yusuf managed to survive the trauma of being thrown inside a well and went on to achieve great things.

The Prophet Muhammad ﷺ also never put a child down whilst praising another; he did not show such preference. He did have a special attachment to Fatima, but he did not convert this favour into action. He was just to all of his children, but she was closest to him in heart.

Whilst some competitiveness between siblings is natural, parents should not fuel the flames by making comparisons. Doing so can cause children to become distant from one another as well as from their parents. Satan is on the lookout to destroy relationships, we need to make sure we are not making it easy for him. The Prophet Muhammad ﷺ made a profound statement in which he said that those who are just with their families will be seated on pulpits of light beside Allah[135]. He also mentioned in the Hadith that the person who dies and cheats his flock will be forbidden Paradise. What is meant by flock here is family; we will be answerable to Allah on the Day of Judgement for depriving our family of their rights and being unjust in our treatment towards them.

A specific preference regarding children which was extremely prevalent in the society surrounding the Prophet Muhammad ﷺ – and still is unfortunately in different cultures around the world – is the preference of sons over daughters. It is due to this reason that we find so many Hadith about the rewards of raising daughters well. The Prophet ﷺ was brought up amongst people whose culture was to show extreme favouritism towards sons, to the point of burying their daughters alive. The Messenger of Allah ﷺ mentioned that whoever is given daughters, treats them with goodness and brings them up well, will have his daughters serve as protection for him on the Day of Judgement. He also said that the one who takes care of three daughters will be given paradise. Another powerful statement of the Prophet ﷺ is that he will be as close as two adjacent fingers are to those who take care of orphans and daughters. He put them on the same level of importance; daughters have been neglected like orphans throughout history. They were not given their due rights or respect and the Prophet ﷺ came to change this.

In Surah Ashura, Verse 49, Allah mentions gifting people with girls (daughters) before sons. There is wisdom behind this in that the mentioning of daughters before sons was to console daughters who had been mistreated or were seen as inferior. Allah also mentions that it is through His will which gender is born, and it is not the will of the parents. Allah chooses and is well-aware of whom He blesses with a daughter, and whom He blesses with a son. Ibn Qayyim also commented on this verse and said that Allah did not use the definitive article when mentioning females, in Arabic this makes it a stronger form of expression but He used the definitive article with the males and by doing so Allah amended the perceived inferiority of females by mentioning them before males and using the stronger form of expression with regards to them.

However, it is sad to see that even in current times people will pray for a son and become upset if Allah gives them a daughter. This also plays into education and the inequal treatment regarding it. Scholars have said that it is the right of both girls and boys to be educated and they must have access to it equally. It becomes an injustice when daughters are not educated to the same degree as sons, even though throughout Islamic history we can see examples of women who were great scholars. Imam Malik's daughter Fatima was the greatest scholar out of all of his children; she had memorised his collection of Hadith and went on to teach many thousands of students.

The scholars understood the value and importance of educating their children equally. They did not differentiate between daughters and sons, leading to those girls becoming great women of knowledge.

Whether preferential treatment comes in the form of an older child versus the younger child, or the gender of a child, or natural attachment, we must remember to be mindful of Allah. We must pay attention to how we treat our children, and we must be aware that we do not become unfair towards them in any capacity.

May Allah make us just with our families and protect us from becoming unjust due to any injustice done to us. Amin.

27

HOW RIGHTS WORK IN MARRIAGE

Mu'awiyah al-Qushayri Narrated: I went to the Messenger of Allah ﷺ and asked him: What do you say (command) about our wives? He replied: Give them food what you have for yourself, and clothe them by which you clothe yourself, and do not beat them, and do not revile them.

ONE OF THE most difficult subjects within the family realm are the rights within a marital relationship, and since it is not possible to address each and every scenario, in order to grasp the overall intent we will look at the overarching framework given to us by the Prophet Muhammad ﷺ. We can learn the basic rights from these frames and build upon the spirit of the Prophet's life (*Sunnah*) with regards to these rights.

I want to begin by mentioning a Hadith narrated by Mu'awiyah al-Qushayri: "I went to the Messenger of Allah ﷺ and asked him, 'What do you say (command) about our wives?' He replied, 'Give them food what you have for yourself, and clothe them by which you clothe yourself, and do not beat them and do not revile them.'"[136]

We see here that the question was particularly directed towards the rights of the wife upon the husband, and the Prophet ﷺ deliberately used strong language in his answer because he understood the intent of the question and knew where the deficiency existed. The Prophet ﷺ could have chosen to simply answer by saying show excellence (*ihsaan*) to your wives, but he was more specific and gave an answer that included physical and emotional rights. He made it a point to mention that a wife should eat the same quality of food as the husband, her clothes should be of the same quality and that she should not be subjected to physical abuse such as beating, nor should she be emotionally abused through feelings such as revilement.

In *Surah Baqarah*, 2:228, Allah says: *"And due to the wives is similar to what is expected of them, according to what is reasonable."* Allah mentions the rights of women as wives before the rights of the husband, and He puts those rights in the same category, meaning that the rights of both the husband and wife are similar. There are differences in regard to the technicalities of those rights, but in general a person should treat their spouse as they would hope to be treated. Ibn Katheer commented on this verse and said that *'bil ma'roof'* has two connotations here, one being according to that which is customary, and the second being in kindness. Many aspects of marriage can and have changed over time and place, and that is why we should look to that which is customary or standard in order to recognise how to carry out these rights or obligations within the standard and with kindness.

Ibn Abbas set a wonderful example and quoted this verse when explaining why he beautified himself before entering the house. He wanted to beautify himself for his wife just as he wanted her to beautify herself for him. Ibn Abbas understood that on the Day of Judgement, Allah would ask each person about their rights and obligations towards one another and doing *ihsaan* whilst fulfilling the rights of others upon you is a way of pleasing Allah. We also should not be too demanding of our rights; however, this does not mean that we wilfully accept injustice or harm. What this means in other words is that we should be forgiving with things that are due *to* us, and we excel in that which is due *upon* us. And that should be our approach in marriage, however, we are human and it is inevitable that there will be gaps.

Allah will compensate the gap on the Day of Judgement; this does not mean that Allah will punish our spouse, but He will compensate generosity with generosity, and forgiveness with forgiveness.

Let us now look at the technical rights of the wife in further detail:

1. The first right of the wife is spending or providing:

- Spending refers to providing acceptable food and clothing, and towards expenses. The word used specifically indicated according to that which is customary. The Prophet ﷺ did not say that a husband should provide a certain amount of money to his wife for expenses every single month, as that would cause many problems. Expenditure is liable to change with time and place and the Prophet ﷺ built this into his answer.

  - The wife is not asked or expected to contribute financially towards the house, however, if she does then that is excellence on her part. One such example can be found through Zainab, the wife of Ibn Mas'ud, who paid her obligatory charity (*zakah*) to him.

  - If a husband is being stingy and not providing for his wife, the wife has the right to take from him without permission, but it must be reasonable and only the amount which will suffice her and her children. The Prophet ﷺ said to Hind when she came complaining that Abu Sufyan was cheap with her, "Take from him what suffices you and your child within reasonability." However, most scholars have said that reasonability is subjective, and a woman should go to a judge or scholar before taking from her husband, in order to determine what is reasonable in her situation. The position of Imam Ahmad in this regard is the most lenient as he said a woman can take from her husband within reasonable means without the need to go through a judicial process.

2. The second right of a wife is housing:

    - One of the most famous Hadiths of the Prophet ﷺ is in which he said, "Oh young men, whoever among you can afford it, let him get married."[137] According to Ibn Qayyim, the technical definition of 'afford' here is the ability to provide a home, food and clothing.

    - If others live in the same home, it is the right of the woman to ask for her own private living arrangement. If, however, she allows others to live with them (such as parents), then it is excellence (*ihsaan*) on her part.

3. The third right of the wife is intimacy:

    - The right to intimacy is not just limited to the husband.

    - Scholars have different opinions on how often a husband must make himself available to his wife, and the reason for this is that they used different forms of analogy to come to their conclusions. Some scholars said that a husband must make himself available once every four nights, whilst some said at least once a month.

    - The husband must also use his own initiative to exercise the reasoning given by scholars as the consensus is that the wife also, cannot be denied by her husband just as the husband cannot be denied by the wife.

4. The fourth is that the wife also has emotional rights:

    - The Prophet Muhammad ﷺ mentioned that a husband should not belittle, mock or harm emotionally his wife.

    - The Prophet Muhammad ﷺ led by example; there are numerous examples from the life of the Prophet ﷺ that show his sensitivity to the emotional well-being of his wives. For example, he could tell when Aisha was upset with him as she would take oaths, or swear by the Lord of Ibrahim, instead of the Lord of Muhammad ﷺ (which she did when she was happy). He paid attention to what she was saying and how she was feeling. This goes beyond the realm of rights; he went over and above in showing love and consideration towards his spouses.

- Another example is of Aisha, may Allah be pleased with her, wanting to see the Abyssinian war dances, the Prophet Muhammad ﷺ took her and she put her head on his shoulder and she watched them in that position for quite some time, after which the Prophet ﷺ asked her, "Are you satisfied?" and she said that she was not. So he waited until she said that she was satisfied before leaving. This shows excellence (*ihsaan*) towards the wife; understanding her emotions and showing love and care goes beyond the basic rights, but it is better for the relationship.

Showing excellence in a marriage

Allah mentions in *Surah an-Nisa* 4:19: *"And dwell with them in kindness."* This verse shows that kindness involves the things that a husband says, overlooking the shortcomings of the wife and going beyond the basic justice or rights. Showing excellence by extra love and care is better for the marital relationship. Another example of the Prophet ﷺ going above and beyond is when Aisha, may Allah be pleased with her, had lost her necklace and he stopped the entire army in order to find it. It was not her right, but he did it out of love.

A Hadith narrated in Sahih Muslim says, "A believing man should not hate a believing woman; if he dislikes one of her characteristics, he should be pleased with another." The Messenger of Allah made a clear point here in saying that a husband should not focus on one thing that he dislikes about his wife, but rather he should focus on what he does like as it will help overlook the flaws, and we all have flaws.

It is also worthwhile mentioning here the right to equal treatment in a polygamous marriage. Allah and His Messenger ﷺ have clearly stated that there must be justice in polygamy. One such Hadith says, "Whoever had two wives and gave preference to one over the other (in their rights), he would come on the Day of Judgement crooked."[138] What is meant by the word crooked here is bent down, or burdened more on one side than the other, and it is for this reason that scholars have said that one must show God-consciousness (*taqwa*) in order to achieve justice in a polygamous marriage.

Moving on now to the rights of the husband upon the wife, there are several similarities in the rights when comparing them with those of the wife, however, we will be looking at the differences too:

1. The first right of the husband is leadership. This is one of the most difficult concepts to grasp, although there are several Hadith that mention this right:

   - The Hadith which mentions the flock confirms that the man, or husband is the guardian of the family – he has a leadership role.

   - Another Hadith mentions the wife's obedience towards her husband earning her a place in Paradise. It is important to note that when translating from Arabic, it can be difficult to translate the words to their full intended meaning. The word obedience often has connotations of superiority of the one that is being obeyed, however in reality no person has absolute authority over another person. We must not focus on the translation, but instead focus on the intended meaning.

   - There is no dictatorship, oppression or lack of accountability in a marital relationship as the Prophet Muhammad ﷺ said, "The best amongst you are those who are the best to their wives."

   - Imam Ghazali said the marital relationship is like the model of the Caliph (*Khilafa*) and the consultation body (*Shura*), in that they function in tandem and are accountable to each other. There is no undermining or belittling or oppressing of one another.

- A wife should follow her husband in that which is not unreasonable or impermissible. As mentioned in a Hadith, "There is no obedience to a creation while disobeying the Creator."

2. The husband's right to intimacy:

    - The husband's right to intimacy does not mean that he can cause harm to his wife or take advantage of her.

    - There are Hadith of the Prophet Muhammad ﷺ which prohibit a woman from not making herself available to her husband as a means of punishing him or showing anger towards him.

    - The right to intimacy is for both the husband and the wife, however, extra emphasis can be found towards the husband within the Hadith of the Prophet ﷺ.

3. The husband also has emotional rights:

    - During the farewell speech, the Prophet Muhammad ﷺ made it a point to say that a wife should not let someone, whom her husband dislikes, enter the house. Nor should she allow someone to enter without his permission. This shows a degree of respect and co-operation towards the husband.

    - When the Prophet Muhammad ﷺ gave advice to men and women about their obligations, they knew the intent was not mean-spirited. Advice could be given frankly because the level of trust and understanding was at such a high level; but when we only read the text without considering the context, we lose that meaning. For example, when Abu Bakr grabbed Umar by the beard, Umar did not get offended by it as they had a relationship strengthened by trust.

In a Hadith narrated by Asma bint Yazeed, she came to the Prophet Muhammad ﷺ in the presence of men and said, "Oh Messenger of Allah ﷺ, how is it that we the women do all this, but the men go out for Salatul Jummu'ah and go out to battle with you and take all the reward. Don't we receive some of the reward?" The Prophet ﷺ said, "Have you heard a speech more beautiful than this woman's speech? Go back to the women and tell them that for them is the same reward as the men."[139] We can see here how the Companions – whether male or female – and the Prophet Muhammad ﷺ had a sense of frankness in their relationship, and that they did not take offence to what was said.

- Showing ungratefulness towards the husband can hurt him emotionally and make him feel inadequate. In another Hadith, Asma bint Yazeed narrated, "The Prophet ﷺ passed by me while I was with some young slave girls belonging to me. He greeted us and said, 'Beware of the ingratitude of those with blessings.' I was the boldest of them in coming forward to question him and I said, 'Messenger of Allah ﷺ, what is the ingratitude of those with blessings?' He replied, 'Perhaps one of them will remain unmarried for a long time with her parents and then Allah provides her with a husband and children from him, and then she gets angry and is ungrateful and says. 'I have never seen any good at all from you.'" The context of the hadith is that of a man who is overall fulfilling his responsibilities but slips up on occasion.

When trying to understand the marital relationship, it is helpful to see what Allah has said regarding it. For example, in *Surah Rum* 30:21: *"And of His signs is that He created for you from yourselves mates that you may find tranquillity in them; and He placed between you affection and mercy. Indeed, in that are signs for a people who give thought."* The rights of the spouse must be fulfilled without a second thought out of the fear of Allah and obedience to the statements of the Prophet Muhammad ﷺ.

In the last will of the Prophet ﷺ, he said, "Hold onto your prayers and treat your wives well."[140] Ibn Qayyim said regarding this statement that our relationships are divided between the rights of Allah and the rights of people. This is enough for us to understand that the thing that should govern these relationships must be aiming for excellence (*ihsaan*). We should go beyond what is required of us to make these relationships truly successful; if we focus on the technicalities of our rights then it is a sign that the marriage is collapsing. A marriage is more than just the basic fulfilment of the rights; the rights are a given. Showing excellence (*ihsaan*) and seeking to inspire *ihsaan* in the other person makes a marriage long lasting, happy and successful.

Imam Ahmad mentioned that he and his wife were married for thirty years and they only argued once, and even then, he was in the wrong. The night that they had gotten married, they prayed together and she gave a speech, or even a sermon, to say how she will do her best to fulfil the rights of Allah and to do her best as a spouse. Imam Ahmad was taken aback by this, and also made a promise to his wife that he would do his best to be the best husband to her.

Every person should look at themselves first and foremost, out of the fear of Allah, and to ensure that they are not slacking in doing their best. A person may be married to someone who is very patient or lenient, however, they should challenge themselves to be a better spouse and not become complacent. This is not to say that there will not ever be a time where we worry about our rights; there may be a time where we need to consult with a third party for counselling or advice but even then the spirit is of seeking help from a third party to get through a difficult situation as opposed to simply complaining about a spouse.

Before I conclude, I would like to make an important point about emotional voids and their impact in marriages. Unfortunately, the world has changed to such an extent that the vast majority of people are isolated to quite a large degree. There is no longer the old village structure which enabled people to access emotional support from people, thus creating many voids and a stronger feeling of isolation. And it is because of this that we have greater emotional voids and needs, but we also then create a greater expectation of marriage being able to fulfil these demands. Two empty souls do not make a marriage complete. Marriage will not fix all the problems and needs that we have and that is not an expectation that we should have of marriage.

When the Prophet Muhammad ﷺ spoke about excellence (*ihsaan*) in marriage, he did not limit it to simply extra acts of kindness towards the spouse. *Ihsaan* in marriage includes things like waking our spouse up for the morning prayer (*Fajr*) or for extra worship at night (*Qiyam al-Layl*), enjoining good and forbidding evil and gently pushing one another to become better Muslims in order to fill the soul and become more complete. When we are spiritually fulfilled, we become more complete as a person and are able to give to others. A well-known principle in Islam is that "He who does not have something, cannot give something." If we do not have peace, we cannot give peace.

Lastly, it is important to understand the needs of the spouse. Scholars have said that in the context of emotional needs, the husband's greatest need is respect, whilst the wife's is love. This concept, however, is not just limited to Islam. The Book of Ephesians in the Bible says, *"Each one of you must love his wife as he loves himself and the wife must respect her husband."* Shaunti Feldhahn – a Harvard graduate and social researcher said, "A man's highest need is to feel respect, whereas a woman's highest need is to feel loved."

These statements do not by any means claim that the wife does not need respect, as the Prophet Muhammad ﷺ clearly said that the wife should not be belittled in any way. However, the point being made is that men tend to underestimate the amount of love they need to show their wives in order to fulfil their need. Similarly, a man also needs love, but his greatest need is to feel respected and appreciated. If both sides fail to fulfil these needs, it stops them from seeking to do *ihsaan* for one another and eventually diminishes both love and respect within the marriage.

May Allah allow us to become the best to our spouses, by fulfilling their rights and needs and protect us from taking advantage of one another. May Allah bless our marriages with understanding, patience and compassion. Amin.

28

THE RIGHTS OF EXTENDED FAMILY

Ali ibn AbuTalib narrated: When we came out from Mecca, Hamzah's daughter pursued us crying: My uncle. Ali lifted her and took her by the hand. (Addressing Fatimah he said:) Take your uncle's daughter. She then lifted her. The narrator then transmitted the rest of the tradition. Ja'far said: She is my uncle's daughter. Her maternal aunt is my wife. The Prophet ﷺ decided in favour of her maternal aunt, and said: The maternal aunt is like the mother.

RIGHTS IN ISLAM are not just limited to the immediate family, but they branch out to extended family members. In this chapter we will look into the rights and responsibilities towards extended families.

The Hadith that I want to begin with is narrated by Ali bin Abi Talib, may Allah be pleased with him, and it is both beautiful and tragic: "When we came out from Makkah, Hamza's daughter pursued us crying,

'My uncle!' I lifted her up and then said to Fatima, 'Take your uncle's daughter.' Fatima then lifted her up. Ja'far – the brother of Ali – then said that he has the greatest right to her, and that he should take her under his care because Ja'far's wife was the maternal aunt of the girl. And so the Prophet Muhammad ﷺ ruled in the favour of Ja'far because of his statement, 'The maternal aunt is like the mother.'"[141]

This incident took place after Hamza had been brutally martyred, his young daughter recognised Ali, Hamza's nephew, as her extended family and approached him in grief after the loss of her father. Fatima, Ali's wife, was Hamza's grand-niece. They wanted to take custody of Hamza's daughter. Zayd bin Haritha had been paired with Hamza as a brother at the time of migration (*Hijrah*), and by that right he also wanted to take care of Hamza's daughter. Ja'far, Ali's brother, was married to Asma bint Umyas, the young girl's maternal aunt. They also wanted to be the ones to care for the girl. The Prophet however ruled in favour of Ja'far because he was married to Asma bint Umays, the maternal aunt.

The Hadith covers the concept of custody of an orphan if such a situation arises, but it also goes beyond this and includes the status of the maternal aunt. The Prophet Muhammad ﷺ recognised the special connection between a maternal aunt and their niece or nephew, and Imam Dhahabi also commented on this saying, "The maternal aunt shares the status of the mother in kindness, in honouring and in keeping ties."

In another Hadith narrated by Ibn Umar: "The Messenger of Allah ﷺ was approached who said, 'O Messenger of Allah ﷺ, I have committed an enormous sin. Is forgiveness possible for me?' The Prophet said, 'Do you have a mother?' He said, 'No.' The Prophet ﷺ said, 'Do you have a *khala* (maternal aunt)?' He said, 'Yes.' The Prophet ﷺ said, 'Then show her kindness.'"[142] This was to say that the man should show his maternal aunt kindness just as he would his mother.

The Prophet's ﷺ wife Aisha, may Allah be pleased with her, complained to the Prophet ﷺ that all of her friends had a *kunya* but she did not, and so the Messenger of Allah ﷺ gave her the *kunya* of Umm Abdullah as she was the maternal aunt of Abdullah bin Zubair (son of Asma bint Abi Bakr). Aisha may not have had any children herself, but she was like a mother to Abdullah because of her relationship to him through her sister. Mothers and maternal aunts in other words, are almost interchangeable.

After the maternal aunt, it is the paternal uncle who is given importance as he is like a father. We can see this in the following two Hadith regarding the Prophet's ﷺ uncle Abbas: When al-Abbas would enter into a room, the Prophet Muhammad ﷺ would stand up and kiss him on the forehead and would sit him on his right side and say, 'This is my paternal uncle, this is my uncle.' Abbas then said, 'Oh Messenger of Allah, I don't deserve for you to say that.' And the Prophet ﷺ replied, 'You are what's left of my father. The paternal uncle is like a father.'

Abu Hurairah narrated: "The Prophet ﷺ said, 'Al-Abbas is the uncle of the Messenger of Allah, and indeed, the uncle of a man is the equal (*sinu*) of his father.'"[143] *Sinu* refers to the equal of the father. The Prophet Muhammad ﷺ was also sometimes referred to as the son of Abu Talib as Abu Talib was his uncle.

Scholars, in regards to this topic, have also mentioned the order amongst the aunts and uncles in terms of status and closeness to a person after their parents: maternal aunt, paternal uncle, maternal uncle and paternal aunt. The reason why the maternal aunt is first in the list is because the mother takes precedence in terms of being shown love and honour, as said in the Hadith by the Prophet ﷺ ,"Your mother, your mother, your mother, your father."[144]

The beauty behind these Hadith is the hidden reciprocation that is yielded from the extended family system. Family holds importance in Islam as it is the family that we can turn to in times of need. Abu Talib needed help with looking after his children due to them being in a situation of poverty, and so Ali was taken in by the Prophet Muhammad ﷺ whilst Ja'far was taken in by al-Abbas. They understood that they had to take care of and help family, because they are so close in relation. The goal is not just to provide from a financial perspective, but from an emotional perspective too. If a maternal aunt or paternal uncle takes custody of a child, their responsibility goes beyond the scope of financially providing for them. They ultimately take on the role of the mother or the father and provide emotional support, as well as a love that is closest to that of a parent.

In Palestine for example, it was common for the paternal uncle to marry the widow of his brother after his sudden death, and the reason for this was to look after the children. Islam does not obligate this, but this example shows that they understood the role of the extended family and that it is essentially a support system. Grandparents, as well as aunts, uncles and cousins take on roles and responsibilities of parents when the situation calls for it.

Furthermore, it is said in *Surah Baqarah* 2:133: *"Or were you witnesses when death approached Yaqub (Jacob), when he said to his sons, 'What will you worship after me?' They said, 'We will worship your God and the God of your fathers, Ibrahim, Ismaeel and Ishaaq – one God. And we are Muslims (in submission) to Him.'"* The Prophet Yaqub was the son of Ishaaq, but they referred to his uncle Ismaeel and his grandfather Ibrahim as his fathers too. This shows that the closeness of paternal uncles and grandfathers was understood much before the time of the Prophet Muhammad ﷺ and that they have always held an important role within families.

There are also many benefits of the extended family system, which we will now look at:

1. In regards to marriage (arranged), it is not just the coming together of two individuals, but two families. Both families use their economic, emotional and human resources to help the newlywed couple if the need arises. One such example is of the Prophet Muhammad ﷺ defusing the situation when Fatima and Ali had an argument. The Prophet ﷺ came home and saw that Fatima was there and was crying, and he asked where Ali was, to which she replied that they had an argument and he left to go to the Masjid. The Prophet Muhammad ﷺ then went to the Masjid where he saw Ali lying down, he walked up to him and said, "Sit up, oh father of dust."[145] He did not show anger towards Ali for upsetting his daughter, nor did he make a judgement because he was not fully aware of what the argument was about. He lightened Ali's mood by making a joke and calling him father of dust, and essentially telling Ali that he is like his son and that he and Fatima should put the argument behind them and move on.

    Unfortunately, on many occasions we do not see family members trying to resolve any issues that have arisen between a married couple, but instead they worsen the situation by becoming possessive about their son or daughter, resulting in the married couple falling deeper into dispute. Families should support them as a couple and help them stay together happily rather than leaving them to solve it themselves or retreating with their son or daughter when a problem arises. The first guidance, before the marriage even takes place, comes from the guardian (*wali*) in the form of looking for compatibility between the two prospective spouses.

2. Scholars have mentioned that such a family system creates a feeling of community; everyone invests and takes interest in each other's welfare. It is the stark opposite of what we see today – especially in western society – in regards to individualism and everyone acting for their own self-interest. There is very little co-operation and sacrifice for the sake of benefiting those close to us in relation. Raising families together, taking advice from one another, investing time, effort and even money in family is like a small community (*ummah*) within the wider Muslim *ummah*. By creating this sense of community from home, it ultimately allows us to understand and benefit the Muslim community on a larger scale.

3. Islam does not stop a woman from working or having a career; it was understood even in the early days of Islam that her earnings belonged to her alone. However, having extended family allows a woman to have easier access to support and allows her to take on multiple tasks at a time.

    By not having a family structural system in place, many women who want to or need to go out and work end up doing so at the cost of children and their home. It is usually a choice between not having children deliberately in order to focus on the career, or leaving their child(ren) with a baby-sitter who is unrelated, and quite possibly not even on the same wavelength in terms of how to bring up children.

4. The concept of elderly people living alone, in care homes or away from family is a very alien thing in Islam. Taking care of each other protects people from growing old alone and dying alone. The very same people who brought us up have the right to be looked after when they reach old age. However,

sometimes a situation can arise that the immediate children do not have the capacity to take care of their parents, and so the extended family steps in to help to ensure that nobody is left alone towards the end of their lives.

In *Surah an-Noor* 24:61, Allah mentions that there is no constraint or blame if we eat at the houses of our fathers, mothers, brothers, sisters, father's brothers, father's sisters, mother's brothers and mother's sisters. This verse indicates that people will frequently meet their extended families, and that they will always be around them.

5. Charity is a huge part of Islam, and Allah mentions that Muslims should give charity to their relatives first and foremost. In almost every book of obligatory charity (*zakah*), the scholars have mentioned that those who are closest to you (extended family) have the greatest right upon that charity, we need to look within our relatives to see if there is anyone who needs help. The Hadith that I mentioned at the beginning of this chapter is a wonderful example of this as it also involves an orphan, and Allah has said that we must look after orphans of close relatives.

This also leads onto the importance of maintaining the ties of kinship. A lot of the time, we choose to ignore the plight of the extended family because we start feeling as though helping them will reduce our provision whilst increasing our responsibilities. However, the Prophet Muhammad ﷺ told us that the opposite actually takes place and that if we want to have our provision (*rizq*) increased, we should maintain the ties of kinship. So, whilst charity also increases our *rizq*, so does maintaining the ties of kinship. It is also worth mentioning here that the word for womb in Arabic is *rahim*, which comes from *Rahman*. Allah says that He is *Al-Rahman*, the Most Compassionate and that if a person maintains the ties of kinship, He maintains a connection with that person, and He cuts that person off if they cut off their ties. We must try our best to maintain our ties and to help those who are our blood relatives, and then those that come afterwards.

An example of looking out for those that are not blood relatives is of Abdullah bin Umar when he was en route to Makkah. He was riding a donkey and he encountered a Bedouin man along the way. Abdullah bin Umar said to the man, "Aren't you so-and-so?" The man replied, "Yes." Abdullah bin Umar then gave the Bedouin his donkey, and the turban from his head saying, "Here, ride this donkey and put this turban on your head." Abdullah's companion Abdullah bin Dinar said to him, "May Allah forgive you; these are mere Bedouins. They would be satisfied with much less than this." Abdullah bin Umar said, "This man's father was a cherished friend of my father Umar, and I heard the Messenger of Allah ﷺ say, 'One of the greatest acts of kindness is for a man to kindly treat the loved ones of his father following his death.'"[146] Abdullah bin Umar was the narrator of this Hadith and he was a living example of it.

Another example is from the Prophet Muhammad ﷺ himself. Long after Khadijah passed away, the Prophet ﷺ would divide any gift that he received and send it to the friends and family of Khadijah. He would also gift Khadijah's sister every time that he heard her voice because her voice sounded like and reminded him of his beloved wife Khadijah. We should take a lesson from this and apply it practically in our lives after our parents pass away by reconnecting with their friends and family to show them appreciation, and to maintain a relationship with them. We are very blessed in the sense that nowadays we are able to send gifts and cards very easily to people through the post, and we should use this to our advantage.

Before I conclude this chapter, I would like to point out why we have not covered the in-laws in depth. The reason behind this is that there are no Hadith about the in-laws; the respect and love that we show them is excellence (*ihsaan*) on our part. There are no such specific rights of the in-laws, but by looking at the examples that the Messenger of Allah ﷺ set (for example the way in which he treated the relatives of Khadijah even after her death), we can try and do our best to treat them with excellence and use this as a means of drawing closer to Allah. When we truly love our spouse, we will love those that are or were beloved to them.

May Allah allow us to fulfil the rights of our relatives and those who are beloved to them, and may Allah make us from those who bring happiness to our communities. Amin.

THE RIGHTS OF THE ELDERLY WITHIN SOCIETY

Abu Musa al-Ash'ari narrated: "The Prophet ﷺ said: Glorifying Allah involves showing honour to a greyhaired Muslim and to one who can expound the Qur'an, but not to one who acts extravagantly regarding it, or turns away from it, and showing honour to a just ruler."

IN PREVIOUS CHAPTERS we have briefly touched on *ihsaan* or excellence in certain situations and relationships, but in this chapter the focus is upon showing excellence, extra compassion and mercy towards the elderly – even if they are not related to us. There is a lot of emphasis in Islam on honouring the elderly outside of our family, and even outside of our religion.

I want to begin by mentioning a very powerful Hadith narrated by Abu Musa al-Ash'ari: "The Prophet Muhammad ﷺ said, 'Glorifying Allah involves showing honour to a grey-haired Muslim and to one who can expound the Qur'an, but not to one who acts extravagantly regarding it, or turns away from it, and showing honour to a just ruler.'"[147]

The first person in line when it comes to honouring the elderly is one who has attained grey hair within Islam, and whilst learning and spreading the teachings of Islam. This ties into the framework introduced by Islam whereby providing for people, for the sake fo Allah, will result in Allah providing for us. The scholars have also included the oppressed in their interpretation of this Hadith and have said that we are taken care of by Allah in accordance to how we take care of those who cannot give anything back to society. In keeping with the topic of the elderly, there are many different types of vulnerability that arise with old age; whether that be the effect on the person physically or mentally such as the memory and pace, or the ability to earn.

There is a very famous Hadith narrated by Abdullah bin Amr in which the Prophet ﷺ said: "He is not from amongst us who does not respect our elders, show mercy to our youngsters, and realise the right of our scholars."[148]

Respecting the elderly is not just limited to symbolic gestures of respect, but it also extends to acknowledging an elderly person's right upon you and allowing them their position in society. Equally, the Prophet Muhammad ﷺ understood the gap between the generations and followed the advice of respecting elders with showing mercy to the youth. There is a wisdom and importance to the recognition of the elderly and establishing respect towards them, whilst dealing with the youth with a sense of compassion and gentle guidance in that it aims to create harmony in society as a whole. There is a fine balance that needs to be maintained so that different participants within society feel accepted and engaged in order to overcome such generation gaps and this is something the Prophet ﷺ fully understood.

In studying the life of the Messenger of Allah ﷺ, we find that most of his Companions were younger than him. It was uncommon to find Companions of the Prophet ﷺ that were beyond forty years of age, a lot of his Companions died in battle in their thirties or younger. With the majority being so young, it could have been very easy for them to lose sight of the elderly and begin to disrespect them because they were so few in number and also because they would not have been able to achieve much physically such as during battle or whilst building the Masjid in Madinah for example.

One such Hadith portrays this situation very clearly for us, and it is narrated by one of the youngest Companions – Anas: "An older man came to talk to the Prophet ﷺ and the people were hesitant to make room for him. The Prophet ﷺ then said, 'He is not one of us who does not have mercy on our young and does not respect our elders.'"[149] This narration gives a clear picture that the Messenger of Allah ﷺ was surrounded by young people, and he disapproved of people not giving the elderly the respect that they deserved. Whilst this is something that was done due to forgetfulness or out of convenience in the sense that they were always trying to learn from and share with the Prophet ﷺ, it is extremely powerful that Anas being a young man himself, is the narrator of such a Hadith.

We will now look at some of the specific lessons that we can learn from these Hadith:

1. How we treat others:

    - Allah says, "Is there any reward for excellence except for excellence?"

    - Most of us will have heard the saying that we are going to be treated by our children the way that we treat our parents. The Prophet Muhammad ﷺ expanded on this and said, "Whoever humiliates or disrespects someone who is elderly, he will not die until Allah sends someone upon him to humiliate him in his old age."[150]

    - There is a weak narration regarding Abu Bakr, may Allah be pleased with him, that when he reached old age, the youth would compete to serve him. He was asked why this was the case, and he recounted that when he was young, he would also rush to do the same for an elderly man.

    - Similarly, there is another Hadith of the Prophet ﷺ in which he said, "No youth treats an elderly person with honour except that Allah sends someone to treat them with honour in their old age." It may not always be the children of an elderly person that honours them, but Allah might instead send them someone else from their extended family or even unrelated who honours them with respect and love.

- Respect itself is subjective, and purposely so, because Islam emphasises and allows us to act according to our customs as long as they do not contradict the *Shari'ah*.

2. Assisting the elderly economically:

    - Ibn Qayyim mentioned in *Ahkam Ahl adh-Dhimmah* (Rulings on how to treat protected non-Muslim minorities): When Umar bin al-Khattab was Caliph, he saw an old Jewish man begging and asked him, "What brought you to this condition that I see?" The elderly Jew said, "The demand of tax (*jizya*), needs and old age." Umar took him by the hand to his home and then called the custodian of the treasury (*bait ul-maal*) to say, "Take a look at his suffering, by Allah this is not justice on our part that we extract from them in their youth and leave them helpless in their old age! I want you to assign a stipend for this man and ensure that he is taken care of."

    - Although the tax on protected non-Muslims (*jizya*) was less than the obligatory charity (*zakah*) due on all Muslims at the time of Umar, he exempted the old man and those like him from paying the tax and introduced a type of social security and retirement benefit. He became visibly upset about the situation and the fact that we take what people contribute to society during their younger years without a second thought, but we forget about them when they reach old age; from a social justice point of view this situation was unacceptable to him.

3. Physically assisting the elderly:

- Umar would compete with Abu Bakr in their good deeds, but Abu Bakr would always precede him. On one occasion, Umar gave half of his wealth in charity and he thought that he did more than Abu Bakr, but Abu Bakr gave the entirety of his wealth. On another occasion, during Abu Bakr's reign as Caliph, Umar went to the outskirts of Madinah to serve the elderly women who lived there in terms of cleaning, bringing food or whatever else they needed help with. When he went to one house, the old lady who answered the door said that someone had already been. When Umar asked her who it was, she said that the person did not want anyone to know. Umar then hid behind her house the next time and saw that Abu Bakr, while dealing with all the responsibilities that came with being the Caliph, was still making time to come and help her.

- Talha bin Abdullah said, "Umar (during his time as Caliph) went out in the depths of the night and entered someone's home. In the morning, I went to that house, only to find an elderly immobile blind woman I said to her, 'Why does this man come to you?' She said, 'He has been visiting me regularly for such-and-such a time. He brings me what I need and removes my waste.' I said to myself, 'Woe to you oh Talha! Are you probing for the flaws of Umar?'"

- These examples prove that it does not have to be a relative that we help; all of the elderly have a right upon society collectively. The elderly should never find themselves in an undignified position, and it is upon us to ensure that we go out and check on them.

4. Emotional rights of the elderly:

- The Prophet Muhammad ﷺ said in a Hadith, "The young person should always initiate salaam to the older person."[151]

- During the conquest of Makkah, the father of Abu Bakr accepted Islam and Abu Bakr carried his father to the Prophet Muhammad ﷺ who said, "You should have left the old man in his home. I would have come to him." The Prophet ﷺ did not like that Abu Bakr brought his old father to him as it would have caused him difficulty.
  In another Hadith, the Prophet Muhammad ﷺ said, "Jibreel commanded me to always put forth the elders."

- The Messenger of Allah ﷺ also said, "I dreamt that I was cleaning my teeth with a tooth stick (*siwak*) and two people came to me. One of them was older than the other and I gave the *siwak* to the younger one. I was told that I should give it to the older one first and so I did."[152] A point to note here is that the dreams of the Prophet ﷺ were always a form of revelation and hence an instruction.

- The Prophet ﷺ would always pay very close attention to such things and there is stress towards giving preference to the elderly, for example, if there are two people waiting to go through a door, the elder person should be given preference over the person on the right. The Prophet ﷺ also mentioned that the eldest amongst a group of people should lead the prayer.

- Rafi' ibn Khadeej and Sahl ibn Abi Hathma reported that Abdullah bin Sahl – a Companion of the Prophet ﷺ – was found murdered in Khaybar, amongst some of the palm trees there. The Prophet Muhammad ﷺ gathered the Companions, Abdur-Rahman bin Sahl and the two sons of Mas'ud – Huwayyisa and Muhayyisa – came to speak to him about the murdered Companion Abdullah. Abdur-Rahman was the youngest of them and began to speak, but the Prophet Muhammad ﷺ said, "Let the oldest speak first."[153]

This Hadith means to show that when there is a gathering, the elders should be allowed to speak first in order to give them their due respect, even if it means sitting there longer.

5. Being gentle in religious obligations:

- Imam Shafi'i said that an elderly person never asked the Prophet Muhammad ﷺ for a concession except that he would give it to them. Not only that, but the Prophet ﷺ would also make them feel better about taking that concession. For example, if an elderly person was not able to stand up and pray anymore, their reward will still be the same as the one who stands, even if they now had to sit and pray. Similarly, if someone finds it difficult to fast and they give the monetary compensation (*fidyah*), their reward will be the same as if they were fasting.

- In a Hadith narrated by Abdullah bin Abbas, a man asked the Prophet ﷺ, "The command of Hajj has come while my father is an old man and cannot sit firmly in his saddle; if I tie him to the saddle, I fear that he will die. Can I perform Hajj on his behalf?" The Prophet ﷺ said, "Don't you think that if your father owed a debt and you paid it off, that would be just as good?" The man said, "Yes." The Prophet Muhammad ﷺ said, "Then perform Hajj on behalf of your father."[154]

From what we have covered so far in this chapter, we can see that there is a lot of emphasis in the Prophetic guidance towards caring for the elderly. We have a collective social responsibility towards them; whether that be towards their financial situation, or physical and mental health. We must give them their due and give them the recognition that they deserve in both public and private settings – this also includes giving them precedence whenever and wherever possible. The elderly must also not be subjected to undue hardship in religion, nor should they be made to feel guilty about not being able to perform religious obligations when they find it difficult, as the *Shari'ah* has concessions for the elderly.

May Allah allow us to honour, respect and love the elders in our homes and communities to the best of our abilities. And may Allah allow us to be treated with honour and respect when we reach old age. Amin.

30

ISLAM'S POSITION ON SLAVERY

Abu Hurairah reported Allah's Messenger ﷺ as saying: "None of you should say: My slave and my slave-girl, for all of you are the slaves of Allah, and all your women are the slave-girls of Allah; but say: My servant, my girl, and my young man and my young girl."

I WANT TO NOW look at a topic that is often misunderstood with questions arising such as, how can we celebrate Bilal and the other accounts of liberation when there appears to be slavery in Islam? From this, come varying different answers and viewpoints. We sometimes have very simplistic declarations about slavery, whilst sometimes we have accusations that try to associate Islam uniquely with slavery. It is due to these confusing and conflicting viewpoints that we must learn what Islam allowed and what Islam forbade.

First and foremost, we must keep in mind that there is no slavery, except to Allah the Most High. One such Hadith that proves this point is narrated by Abu Hurairah: "The Prophet Muhammad ﷺ said, 'None of you should say: My bondman and my slave-girl, for all of you are the bondmen of Allah, and all your women are the slave-girls of Allah. But say, My servant, my girl, and my young man and my young girl.'"[155]

The point that the Prophet Muhammad ﷺ was making here was that we should not refer to anyone as a slave as we are all the slaves of Allah in the true meaning of the word, meaning there is no slavery in Islam except to Allah. The word *abd* is used to describe all humans as slaves to Allah, and it is prohibited to use this word otherwise. The word that is used to describe or refer to apparent 'slaves' is instead *raqeek*, and even then, the Prophet ﷺ told us not to refer to them as slaves as it is not a true representation of their state – which was one of captivity usually under the circumstances of war.

Furthermore, a very important Hadith that sets the tone and talks about the concept of 'slaves' in Islam is narrated by Abu Dhar, in which the Prophet Muhammad ﷺ said: "Allah has made some of your brothers as slaves under your care. So, whoever has his brother under his care, then let him feed him from his food, and let him clothe him from his clothes. And do not give him a duty that he cannot bear, and if you give him a duty he cannot bear, then assist him with it."[156]

Another Hadith mentions, "Whoever kills the one who was placed under his care, we will kill him."[157] The point to note here is that in Islam, those individuals that were in positions of serving others, were not seen as below those that they were serving; the Messenger of Allah ﷺ made it clear from the very beginning that people who served others whilst under their care, were not to be harmed in any way and that they were to be treated with dignity and respect. The Prophet ﷺ also said in another Hadith, "There is no expiation for hitting a *raqeek*, one who has been placed under your care, except for freeing him."

It is due to these reasons that Islam immediately appealed to those who were most downtrodden in society. Five of the first seven people who publicly announced their acceptance of Islam were slaves. The Messenger of Allah ﷺ was told by Allah in the early days that victory will come from the people who have been oppressed; Islam brought a feeling of liberation to them. The Companions understood the nature of Islam as one that emancipates society.

One such example that illustrates this understanding of Islam is of Rib'ee bin 'Aamir who was the ambassador of Umar bin Khattab. He went to Persia to meet their ruler, Rustom, who asked, "Who are you people?"

Rib'ee then answered with an extremely wonderful and profound reply, "Allah has sent us so that we may take people out of slavery to other slaves, to slavery to the Lord of all slaves. And from the constriction of this world to the expanse of the Hereafter, and from the injustices of all the other systems of this world to the justice of Islam."

On another occasion, Salman the Persian was describing all the times that he had switched hands from lord to lord, master to master. Abu Hurairah interjected and informed him that the Prophet Muhammad ﷺ forbade calling slaveowners master or lord, instead he said that we should refer to them as *maula*, or one who is in charge or one who has been entrusted.

The term slavery is loaded with many different connotations that are not accurate Islamically, so much so that the term in a general operational context has become defunct. Because of the transatlantic slave trade, America has been one of the biggest slave holder nations in the world. The slave trade is very well-known across the world, and it unfortunately becomes associated with slavery in Islam. Although the Prophet Muhammad ﷺ taught his Companions that they were not to be called slaves, they were not to be dressed differently from themselves, they were not to be hit, they were not to be fed anything less than what they fed themselves, they were not to be burdened, there is still a major misrepresentation of Islam's viewpoint on slavery. It has become impossible for us to separate in our minds the institution of 'apparent slavery' that existed in the time of the Prophet ﷺ due to war captivity and how Islam aimed to deal with it and the image of slavery as we know it in terms of the transatlantic slave trade and all the associations it has with racial discrimination, brutality and oppression.

Rudolf Ware has written on the abolishment of slavery in Islam in a book called *The Walking Qur'an*. In this book he made some very insightful statements showing how between the nineteenth and twentieth century - the West, post-enlightenment - aimed to denigrate African and Muslim societies. There was a shift in the historiography and the way that Africa and the Muslim world was represented in Western post-enlightenment literature. The goal was to make Europe or the West synonymous with liberation, whilst making the East synonymous with barbaric regressiveness. The West was made to seem forward-thinking, and the East was represented as a backwards society.

Another major point, or flaw, regarding the history of slavery, is that the majority of it is written by Europeans or Americans, as mentioned by the Harriet Tubman Institute. In fact, Michael Zeuske commented on this and said that most of the religious rhetoric that stemmed from Western historians has been nothing more than 'Christian-globalist pamphlets directed against "Islamic slavery"'.

However, questions still arise from those who see conflicting evidence. Whilst there is historical evidence to show that Islam is a religion of abolishing slavery, why are there more recent incidents in Muslim countries of both Muslims and non-Muslims being targeted and being forced into slavery? The question exists as to whether there is a standardised position in Islam.

Firstly, conventional Islamic sources have a lot of inspiration against slavery and exploitation, more so than any other religious texts. Secondly, whilst we find that Muslim countries such as Mauritania and Saudi Arabia were both from the last countries to abolish slavery, Tunisia on the other hand abolished slavery in 1846 – nineteen years before the thirteenth amendment was ratified in the United States of America. We can therefore say that it is unfair to associate the true rulings and practice of Islam with certain countries.

Furthermore, we are not focusing on the conditons of slavery to downplay abuse and aggression in the past. Rather, we are focusing on the conditions to recognise the abuse and aggression in the present. There is more human exploitation, abuse and inequity today than there ever has been in the history of the world. Today we can see huge amounts of exploitation and slavery through human trafficking. The state of Texas accounts for almost a third of human trafficking that takes place in the United States of America. There is an extraordinary amount of modern-day slavery in Texas; even without the legal ownership of the past, more people live in conditions of slavery today than in any other time in history. Brutal working conditions for migrants, prostitution and human trafficking are all forms of bondage. The United States also has more prisoners than any other nation in the world, and possibly even in the history of the world.

There is visible inequality in the United States with African Americans suffering the most. There has been little to no progress for them in terms of home ownership, employment and incarceration. Whilst the country boasts progressiveness, it has in fact regressed in many ways such as not providing certain ethnic groups with the rights that they deserve.

It should also be taken into account that no other religion or its texts are scrutinised like Islam in regards to slavery. For example, if we are to look at the double standards in other religions, we can begin with Christianity.

The Bible says the following: *"However, you may purchase male or female slaves from among the foreigners who live among you. You may also purchase the children of such resident foreigners, including those who have been born in your land. You may treat them as your property, passing them onto your children as a permanent inheritance. You may treat your slaves like this, but the people of Israel, your relatives, must never be treated this way."* (Leviticus 25:44-46)

In addition to this, Exodus 21:20 says: *"When a man strikes his male or female slave with a rod so hard that the slave dies under his hand, he shall be punished. If, however, the slave survives for a day or two, he is not to be punished, since the slave is his own property."*

We can see that the Bible holds a different – and harsher – view on slaves, and whilst the point is not to attack the Bible, it is important to acknowledge the double standards, whereby especially in regards to this topic the Qur'an and *Sunnah* are questioned a lot more than any other world religion. There is not a single verse in the Qur'an or a single Hadith of the Prophet ﷺ that encourages slave trading. As far as the institution of slavery is concernd, Allah makes a profound statement in the Qur'an which is far different from what Islam is accused of: *"Shall I not tell you what the Straight Path is, it is to free the neck of a slave."* The Prophet Muhammad ﷺ was unlike anyone else, and he died having freed every slave that served him, yet he is treated differently from the Prophets Abraham and Solomon, and others mentioned throughout the Old Testament.

When images from Libya were released in regards to their slave trade, a particular point that we can notice is that many of the slaves were pictured reading the Qur'an; this is because they were Muslims. The slave trade there is historic, it is racialised; however, the problem is that whenever an Arab country or Muslim country is reported to have been involved in something of this nature, the general population has a negative attitude towards Muslims and associates Islam with the slave trade. But, the Pigmy population in Congo are ignored because it does not feed into the Islamophobic rhetoric. These are double standards; if we are to understand the relevance of all this to the religious lens, it is that all other religions should also be examined for their overall views on human rights in order to gain a complete picture of the subject.

It becomes confusing when we have the Hadith clearly prohibiting slavery and many other things that can be included in modern-day slavery such as human trafficking, forced marriages and unfair labour practices, but at the same time we witness these things occurring in Muslim societies. It is imperative that we begin focusing on how to deal with the presence of practices that amount to slavery in the Muslim world today. Certain countries in the Middle East for example treat their foreign workers unfairly, they are practically enslaved; this is wrong and should be called out as wrong.

ISIS too, is uniquely deviant in many different ways. Their violence and extremities have been witnessed at an acutely high level. No other Islamic movement, no matter where it falls on the spectrum of orthodoxy, has called for a re-introduction of slavery. Hizbul Tahrir have called for the establishment of a Caliphate and have clearly stated that "Islam has abolished slavery and there are no situations where slavery would return in a future Caliphate." Furthermore, Sayyid Qutb – one of the founders of the Muslim Brotherhood – said, "And concerning slavery, that was when slavery was a world-wide structure and which was conducted amongst Muslims and their enemies in the form of enslaving prisoners of war. And it was necessary for Islam to adopt a similar line of practice until the world devised a new code of practice during war other than enslavement." He also went on to mention that the Prophet Muhammad ﷺ never took prisoners of war as captives unless the opposing army took captives. Islam allows the captivity of a person who is fighting against Muslims, but Islam does not allow the abduction of people.

In 2014, a letter was addressed to the leader of ISIS from hundreds of prominent Muslim scholars around the world, saying that "No scholar of Islam disputes that one of Islam's aims is to abolish slavery… After a century of Muslim consensus on the prohibition of slavery, you have resurrected something that the *Shari'ah* has worked tirelessly to undo and has been considered forbidden by consensus. Indeed, all the Muslim countries in the world are signatories of anti-slavery conventions." The strength of this statement and its signatories suggests that there is no room for the re-introduction of enslaving practices according to the most prominent Muslim scholars.

Talking about these conditions, talking about exploitation as its exists today, not allowing our outrage to be directed by media or agenda-driven politics, not allowing ourselves to fall victim to epistemology rather than historical reality and our present day reality is extremely important when addressing these issues within a framework of addressing oppression and inequity in the world today.

The Prophet Muhammad ﷺ was the most progressive man in the world on the laws of slavery. His teachings resonated initially with the slave class because of the rights, justice and respect that Islam gave. Islam gave slaves so much dignity that they technically were not even slaves anymore; they were part of the family.

May Allah allow us to treat everyone with respect and dignity and protect us from causing harm or injustice to anyone. May Allah allow us to help those who are enslaved and protect those who are treated unfairly. Amin.

31

ISLAMIC ETHICS REGARDING ASYLUM, REFUGEES AND MIGRATION

Abu Hurairah (ra) reported: The Messenger of Allah ﷺ said, "He who gives respite to someone who is in straitened circumstances, or grants him remission, Allah will shelter him in the shade of His Throne, on the Day of Resurrection, when there will be no shade except its shade."

FOLLOWING ON FROM the previous chapter on slavery, another major issue that exists today is that of refugees and asylum. If we look at the world today, the majority of people only migrate because they are forced by their circumstances; they migrate as refugees or as asylum seekers. In fact, there has never been a refugee crisis worse than the one we have currently. There is such a large swathe of people trying to find somewhere on this earth where they can survive and live in relative safety. The people of Rohingya, Syria, Palestine and several countries of Africa have been forced into displacement with little to no outcry from the rest of the world.

However, because it is so easy to get drawn into the modern debate, I want to focus more on the Islamic perspective of this topic. I want to begin by quoting a Hadith which was narrated by Abu Hurairah: "The Messenger of Allah ﷺ said, 'He who gives respite to someone who is in difficult circumstances, or grants him remission, Allah will shelter him in the shade of His Throne on the Day of Resurrection, when there will be no shade except its shade.'"[158]

This Hadith, like those we have covered previously, portrays the true essence of Islam in the sense that Muslims are expected to look out for others. We are not taught to be selfish, but rather the example, *Sunnah* of the Prophet ﷺ teaches us to be selfless towards our family, community and the wider population.

When we look at the tribal system before Islam, we disapprove of it almost straight away because a person would only have been given social and economic rights if they were part of the tribe. Those who did not belong to that tribe, or those who belonged to a lower classed tribe, were not treated fairly. However, the state of the present world is no better, we could even say that it is worse. People who are born in a certain country, or hold a certain passport are given more freedom and benefits than those who are not official citizens. It is sad that so much preference is given to a passport or nationality, thus making other people seem less valuable. They are not able to access healthcare, schools and other public services because of their nationality or passport.

In present day society, human rights are almost always referred to in the context of freedom of expression and liberty. The focus of human rights is more upon individuals being able to express themselves or live in a certain way, which then leads to particular groups of people becoming more privileged than others. In contrast to this, human rights in Islam begin with the right to a dignified existence. The refugee crisis that we are witnessing currently should be viewed within this context, they should have the right to live a dignified life.

People do not leave their homes, livelihoods and everything that is dear to them for the sake of it; it is due to unfortunate and difficult circumstances that they make the tough decision to leave. Allah has likened refugees, or people forced from their homes to death, as in *Surah an-Nisa* 4:66: *"And if We decreed upon them, 'Kill yourselves' or 'Leave your homes,' they would not have done it, except for a few of them."* Asking someone to leave their home would be like asking them to kill themselves.

The aforementioned Hadith promises the reward of shade under Allah's Throne on the Day of Judgement; this reward is a form of protection in return for giving protection to others in this world (*dunya*). It is also worth recalling a Hadith we covered in a previous chapter which mentions the basic rights of a person: "The Prophet Muhammad ﷺ said, 'There is no right for the son of Adam except in these things: a house in which he lives, a garment to cover his nakedness, a piece of bread and water.'"[159] If a person has these rights taken away from them, they will almost certainly leave to find a place where they are given these basic rights. The right to shelter is applicable to everyone, and we must do whatever we can to accommodate this right for others.

If we look at the history of Islam, the first migration done for the sake of safety during the life of the Prophet Muhammad ﷺ, was of the early Muslims to Abyssinia. The Messenger of Allah ﷺ knew that Najashi was a just person and would not send them back to their home in Makkah as they were facing persecution there; this quality was highly praised as it is something that is expected from Muslims. Even when Amr bin 'Aas went to Najashi to demand that the Muslims be returned to Makkah, Najashi did not let him take them.

The first group of refugees that migrated to Abyssinia also included the daughter of the Prophet Muhammad ﷺ, Ruqayyah.

One example that stands out during this time is of Abu Bakr when he was on his way to Abyssinia. He was stopped by a chief named Ibn ad-Daghinah from the outskirts of Makkah who asked why he was leaving. Abu Bakr replied, "My people kicked me out, so I desire to explore the earth and worship my Lord freely." Abu Bakr's answer shows us that he believed that he had the right to travel where he pleased as the world belongs to Allah, and to worship Him freely. Ibn ad-Daghinah said that this was unjust, and that Abu Bakr was a valuable asset to the people of Makkah, and he granted him asylum.

The right to migration is embedded in our religion; it is not limited to seeking refuge or asylum, but it also expands to migrating for the sake of betterment for you and your family in terms of practicing Islam and even improving finances. The concept of borders, nationalities and restriction to the movement of people and goods is not something conceived of in Islam. The value, or lack of value, brought to an area with the arrival of refugees should not put local residents off, nor should they concentrate on this aspect as it does not allow them to take care of refugees in the proper manner.

Refugees must be treated with respect and love; they have left everything that was familiar to them behind in the search for safety and wellbeing for themselves and their families. One particular Hadith puts the treatment of refugees into perspective: "Are you given victory and sustenance except by the way you treat the most vulnerable?"[160] By treating vulnerable people such as refugees with care and dignity, we can expect to be rewarded by Allah in the form of victory in the Hereafter and an increase in sustenance in this world.

In another Hadith, the Prophet Muhammad ﷺ said: "There is no leader who closes the door to someone in need, one suffering in poverty, except that Allah closes the gates of the heavens for him when he is suffering in poverty."[161] This is a powerful statement saying that if we turn someone away in their time of need, we will be turned away by Allah in our time of need. This applies to nations as much as it does to individuals; if a country shuts it doors on vulnerable people in need, it will ultimately lead to a loss for the country in terms of blessings, wealth and safety.

Umar bin Abdul Aziz is a great example of someone who would grant asylum to everyone, as he understood the importance of it in Islam. When he was the governor of Madinah, he would grant asylum to Muslim refugees who were feeling from Hajjaj bin Yusuf. There was no concept of refugee camps during his reign, instead, he expected and told the citizens of Madinah to take it upon themselves to take care of the refugees as they would with family. The reign of Umar bin Abdul Aziz was one of the greatest in the history of Islam - it was the most stable in terms of the wealth of the nation, social welfare within the nation and policy matters leading to safety of the citizens - as he dealt with matters justly. He would not turn people away and would take care of those in need.

Allah says in *Surah al-Hashr* 59:9: *"And (also for) those who were settled in al-Madinah and (adopted) the faith before them. They love those who emigrated to them and find not any want in their breasts of what the emigrants were given but give them preference over themselves, even though they are in privation. And whoever is protected from the stinginess of his soul, it is those who will be successful."*

The verse praises and talks about the people of Madinah (*Ansaar*) being welcoming and loving towards those who migrated to them. It is with faith that people are able to adopt such a warming attitude towards others, otherwise generally, once local residents begin to feel a burden from looking after refugees, they also begin to resent them. An example that many of us will be familiar with is people blaming refugees for taking their jobs. The *Ansar* on the other hand, did not know the migrants personally, but took care of them with love and respect because they knew that by doing so, they would be earning the pleasure of Allah.

Allah then goes onto say in the same verse that the *Ansar* had no ill feelings towards the migrants and what they were given; in fact, they preferred the migrants over themselves even though it may have put them in a position of hardship. This is a characteristic that we rarely see in modern times when people are more prone to being selfish rather than selfless. Refugees are not always welcomed with open arms, nor are they given any preference because of the difficulties that they have endured. We are also taught in the Qur'an that travellers who have lost their wealth or have seen it reduced, are deserving of charity (*zakah*).

Taking care of migrants or refugees is not just limited to those who are Muslims, but this act also extends to those who are non-Muslims. Allah says in *Surah at-Tawbah* 9:6: *"And if any one of the polytheists seeks your protection, then grant him protection so that he may hear the words of Allah. Then deliver him to his place of safety. That is because they are a people who do not know."*

Imam Awza'i was once asked about this verse with the question, "And where is his place of security? Do you think if he says, 'My place of security is in Constantinople,' we should take him there?" Imam Awza'i answered this by saying, "If he reaches one of their fortresses or one of their strongholds, this would be his place of security." After this, he was asked, "What if the polytheists are met by a Muslim patrol in their country before they reach their place of security?" He answered, "The patrol should not stand in their way."

He was then asked about the enemy who enters a Muslim land under a safe conduct which is valid until his return, but on the way back to his homeland, he climbs a mountain that falls into their territory and is forced by strong winds to return to Muslim land. Awza'i then answered by saying that he was of the opinion that the enemy would be entitled to protection under the safe conduct even if he was forced back.

We cannot discriminate against non-Muslim refugees and migrants because they do not belong to the same belief as us. Treating them with respect and care can give them the opportunity to learn about Islam. By showing good character, we show Islam, and there is no greater opportunity to showcase Islam to refugees or migrants than by taking care of them in the way that the Qur'an and *Sunnah* teach us.

We can conclude that asylum (*istijarah* or *talab al-jiwar*) is a human right in Islam. A refugee must be given the same rights and responsibilities as a local or national once they have been granted asylum. A refugee should not be seen as less worthy or less capable; they should be seen as equals and be given access to the same things as those who are local. Modern refugee law, however, does not recognise the right to asylum unfortunately. It also does not recognise the right to any permanent or liveable accommodation for refugees; many refugees are left homeless or in horrific living conditions. By stripping people of their right to safety, and not allowing them to know if they will be safe in a home soon because of a lack of paperwork is viewed as a crime in Islam.

Yet, when we look into history, we find that the Prophet Ibrahim and his family, peace be upon them, were refugees, Prophet Musa, peace be upon him, was a refugee, and even the Prophet Muhammad ﷺ was a refugee. The concept of migration is ingrained in the Muslim psyche. Najashi survived a revolt against him, but due to him accepting the Muslim refugees and granting them rights and safety, Allah blessed his reign as ruler and his homeland of Abyssinia. Similar to how Islam teaches us that charity does not diminish our wealth, Islam also teaches us that accepting, taking care of and granting rights to refugees or migrants will not reduce the overall wealth and blessings of our country.

May Allah allow us to fulfil the rights of refugees, and open our hearts towards them, allowing us to help them and grant them protection to the best of our means. Amin.

32

RACISM, SUPREMACISM AND TRUE PATRIOTISM

> *Abu Hurairah (ra) reported: The Prophet ﷺ said: Allah, Most High, has removed from you the pride of the pre-Islamic period and its boasting in ancestors. One is only a pious believer or a miserable sinner. You are sons of Adam, and Adam came from dust. Let the people cease to boast about their ancestors. They are merely fuel in Jahannam; or they will certainly be of less account with Allah than the beetle which rolls dung with its nose.*

FOLLOWING ON FROM the previous chapter on migrants and refugees, we will now look at some of the main factors that contribute towards the negative treatment of refugees: racism, supremacism and nationalism.

Islam is completely anti-racist, and it has been mentioned explicitly that there is no place for racism in the religion. There are numerous Hadith that speak against racism; however, I want to begin with a Hadith that covers the themes of both racism and nationalism.

Abu Hurairah reported: "The Prophet Muhammad ﷺ said, 'Allah, Most High, has removed from you the pride of the pre-Islamic period and its boasting in ancestors. One is only a pious believer or a miserable sinner. You are sons of Adam, and Adam came from dust. Let the people cease to boast about their ancestors. They are merely fuel in Jahannam; or they will certainly be of less account with Allah than the beetle which rolls dung with its nose.'"[162] It is worth remembering here that the Prophet Muhammad ﷺ avoided the use harsh or strict language unless he really wanted to make a specific point regarding a subject.

This Hadith has several themes running through it:

1. A paradigm shift in the way that people are viewed (you can either be a pious believer or a miserable sinner).

2. Unity between all human beings (we are all the children of Adam).

3. The concept of humility (Adam came from dirt).

4. The comparison between the arrogance of racism and the disgrace of rubbing your nose in dirt or dung to the beetle. It is seen as a disgrace to be racist.

Dr Abdullah Hamid Ali wrote an article called '*Beyond Race*' in which he mentioned that in the pre-modern era, race and group membership were determined more so by cultural traits such as language and shared customs rather than skin colour. Most of the Arabs during the time of the Prophet Muhammad ﷺ had a dark complexion, but the people of Makkah and the Hijaz area in the seventh century were not defined by the colour of their skin. The people of Makkah were defined by their tribe, their language, their customs and their lineage, and this can be seen through the varying descriptions of the same person. They did not pay much attention to the skin colour, however there were instances when they would make comments about the skin colour in an offensive way. For example, Abu Dharr was a black man, yet he still insulted Bilal by saying, "Oh son of a black woman", because Bilal was a non-Arab black man.

The Prophet Muhammad ﷺ compared boasting on the basis of these things (such as thinking of your lineage as superior, and even the colour of your skin) to filth. In one Hadith, the Prophet ﷺ condemned the use of tribalism or nationalism to belittle others by saying, "Leave it because certainly it is filthy."[163] Structural racism also penetrates culture; people may see it as something purely political, but it is also sociological. One example of this is that the Prophet Muhammad ﷺ lived in a society that regularly swore by their forefathers, the Prophet ﷺ commented on this and said, "Whoever swears by something, let him not take an oath except by Allah. Do not swear by your forefathers."[164]

Oftentimes, when people of different customs and beliefs dwell in peace, there will be someone who will create divisions between them by introducing labels and structural racism. An example of this in recent history is the partition of India and Pakistan where the British played a large role. The partition caused unimaginable amounts of death and destruction because identities were created, and people became divided resulting in them killing each other over those identities. The Prophet Muhammad ﷺ made a profound statement regarding this kind of behaviour in a Hadith narrated by Jundab bin Abdullah: "The Messenger of Allah ﷺ said, 'Whoever fights for a cause that is not clear, advocating tribalism and dying for the sake of tribalism, then he has died a death of *jahiliyyah*.'"

The Messenger of Allah ﷺ referred to the days of ignorance (*jahiliyyah*) because people used to kill each other over their tribes; the tribal wars were prevalent in Arab society before the Prophet Muhammad ﷺ was even born. It was for this reason that the population of Madinah was mostly under forty years of age, as their fathers had killed each other. The Prophet ﷺ made it a point to say that there is no nobility in fighting under the banners of tribalism or nationalism. And referring back to the incident of Abu Dharr calling Bilal the son of a black woman, the Messenger of Allah ﷺ admonished Abu Dharr by saying that he still had ignorance (*jahiliyyah*) within him.

In another Hadith, the Prophet Muhammad ﷺ mentioned that traces of ignorance will remain in the Muslim community (*ummah*). It is narrated in Sahih Muslim: "There are four traits of the Days of Ignorance (*jahiliyyah*) that will always remain in the *ummah*:

1. Boasting about one's ancestors' deeds and virtues.
2. Defaming others on the basis of their lineage.
3. Seeking to be given rain by means of the stars (referring to superstitions).
4. Ritualistic mourning and wailing over the dead."

The manifestations may change but these diseases will remain; though ideally they should be eradicated, unfortunately, there has been and always will be some form of racism or nationalism within the Muslim community.

We also, however, come to learn through the teachings of the Prophet Muhammad ﷺ and the Qur'an that a person's true value is based on their spirituality and piety (*taqwa*). The Hadith of the Messenger of Allah ﷺ do not just negate the ugliness of tribalism and racism, but they also affirm spiritual equality. Allah also ties the two together in the Qur'an, as we find in in Surah *al-Hujurat* 49:13: *"Oh mankind, indeed We have created you male and female and made you nations and tribes that you may know one another. Indeed, the most noble of you in the sight of Allah is the most righteous of you. Indeed, Allah is Knowing and Acquainted."* This verse was revealed in response to the comments made about Bilal, and it can clearly be understood that whilst there are indeed different tribes of people, the only thing that distinguishes a person is their piety, or righteousness. The colour of our skin, our lineage, our social class and our nationality, hold no importance in the sight of Allah, it is only the level of our faith and piety.

The Companions of the Prophet ﷺ took some time to fully understand and appreciate what this meant, and how to put it into practice. An example of this can be found in a Hadith narrated by Abu Hurairah: "The people said, 'Oh Messenger of Allah ﷺ, who is the most honourable amongst the people in Allah's sight?' He said, 'The most righteous amongst them.' They said, 'We do not ask you about this.' He said, 'Then Yusuf, Allah's Prophet, the son of Allah's Prophet (Yaqoob), the son of Allah's Prophet (Ishaac), the son of Allah's Khalil (Ibrahim).' They said, 'We do not ask you about this.' He said, 'Then you want to ask about the descent of the Arabs. Those who were the best in the pre-Islamic period of ignorance will be the best in Islam, provided they comprehend the religious knowledge.'" What we see here is that the Prophet ﷺ was telling them that in terms of lineage , there is not going to be any greater example of noble lineage than of Yusuf through to Ibrahim. However, the people were more interested to know about themselves, the Arabs. And so the Messenger of Allah said to them that the best amongst them in the Days of Ignorance would be the best amongst them in Islam, but only if they gain religious understanding, meaning to say, the only way that the transition of nobility can take place is if faith and piety are achieved. If there is no religious understanding, then there is no nobility. Abu Lahab and Abu Jahl are prime examples of this; whilst before Islam and the Prophethood of Muhammad ﷺ they were considered the most noble of Arabs, they were in fact not noble at all. The only thing that characterised them was ignorance and humiliation.

Another interesting and important point to note is that the Prophet Muhammad ﷺ pointed to his heart and said that piety (*taqwa*) exists in the heart. Piety cannot be seen or accessed by anybody else , and so we must treat everyone equally. Human beings cannot know who is higher in the sight of Allah because only Allah can distinguish us; we do not have the right to treat some people better or worse than others.

This brings me onto the point of racism in society. Racism is such an evil thing that it has led to genocides, enslavement and apartheid throughout history, and even to the present day. On a personal level, one of the greatest acts of evil that I learnt about was at the apartheid museum during my visit to South Africa. They had colour grading systems which determined the neighbourhood or district that a person would be allowed to live in, it determined where they would stand in a queue and even what services that they were allowed to access. It was not a simple case of only black versus white, but it was based on the colour grading system and where their complexion fell on that spectrum.

Racism is a disease, and the manifestation of it is that a particular group of people can be designated as the 'out group' or 'unacceptable group', or all but one group of people are designated as the 'in group'. This highly unfair approach taken by racism results in a massive imbalance in society across all levels.

The first act of racism was carried out by (*Shaytan*) the devil. He refused to obey Allah because he believed he was better than the Prophet Adam, and it was not only due to the superiority of fire over dirt, there were many other factors. Racism is not based on the superiority of appearance alone, there is much more behind it that draws on all forms of privilege and is usually socially engineered. Looking at more recent times, people in Dallas would become more upset with the removal of the statue of Robert E Lee who advocated white pride and supremacy, than they would have done if someone was to remove a statue of Jesus. White supremacy is worshipped more over Christ, and in states like Texas, people are still holding onto a sense of privilege and entitlement because of the colour of their skin and their history.

Such racism has many implications, and there are several lessons we can take from this. The main question here is: is there a positive form of nationalism or tribalism in Islam?

- We are meant to belong to the faith (*ummah*) rather than the nation, however defending the land we live on from an attack is perfectly acceptable and is as such a positive manifestation.

- Wanting to do good for your people, i.e. your tribe or nation (*qaum*) is a positive quality. However, the betterment of your people should not come at the price of disadvantage towards others, nor through unfair privileges and entitlements. It should instead come through helping others and living up to our ideals of justice and equity towards all of humanity.

- The Prophet Muhammad ﷺ loved his tribe (*qaum*); although he was the Messenger of Allah to all of mankind, he never stopped being a Hashimite. His love for his *qaum* however did not mean that he denigrated other tribes, or gave preference to Banu Hashim when it came to acts of humanity or access to certain 'services', his love was something that showed a bond which is appreciated in Islam.

  During battles, the Prophet ﷺ would allow people to fight alongside their family or tribe members. He also used to send people to their own tribes in order for them to call people to Islam, as he knew that they would be more likely to respond to the call of faith from a fellow tribesman than from a foreigner.

- Allah praises the attitude of wanting good for your people. For example, the Prophets would refer to the people of their nation as 'my people,' even if they had not yet accepted their message and call towards faith.

- The Prophet Muhammad ﷺ validated the identities of the Aws and Khazraj tribes of Madinah; he only condemned them when people used their identities as calls against each other, thus leading to strife and civil war.

- Dr Salah al-Sawy said the following: "Religious loyalty (*walaa'*) and all it entails of love and support for co-religionists does not conflict with national identity and the love and affection its social bonds naturally generate. We believe that we are a part of the Muslim *ummah* (global community) in light of our religion, and a part of our respective local societies in light of our citizenry and human relationships. We do not believe there is an inherent conflict between a religious and national identity, so long as one's country does not criminalise religiosity or curtail the right to practice one's religion or call to it. We also believe that living together should naturally weave a social fabric between a people of a shared homeland allowing for a harmonious co-existence between them, regardless of how different their beliefs may be. This involves an ethos of kindness, justice, and security against harm. It also necessitates a reciprocation of social responsibility that is shared by all, and observes the sanctity of people's lives, wealth, honour, and public spaces which cannot be touched except by the current laws or governing bodies of that land."

The point being made here is that there is a difference between religious loyalty that we feel towards our Muslim brothers and sisters around the world, and the loyalty we feel towards people that we share an identity with, by whatever virtue that may be. It does not become harmful until that loyalty manifests itself through bigotry or discrimination against others.

- The Prophet Muhammad ﷺ would call tribes to live up to their best values. For example, if people of a certain tribe were known for their generosity, he would encourage them to exhibit that quality and live up to that cultural identity. However, this does not mean that they can expect privilege as a result of that or denigrate others.

- Racism is quite often disguised as nationalism, ethno-nationalism, and it is usually just another form of white supremacy. If a white American nationalist has more loyalty to a refugee coming from a predominantly white country such as the Netherlands, but little to no loyalty towards an African American that lives right next door, they are a false nationalist. This behaviour should instead be categorised as racism.

- Whilst a Muslim should believe in the superiority and correctness of Islam, they should not act intolerantly towards those of other faiths, nor view others as inferior. We cannot demonise non-Muslims or act unfairly towards them, it may just be that having a positive and just attitude towards them will pull them towards Islam.

- Malcom X wrote in his '*Letter from Mecca*': "America needs to understand Islam, because this is the one religion that erases from its society the race problem. Throughout my travels in the Muslim world, I have met, talked to, and even eaten with people who in America would have been considered white – but the white attitude was removed from their minds by the religion of Islam. I have never before seen sincere and true brotherhood practiced by all colours together, irrespective of their colour."

Malcolm X understood that the problem was not with the complexion of a person, but with their mind and adopting a 'white minded' approach. Furthermore, his comment stating that Islam erases racism from society, was calling to attention what many liberationists struggle for – an anti-racist society and tradition. The explicit anti-racist tradition of Islam is unique, and it is something that all Muslims should take pride in and aim to achieve. Although Malcolm X did experience racist Muslims on his travels, he was speaking to the philosophy and structure that Islam was setting up in it rituals and guidance to humanity. Hajj gave him a true glimpse into the Islamic approach and the potential of an anti-racist society.

- Gandhi, who was a staunch Hindu, also felt that Islam was superior in the sense of having an uncompromising and clear vision of human brotherhood. When he wrote about

Islam's contribution to India, he said: "Islam's distinctive contribution to India's national culture is its unadulterated belief in the Oneness of God and a practical application of the truth of the brotherhood of man for those who are nominally within its fold. I call these two distinctive contributions. For in Hinduism the spirit of brotherhood has become too much philosophised. Similarly, though philosophical Hinduism has no other god but God, it cannot be denied that practical Hinduism is not so emphatically uncompromising as Islam."

There were times in Muslim history when black people struggled, however, unlike Europe and America, black Muslims were able to rise to high positions in society. The Prophet Muhammad ﷺ paid very close attention to how Muslims of different races were treated, and it was due to this approach that racist attitudes were overcome and the mindset penetrated society in such a way that black Muslims were able to progress in life with more ease and respect.

- One of the first examples is of the Prophet Muhammad ﷺ appointing Bilal to be the first to call to prayer (*mu'adhin*). Another example is of 'Ataa bin Abi Rab'iah being the first Mufti of Makkah – proving that black Muslims could reach top levels of scholarship, whilst other examples include black Muslims running the Mamluk Dynasty and leading armies, like Tariq bin Ziyad.

- Bilal, although being an Abyssinian, married Halaa bint Awf who was from one of the noblest of Arab families at the time. The Messenger of Allah ﷺ in fact proposed for the marriage on behalf of Bilal. He was also made head of the treasury – a great responsibility.

Other examples of black Muslims being honoured include Umm Aymaan (Barakah), whom the Prophet Muhammad ﷺ referred to as his mother after his mother. Sumayyah, the first martyr of Islam was a black woman. Zayd, the adopted son of the Prophet ﷺ was black. The first martyr of the Battle of Badr was a black Muslim named Mihja'. Usama bin Zayd, a black Companion of the Prophet ﷺ, was the first commander of an army after the Prophet Muhammad had passed away, and whilst some Companions did complain that he was appointed as commander, it was not because of his skin colour, but because of the fact that he was only seventeen years of age.

- There is a wonderful story of Ubadah bin as-Saamit, who was one of the inhabitants of Madina *(Ansar)* and was also a black man. He accompanied the Messenger of Allah in every battle and was one of the scribes of the revelations of the Qur'an.

In this particular incident, the Muslim army during the Caliphate of Umar laid siege to a Babylonian Fortress in 641CE (the area which is known as Coptic Cairo). The Egyptian ruler al-Muqawqis, called for a Muslim delegation and asked them to send their best man forward to him. Amr bin al-'Aas sent a delegation that was headed by Ubadah bin as-Saamit and when al-Muqawqis saw that the one leading was a black man, he was taken aback and did not want to speak to him. He said, "Take this black man away from me and let someone else come and speak to me!" The others in the delegation responded to this by saying, "This black man is the best of us in knowledge and wisdom. He is our leader and the best of us and has been appointed over us. We all defer to his opinion and Umar bin Khattab has appointed him over us and ordered us not go against him. And to us, a black man and a white man are the same!"

Al-Muqawqis said to delegation, "How could you accept this black man as the best among you? Rather he should be the least among you."

To this they said, "No; even though he is black as you can see, he is the best in status among us, one of the foremost among us and one of the wisest." Al-Muqawqis then spoke to Ubadah and said, "Come forward, oh black man and speak to me gently, for your blackness alarms me, and if you speak harshly that will alarm me further." He was still insulting Ubadah even though he had heard what the delegation had to say about him.

Ubadah went forward and said, "I have heard what you said. Among my companions whom I left behind are a thousand men who are all as black as me, and even blacker than me and more terrifying to behold. If you saw them you would be even more alarmed. My youth has gone, but nevertheless I would not be scared if one hundred men of my enemy wanted to face me all at once, and the same is true of my companions, for our hope and our desire is to strive in jihad for the sake of Allah, seeking the pleasure of Allah."

Upon hearing this, al-Muqawqis said to those around him, "Have you ever heard anything like what this man is saying? His appearance alarmed me, but his words alarm me more. Allah sent this man and his companions out to destroy the world! I think they are bound to prevail over the entire world."

- When we look at Sa'd al-Aswad, we find that he was a black Arab from Bani Sulaym. He came to the Prophet Muhammad ﷺ and asked him if his dark complexion would prevent him from entering Paradise (*Jannah*); he believed himself to be unpleasant looking because of his complexion. The Messenger of Allah ﷺ said to him that his complexion would not prevent him from entering Paradise (*Jannah*), entering Paradise is by virtue of a person's mindfulness of Allah. The Prophet ﷺ built up Sa'd's self-esteem and proposed on his behalf to the daughter of Amr bin Wahb, a recent convert to Islam from Bani Thaqif who was also from the most noble of Arabs.

- Julaybeeb was a Companion who was looked down upon for various reasons such as his social class and his appearance. Julaybeeb had a very dark complexion, he did not belong to any tribe, nor did he have any family, however the Messenger of Allah ﷺ would always be looking out for him, making sure his confidence was bolstered and that he felt included. Nobody would consider Julaybeeb for marriage, and so the Prophet Muhammad ﷺ went to the father of a beautiful and righteous woman and said, "I would like to marry your daughter, not to myself but to Julaybeeb." The mother started to scream that she would never allow Julaybeeb to marry their daughter, but the daughter heard the recommendation of the Prophet ﷺ and insisted on marrying him. Uthman bin Affan then paid the dowry for Julaybeeb.

Soon after, Julaybeeb took part in a battle and the Prophet ﷺ asked every tribe if they were missing anybody, they said no, but the Prophet Muhammad ﷺ said that he was missing Julaybeeb and asked where he was. They went looking for him and found him laying dead next to seven men of the opposing army. The Prophet ﷺ stood over him and began to cry, praising his effort and saying three times, "Oh Allah, this one is from me and I am from him." A man that was mistreated his entire life was given so much respect and love by the Messenger of Allah ﷺ, who then picked Julaybeeb up in his arms, dug his grave and buried Julaybeeb himself.

It is clear to see that Islam and the Messenger of Allah ﷺ sought to erase racism structurally within society, and he did this by leading by example. The Prophet ﷺ and the Caliphs put those who were looked down upon due to their race in positions of religious and political leadership, they brought Muslims together through marriage and social interactions. The Prophet ﷺ taught everyone to find their value through their piety (*taqwa*), and to not denigrate others based on their class, or tribe or race.

Umm Mihjan was a black woman who cleaned the masjid, but the Prophet ﷺ did not see her as insignificant and prayed for her after she had passed away. Jibreel was sent to the Prophet ﷺ to inform him of the passing away of Najashi so that he could lead a funeral prayer for him. Muhammad bin Maslama, another black non-Arab was made governor under all of the four righteous Caliphs.

All of these points lead back to the initial Hadith that I mentioned at the beginning of this chapter, which said, "One is only a pious believer or a miserable sinner." Race plays no part in a person's piety and will play no part on the Day of Judgement. May Allah make us pious believers and allow us to be a part of eradicating the disease of racism from within our families and societies. May Allah protect us from this disease and allow us to be makers of change. Amin.

33

STEREOTYPING AND COLLECTIVE GUILT

Abdullah ibn Mas'ud reported: The Messenger of Allah, peace and blessings be upon him, said, "Do not return to unbelief after me by striking the necks of each other. No man is to be punished for the crimes of his father or his brother."

CONNECTING BACK TO the topics of the previous chapters, we will now look at stereotyping and collective guilt. Whilst not all stereotyping is racism and vice versa, they are interconnected and racism is a form of stereotyping – in fact, it is the most evil form of stereotyping.

A very common way in which a person develops racist tendencies is by taking the worst sample of a group of people and making that sample representative of that entire particular race. They use the one bad example to justify their racism and mistreatment towards that group of people. This approach then manifests itself in to discriminatory policies that are brought in by those in power to exploit certain groups and bring them down, whilst favouring those whom they wish.

There are several Hadith that are specific to the concept of stereotyping and collective guilt, however the one that I wish to mention connects killing one another (the worst type of division) to the practice of applying collective guilt. Abdullah bin Mas'ud narrated that the Messenger of Allah ﷺ said: "Do not return to unbelief after me by striking the necks of each other. No man is to be punished for the crimes of his father or his brother."[165]

The wording of the Prophet ﷺ in this Hadith takes the concept of collective guilt a step further by saying that it cannot even be applied to a family, let alone an entire group of people. The Prophet Muhammad ﷺ also showed an example of this in the case of Ikrima, the son of Abu Jahl. Ikrima accepted Islam after the conquest of Makkah, and despite all the crimes and oppression that he and his father Abu Jahl committed against the early Muslims, the Prophet ﷺ told his Companions not to even mention Abu Jahl in his presence in order to not hurt Ikrima's feelings. If we take into account the time and atmosphere at the point, this would have been a difficult task for the Companions because they knew the atrocities that Ikrima and his father had carried out, yet they followed through with the order of the Prophet ﷺ. This was excellence on the part of the Prophet ﷺ and his Companions.

There are several lessons that we can take from the Qur'an and Prophetic tradition in regard to this topic:

1. Allah says in *Surah an-Najm* 53:38: *"And no bearer of burdens will bear the burden of another."* This verse further solidifies the Hadith in which the Prophet ﷺ said that we cannot punish a man for the crimes of his father or brother.

2. When Allah created Prophet Adam, may the blessings of Allah be upon him, He gave him a leadership position on the earth. The Angels asked Allah, "Are you going to place on this earth a creation that will spill blood and spread corruption?" The Angels based this assumption on their experience with the Jinn – another creation of Allah with free will – who are known to have used their free will for evil and corruption.

Whilst the assumption of the Angels does have some accuracy to it, Allah answered their question by saying, "Indeed, I know that which you do not know." The righteous offspring of Prophet Adam would counter those that spread corruption, and they consisted of the likes of Nuh, Musa, Ibrahim, Isa and Muhammad ﷺ. Allah was telling them that there would be gems from mankind, unlike from any other creation of Allah. There have always been people who shed blood and behave corruptly, but Allah has also created people who are righteous.

- There is a Hadith in Muwatta which says, "When you hear a man say, 'The people are ruined,' he himself is the most ruined of them all." What is meant here is that what we see in others is a projection of ourselves.

- Painting everyone with the same brush is something that the Prophet Muhammad ﷺ and Allah have told us not to do. Allah says in *Surah al Imran* 3:113: *"They are not all the same; among the People of the Scripture is a community standing in obedience, reciting the verses of Allah during periods of the night and prostrating in prayer."* This verse was revealed in response to the Companions who were making generalisations about the People of the Book. Allah also mentioned in another verse (*Surah al Imran* 3:75) that there are some people of the Book whom we can trust with a possession, whilst there are some whom we will find not to be trustworthy. They are not all the same regarding their integrity, their trustworthiness or their spirituality.

    If we assume everyone to be the same, how then is it that the Chief Rabbi of Madinah accepted Islam? If all the Jews of Madinah were the same and plotted against the Prophet Muhammad ﷺ, their leader would never have become a Muslim. We cannot decontextualize verses in the Qur'an such as, *"And never will the Jews or the Christians approve of you until you follow their religion."* (*Surah al-Baqarah* 2:120) If this were the case there would be no point to Da'wah – a fundamental action that Muslims are expected to engage in to call people to Islam.

- When we read the verses about Bani Israel in the Qur'an, we should understand that there is a lesson that Allah wants to teach us. By talking about Bani Israel, the nation that came before this *ummah*, we are expected to learn to distinguish good from bad, and we are warned about the mistakes that they made, but we also learn that there were righteous people from that nation that held onto the truth even as deviation took over their community. The Prophet Muhammad ﷺ also said that the largest nation after his on the Day of Judgement would be the nation of the Prophet Musa.

We should focus on ourselves and try not to deviate like much of Bani Israeel, but we should also be wary of criticising that nation. A beautiful example is of Hudhayfa, may Allah be pleased with him, was someone that the Prophet Muhammad ﷺ used to confide in and who was even told the names of the hypocrites. He also used to ask the Messenger of Allah ﷺ about bad qualities and bad characteristics so that he could avoid them and become a better Muslim. Hudhayfa heard some Muslims criticising Bani Israeel and chastised them for behaving as though they were inherently righteous by saying, "What great brothers you are to the Israelites; you claim as if every sweet quality is yours and every bitter quality is theirs! By Allah, you will certainly tread their path, footstep by footstep."

- In another Hadith reported by Aisha, may Allah be pleased with her, the Prophet Muhammad ﷺ said, "Certainly, the greatest liar amongst the people is a man who insults another man by disparaging the entire tribe."[166]

The Arabic word that is used in this Hadith is *hijaa'* which referred to smear poetry (smearing or putting someone down in a poetic way). *Hijaa'* is something that is very similar to what the media in current times does; they take a small group of people or even an individual, and begin to smear the entire community or population of people that belong to the same identity.

Very often, we can see that unfair policies come about from discrimination, stereotyping and collective guilt towards certain people. In the current climate, Muslims are widely targeted and called terrorists. Whilst we can believe and agree that there will be a few Muslims who commit acts of terrorism, these small number of people are used to generalise all Muslims. Even though Muslims are not more prone to violence and terrorism than others, this common assumption is unfortunately propagated due to the media and certain people who have widespread influence. We could show all the factual data in the world regarding terrorist acts, but there will be people who wholeheartedly believe that most terrorism is committed by Muslims as the image has been engraved into their minds.

However, just like not all Muslims are terrorists, not all non-Muslims think bad of us. One example is of a man I met at an anti-Islamophobia rally; he was a victim of the bombing in Boston, and whilst many people would jump at the opportunity to use the bombings as a way to defame the Muslims further, he made it a point to attend a rally that was against Islamophobia. Although his leg had been amputated by the bombings, he did not let the evil of those few who acted inhumanely in the name of Islam to affect his understanding.

When it comes to generalising entire groups of people, there are a few points to note:

- People characterise entire groups of people because of an unfortunate personal experience that they had, or because they have been fed toxic lies and notions about a certain group of people on a consistent basis. When this kind of thought process and behaviour is present within society it has much wider implications than just insensitivity towards a people: it finds its way into the political sphere and policies of a nation. Groups of people are stereotyped and discriminated against as a result of that stereotyping; Muslims are seen as terrorists, Jews and Catholics are seen as disloyal, Mexicans are seen as rapists whilst the black community are all seen as criminals.

- Not only does this labelling cause certain political policies, it can also lead the victims of this discrimination to channel their frustration by doing the same to others. For example, some Muslims become so upset and angry with the terrorist label that they label all Buddhists as terrorists because of the atrocities being committed against the Rohingya. Stereotyping and mischaracterising groups of people is an effective strategy of pitting people against each other, and we as Muslims should be wary of this and not allow ourselves to fall prey to it.

- We should bear in mind that Allah distinguished between people even on the basis of their degrees of evil. One such example is of the brothers of Prophet Yusuf, with the least evil brother saying not to kill Yusuf, but to throw him into the well so that he may be found and sold into slavery by someone. Allah made a distinction here between the brothers, whilst the rest were happy with ending Yusuf's life this particular brother showed some sympathy towards him. The Prophet Muhammad ﷺ also made a distinction at the Battle of Badr between his enemies. He referred to Umayyah bin Khalaf as being the one with some good in him because he showed hesitation regarding going forth in the battle. The Messenger of Allah ﷺ understood that some people are pressured into committing evil by others and this should be taken into consideration. He understood that some of the people did not want to fight or kill the Muslims and they were literally forced out of their homes to fight. The Prophet's ﷺ uncle Abbas was one of those people who surrendered quickly because of their hesitation to fight.

- There is shirk involved in stereotyping in that the concept of a natural disposition (*fitrah*) towards good is innate in every human being, and by writing people off based on their identity – religious or ethnic – is essentially claiming that they do not have this natural dispositon (*fitrah*). One of the main points of da'wah is to bring people back to their *fitrah* because they have been influenced away from it. Da'wah is to try and connect them again to the natural disposition of doing good and belief in the Oneness of God, and by saying that entire groups of people no longer have a *fitrah*, it is also saying that there is a deficiency in the creation of Allah.

- There is also hypocrisy in stereotyping – by assuming the best of ourselves and the worst of others. We choose to overlook our own shortcomings and mistakes but are quick to find the faults of others, to the extent that we even become obsessed with focusing on their mistakes.

- Stereotyping can very easily lead to dehumanising and demonising other groups of people. It stops us from doing good to others because we wrongly believe that they do not deserve to receive any good. We allow ourselves to not accept the responsibility to seek justice for people and do good to them.

- We lose sight of the oppressors who create such conditions that result in people killing each other. They create war zones and ghettos, and then step back saying that they have nothing to do with the situation. We do not want false propaganda against ourselves, but we should also be careful not to buy into the narratives against other groups of people. Instead, we should focus on dealing with the conditions that lead to bad behaviour, for example the Prophet Muhammad ﷺ said that poverty can lead to disbelief (*kufr*). When people are forced into harsh conditions such as poverty, it opens the doors to manipulate and divide them more easily.

- A revolutionary concept was introduced during the time of the Prophet Muhammad ﷺ in regard to war ethics: women, children, elderly, worshippers such as monks and even trees were forbidden from being harmed during a war. Since they are not party to the battle they are not to be punished for the actions of the real enemy. The entire group is not to be considered guilty for the actions of a section of that group. A prime example of this is after the Battle of Uhud, the Prophet Muhammad ﷺ came across a woman from the opposing side who had been killed and he became infuriated. Although the Prophet ﷺ had just lost Hamza – a dear family member – in battle, he was disturbed and took out the time to question why a woman from the other side had been killed.

- The Messenger of Allah ﷺ disapproved and condemned people who demeaned others because of their identity, whether it was because of their ethnicity or lineage. Nobody is given a choice in who their parents are or what their ethnicity is; it shows a high level of arrogance to demean another person for these things. As well as the infamous incident of Abu Dharr and Bilal, there was also another incident in which Hafsa called Safiyyah the daughter of a Jew. The Prophet Muhammad ﷺ did not deny the fact that she was the daughter of a Jew, and instead gave the best examples of Bani Israel as her ancestors by saying, "Indeed, you are the daughter of the Prophet Musa, your paternal uncle is the Prophet Haroun and you are married to a Prophet. So, on what basis does she demean you?" The Prophet Muhammad ﷺ did not negate that she belonged to a Jewish family and was now a Muslim, as that would have reinforced the language and tone of Hafsa.

Muslims are unfortunately a stereotyped group and we are held collectively guilty for the crimes that a select few have committed, but we should not allow this to become an excuse for us to wrong people of other religions, nor should we wrong Muslims of other ethnicities. Islam is a very diverse religion and we should respect each other, regardless of the generalisations that may be given to us.

May Allah protect us from division and from wronging others. May Allah allow us to see the good (*fitrah*) in everyone and to see and rectify our own shortcomings. Amin.

34

GENDER EQUITY IN ISLAM – REGARD FOR WOMEN

Aisha (ra) narrated… [The messenger] said: Yes. Women are the twin halves of men.

IN THIS CHAPTER we will shift our focus towards a different issue to the previous few chapters and that is of gender equity. The topic of women's rights is quite sensitive and is something that can be difficult to discuss within the context of justice as some of the reforms that Islam introduced are not considered in the same light in Western society. Other reforms however, such as opposing racism, were clear solutions to injustices and no one would dispute that. Edward Blyden in the eighteenth century for example, identified Islam as a liberating theology – Islam was recognised as being justice-based.

However, when we look at the discussion of feminism, or the liberation of women we find that it is a hotly debated topic. Whilst we would say that Islam has the solutions to the inequities experienced by women, there are certain ideologies or iterations within feminism that would view the Islamic reform as being regressive. It becomes difficult to find reconciliation between a religion that is timeless and ideologies that are constantly evolving.

There are also many questions that arise when looking into this subject, but one that I wish to start off by answering is: what did Islam do for women? If we are to honestly acknowledge what Islam has done for women, we will be aware that the greatest contribution that Islam made to women's rights is recognising the full humanity of a woman. This was revolutionary at that point in time, and even more so from a theological perspective.

Feminism is something that is becoming increasingly extreme in modern times; empowerment and equality have taken on very different meanings. One such example is the debate surrounding the disproportionate amounts of nudity of women when compared to men in adverts and movies and its cognitive impact on society. We may feel that the fact that this has been recognised and is subject to debate as objectification of women is encouraging and may lead society to appreciate that this culture is regressive rather than progressive. However, rather than calling for an end to the objectification of women, the solution that some modern feminists have come up with is to objectify men more often and have them be portrayed in a similar way in advertisements and movies to redress this disbalance.

Islam does not consent to the objectification of any human being – male or female. Furthermore, it recognised the full humanity of a woman; not seeing a woman as any less human than a man and this was a massive reformative step.

While trying to find an answer to what empowerment meant to women, I found that the book *Women in the Nation* by Dr Jamillah Karim and Dawn-Maree Gibson provided a wonderful outlook on the transition of women from the Nation of Islam into Sunni Islam. One of the most distinctive features of the Nation of Islam was discipline; that discipline also involved a strong emphasis on gender roles. The book itself narrates the experiences of different women and how they viewed empowerment. Some women felt empowered with the way that the Nation of Islam viewed women, whilst others felt that it was degrading.

One such example is from one of the speeches of Malcom X whilst he was in the Nation of Islam, in which he said, "The most disrespected woman in America is the black woman... We will kill you for our women." This form of protectiveness could be viewed as belittling to some whilst others could take pride in it. Furthermore, when should remind ourselves that the socio-historic influences particularly of the Jim Crow era meant that black women had become extremely aggrieved by the emasculation of black men and seeing black men undermined, that the empowerment of black men meant to them the empowerment of the black human being.

The point being that ideologies can sometimes be very short-sighted – especially in modern times where ideology is more fluid – and can also be restricted to one socio-cultural context. It is important to understand that there will always be differing views due to people's different experiences, social class, culture and time periods. A rich woman in America will have very different views to a poor woman living in Gaza, Palestine in terms of what empowerment is and what is diminishing. If two people living in the same time era can have different experiences, there are bound to be differences in people who live, or have lived, in different times and contexts. Knowing this, the best way then to decide whether Islam is empowering or diminishing, is to see how women in seventh century Arabia felt with the advent of Islam and how men viewed women as a result of the revelations of the Qur'an and the *Sunnah*.

The Yaqeen Institute has also published four papers regarding women's rights in Islam and I would like to touch briefly on their topics here too. The latest paper was on honour killings by Dr Jonathon Brown, and it is interesting to note that most people characterise South-Asian Muslims as being the most associated with honour killings, whereas the South American country El Salvador has the highest number of honour killings per capita. Our views have become skewed in regard to the situation of women around the world, and more often than not, it has been internalised that Muslims are more backwards than anyone else when it comes to women's rights. The truth, however, is that most of the injustices committed against women are due to regional or cultural causes, not religious.

Another paper is on the topic of feminism and is titled, '*Why ideological bandwagons are failing Muslims.*' The third paper is on '*Examining myths in Islamic Law about women*', which discusses the issues of inheritance, testimony and domestic violence. And the fourth paper covers a topic which I would like to go into more detail on, '*We used to have no regard for women – gender equity in the advent of Islam.*'

To begin with, there is a very befitting quote from Umar bin al-Khattab, may Allah be pleased with him, who said, "In the days of ignorance, we used to have no regard for women whatsoever. Until Allah revealed about them what He revealed and allotted for them what He allotted." Umar had a very proud personality, especially prior to Islam and he was known for his harshness, however he prioritised the inherent value of women in this quote before he mentioned the legal aspect of their rights.

The main Hadith that I wish to mention in this chapter, although short, allows us to gain a better understanding of the position of women in Islam. Aisha, may Allah be pleased with her, narrated that the Prophet Muhammad ﷺ said: "Women are the twin halves of men."[167] The wording that the Messenger of Allah ﷺ used was to speak about the essential value of women and that the default is that everything, even in regards to the law, is equal amongst men and women, unless a difference is specified. And even when a difference is specified, the difference is not based on the value or worth of the gender.

The female Companions, or *sahabiyaat*, had never complained or believed that Islam diminished them, rather they believed that Islam empowered them. An authentic narration from several female Companions of that time says, "Allah and His Messenger ﷺ are more merciful to us than ourselves." Islam allowed women to feel human and valued, it restored their humanity and treated women as people rather than as mere objects. This also led to women and men both witnessing the spirit of the law as ordained by Allah, and everything was viewed and based off of that spirit. This was the paradigm shift that was taking place in the mind of society, and we see an example of this paradigm shift through the lens of a person like Umar, may Allah be pleased with him.

There is also a powerful narration from Umm Salamah in which she said to the Prophet Muhammad ﷺ that in all the verses of the Qur'an that had been revealed thus far, the believers were referred to as '*Mu'mineen*,' even though in the Arabic language that refers to both men and women, and there was no specific acknowledgement of the believing women which would be '*Mu'minaat*.' After she had mentioned this to the Prophet ﷺ, a revelation come to him, it was the following verse from *Surah al-Ahzab* 33:35: *"Indeed, the Muslim men and Muslim women, the believing men and believing women, the obedient men and obedient women, the truthful men and truthful women, the patient men and patient women, the humble men and humble women, the charitable men and charitable women, the fasting men and fasting women, the men who guard their private parts and the women who do so, and the men who remember Allah often and the women who do so – for them Allah has prepared forgiveness and a great reward."*

Hadiths and verses from the Qur'an restored the humanness of women and brought about the understanding that men and women have the same rights and responsibilities. There is no differing of these rights and responsibilities based upon an inherent superiority of one gender over the other.

Before Islam, women were viewed as lesser beings in many different societies. Aristotle who is known for his philosophical quotes also spoke regarding women and said, "A woman is defective and a misbegotten man." Another example is from the oldest book of law, Hammurabi, in which it is stated that if a man strikes a pregnant woman and causes her to miscarry and die, the assailant's daughter shall be put to death. The attacker himself would not be held accountable or punished, but his daughter would be. The life of a woman was viewed as less valuable than that of a man. And yet another example is from Judaism and the Niddah laws which discuss whether a menstruating woman contaminates utensils, and if she should be isolated and forbidden from supplication, and even if she should 'atone' herself by casting a stone when she finishes menstruating. What we see here is that the value of women has been diminished through such laws and cultures. Whilst Islam also has guidelines for menstruating women it does not make women feel degraded or punished for a normal and natural process.

Before Islam there were discussions in the Council of Macon in the year 585 on whether or not women even had souls; this was the extent of their degradation. Yet when we compare this attitude to that of Islam, Allah says that we are known by our piety, and we find this in *Surah al-Hujurat* 49:13: *"Oh mankind, indeed We have created you from male and female and made you peoples and tribes so that you may know one another. Indeed, the most noble of you in the sight of Allah is the most righteous of you. Indeed, Allah is Knowing and Acquainted."* The equity and equality in terms of salvation and reward between men and women can clearly be seen here. Allah does not differentiate between men and women except on the basis of their piety.

Unfortunately, it is known that the poorer Arab tribes would bury their daughters alive because they would not view them as worthy offspring. Allah condemned this practice in *Surah at-Takwir* 81:8-9: *"And when the girl who was buried alive is asked, for what sin she was killed."* Allah also mentioned and admonished those who felt a sense of shame at the birth of a daughter in *Surah an-Nahl* 16:58: *"And when one of them is given the good news of (the birth of) a female, his face becomes dark and he suppresses grief."* What is meant here is that even before carrying out the despicable act of burying a daughter alive, they had already buried her value, and this is the attitude that allows a society to accept and become accustomed to such evil practices.

The extent of their ignorance, however, was not limited to burying daughters alive it extended to their marital schemes also. Imam Tabari for example, narrated that Ibn Abbas said, "When a man's father would die, he would be most entitled to his wife. If he wished, he would keep her for himself, or hold her until she was ransomed with a bridal dowry. Or she died and he took her wealth."

Not only that, but men would also send their wives to be intimate with other men in order to have children from a more noble tribe and would even enact contracts around this concept. Then, all of a sudden, these ignorant and evil practices were ruled against during the Prophethood of Muhammad ﷺ. The Messenger of Allah ﷺ told a young girl who approached him to complain about her father marrying her off without her consent, that she had the right to leave that marriage if she was not happy and that her consent was necessary. There was a huge paradigm shift from a society that found it normal and acceptable to trade wives, to a society that gave women more rights and respect than ever before, even to the extent of the language used for marital relationships.

Furthermore, when we look into the concept of *iddah*, the waiting or mourning period for a woman after the death of her husband, Islam does not blame or punish the woman in any way. The *iddah* is out of consideration for the woman and her well-being after the passing of her husband. On the other hand, during the times of ignorance (*jahiliyyah*), the waiting period for a widow was called *iftidaad* and is explained by Zainab, may Allah be pleased with her, who said, "When a woman's husband died, she would be confined to a small dark room. She would don her worst clothes and not touch perfume or anything similar until an entire year passed. Then after the year had passed, she would come out of the room and she would be brought an animal such as a donkey, bird or lamb and do *iftidaad* by wiping her private part with it and then casting it as a sign of her bereavement." This was an extremely difficult practice in which a woman was ultimately punished for the passing away of her husband. It was due to these very ideologies that women were viewed as a curse upon the family simply by virtue of their existence.

Menstruation, or *hayd*, was also viewed in a different light with the advent of Islam. Many different cultures around the world viewed – and in some places still view – women as impure when they are menstruating. The Prophet Muhammad ﷺ clearly stated that a believer is never impure, meaning that ritual impurity such as menstruation does not mean spiritual impurity – women are not soulless, nor should they be punished for something that is natural. The Hadith mentioned before (women are the twin halves of men), comes into this discussion of ritual impurity for men and women. The Prophet Muhammad ﷺ was saying that ritual impurity is essentially the same for both genders with slight differences.

The Messenger of Allah ﷺ would show affection and kindness towards his wives whilst they were menstruating, whilst the People of the Book in Madinah would sleep in different rooms to their wives when they were menstruating. This was a revolutionary attitude not just for the Arabs but for Christians and Jews too. The Prophet ﷺ told his wife Aisha, when she cried during Hajj, that her ritual impurity is not a curse, "You are not cursed; this is merely something given to the daughters of Adam." Up until then, there had been lots of theological literature that had belittled women beginning with Eve (*Hawa*).

Islam had changed the entire perspective towards Adam and Eve. In order to restore humanity, it was essential to go back to the roots of humanity. Eve was not to be blamed for the action of Adam; if Islam also blamed the woman for the action of man from the very beginning, it would allow the continuation of these ideas and open doors to blaming and punishing women in many different areas such as menstruation (*hayd*), the waiting period after a husband's death (*iddah*), pregnancy (miscarriage or gender of baby) and others.

When we think about the barbaric treatment of women, we must ask ourselves if women in the twenty-first century are any less objectified than they were in Makkah in the seventh century? Prescriptive secularism is far more oppressive than any religious system in modern times and history. If we look back to the twentieth century, Nazism, Communism, imperialism and American Dollarism as Malcolm X referred to it were all very oppressive.

People may be talking about France in years to come, how their attitude towards women who chose to cover their skin was oppressive, with the police apprehending and fining them. People talk about the ignorance of the seventh century Arabs and complain about their ways, but they fail to reframe the conversation to current society, and thus fail to see the oppressive stances towards women now. Women in England and France were prohibited until the nineteenth century from reading the New Testament after the English Parliament during the reign of Henry the Eighth, ruled that women were inherently impure. Women were seen as of such little value that until the year 1805, English law permitted men to sell their wives for as little as six pennies.

When it comes to the matter of inheritance, Islam was the first religion that introduced and assigned inheritance to women. However, some people still question whether Islamic law is regressive due to the most famous concept of a woman inheriting half of what a man inherits. To this, many people may answer that a man is obliged to provide for and spend upon his family, which is why he inherits double, but few people are aware that in thirty out of thirty-four scenarios, it is the woman who inherits more than a man.

The law of inheritance is not plain black and white; Islam not only considers the average situation, but it also considers the individual situations of people. This is similar to the concept of testimonies - a woman's testimony is not simply, or always, half of a man's testimony. There are some situations in which this is true, however, there are cases where a woman's testimony will be equivalent to a man's, whilst in others it can be seen as even stronger than a man's (such as issues regarding breastfeeding).

Rather than getting caught up in the details and exceptions of the law, we should instead look at how the law is conceived. Is Islamic law really conceived in a way that belittles and diminishes women?

Dr Jonathon Brown wrote an article about honour killings, and whilst many people associate Islam with honour killings, his article helps clear this misconception. He said that Islam is not the cause of honour killings but is part of the solution. He also mentioned a historically accurate scenario that took place in the British colony of Nigeria in 1947, in which British judges overturned what they viewed as a backward ruling of a local Islamic (*Shari'ah*) court. A man had been sentenced to death by the *Islamic* court for the murder (honour killing) of his wife. The British court overruled this and claimed that this was a crime of passion, and such a crime was not punishable by death. So, whilst the Islamic (*Shari'ah*) court was intent on providing justice to the woman, the British court was not and was finding excuses for the man.

Islamic history and the current state of the Muslim community (*ummah*) should not be romanticised; it is not sufficient to say that Islam helped women realise their rights in the seventh century. It is far more complicated; there are legitimate grievances too, which lead to illegitimate agendas exploiting the legitimate grievances. It is insufficient to simply deconstruct the illegitimate agendas presented by certain ideologies and show their incoherence, we should also use the empowering nature of Islam to address legitimate grievances in ways that conform to the Qur'an and the Prophetic tradition (*Sunnah*). Taking us back to the paradigm shift, Islam came at a time when females were buried alive and were seen as a curse. Then, within the same generation of people, Islam enabled females to become scholars and speak with authority to the entire generation of the Prophet Muhammad ﷺ - such as his wife Aisha. Umar bin al-Khattab chose to appoint two women to overlook the marketplace of Madinah in order to keep a check on everything and everyone. Women were elevated in their position in society as a result of the reorientation of the way in which women were viewed after Islam.

May Allah allow us to fulfil the rights of women and protect us from causing injustice and harm to them. Amin.

35

HOW THE PROPHET MUHAMMAD ﷺ TREATED THOSE WITH MENTAL ILLNESS, DISABILITIES AND SPECIAL NEEDS

Anas reported that a woman had a partial derangement in her mind, so she said: Allah's Messenger, I want something from you. He said: Mother of so and so, see on which side of the road you would like (to stand and talk) so that I may do the needful for you. He stood aside with her on the roadside until she got what she needed.

WE NOW MOVE on to look at how the religion of Islam has very beautifully taught us that society has an obligation towards each and every one of its citizens; having disabilities or special needs does not deny a person justice within an Islamic framework.

When we look at the attitudes within pre-Islamic Arabia, we find that the Arabs used to associate people with special needs with curses and bad omens. The Prophet Muhammad ﷺ came and changed this entire outlook by insisting that his Companions should eat with those who have special needs or disabilities because they were wrongly viewed as being a burden upon society, and even cursed. People would stay away from those with special needs and would never invite them for a meal as they believed that they might be afflicted by a curse.

This attitude, however, was not limited to the Arabs, but also the Ancient Greeks and other civilisations. Plato, for example, said that they are a malicious category constituting a burden on society and a damaging factor to a Republic. A much later example is from the English philosopher Herbert Spencer who lived in the nineteenth century; he called on people to deny those with special needs any kind of help, and he claimed that this category of people constituted a useless and heavy burden for society to carry. By delving deeper into the history of the West and how it treated those with disabilities, we find that there was blatant neglect and persecution of those with special needs and it even led to the killing of disabled babies in some European societies.

The practice of the Prophet Muhammad ﷺ was the opposite, I have mentioned the Companion named Julaybeeb in a previous chapter; he was deformed and as a result of this, he was bullied and ostracised by society. However, the Prophet Muhammad ﷺ made it a point to treat him well, eat with him and referred to him as his family. The Messenger of Allah ﷺ taught us how to be a society that treats people with disabilities or special needs, and these lessons factor into the discussion of social welfare within our current societies. It was not just seventh century Arabia, these views still exist today among many cultures, even among some educated communities.

The Hadith that I have chosen for this chapter is narrated by Anas, may Allah be pleased with him: "There was a woman who had a mental disability, she shouted to the Prophet ﷺ, 'Allah's Messenger, I want something from you.' He said, 'Mother of so-and-so, see on which side of the road you would like (to stand and talk), so that I may do the needful for you.' He stood aside with her on the roadside until she got what she needed."[168] It can clearly be seen from this Hadith that the Prophet ﷺ responded to her in a way that dignified her, and he did not dismiss her by asking someone else to take care of her. The Messenger of Allah ﷺ stopped whatever he was doing previously to listen to the woman and do whatever he could to help her, even though she was in a difficult mental state. Anas reports that she did not even have a particular direction in mind that she wanted to take and the Prophet walked various routes with her until she was satisfied. He demonstrated mercy and compassion so that we could take heed and follow in his footsteps; acting with justice is the minimum that is asked of us in Islam, whilst mercy is something that we should all aim to achieve.

As a leader, the Prophet ﷺ understood his responsibility as a shepherd to his flock, or followers, and he showed humility and care towards every person, no matter what their needs or mental state. Rulers, or leaders, are obligated to take care of people with special needs – whether that be for social, economic, psychological or physical reasons – and to take time out to understand and fulfil their requests. There is a lesson on this in the Qur'an also; a famous story involving Abdullah bin Umm Maktum whereby Allah sent down a revelation for the Prophet ﷺ. While the Messenger of Allah ﷺ was preoccupied in trying to reach and persuade the chiefs of the influential tribe of *Quraysh* with his message, Abdullah bin Umm Maktum unknowingly and unintentionally interrupted the Prophet ﷺ. Abdullah was a poor blind man, he could not perceive what kind of gathering was taking place at that time, and so he approached the Prophet ﷺ to ask, "Teach me from what Allah has taught you." The Prophet Muhammad ﷺ frowned (the word that is used to describe this frown indicates that he did not make any sound out of anger or sadness, but he simply moved his eyebrows closer to each other which formed a wrinkle on his forehead), and he turned away to carry on speaking to the *Quraysh*. Allah then revealed in *Surah 'Abasa* 80:1-4: *"He (the Prophet) frowned and turned away, because there came to him the blind man (interrupting). But what would make you perceive (Oh Muhammad), that perhaps he might be purified or be reminded, and the remembrance would benefit him?"*

If we had been observing the situation we may not have even considered that the Prophet ﷺ had done anything wrong; he did not rebuke the man or physically remove him, he did not even sigh or make a sound. A wrinkle appeared on his forehead and he simply carried on with what he was doing. Furthermore, since the man was blind, he would not have even seen the frown himself. However, through this revelation, Allah wanted the Prophet ﷺ to understand that he should not discount

Abdullah's spirituality and his access to spirituality, even though it would have little or no tangible benefit on society. Allah wanted His Messenger ﷺ to know that a man of his calibre should have a much higher standard of mercy and compassion, as he was a mercy to all of the world. After this incident took place, the Prophet Muhammad ﷺ would greet Abdullah bin Umm Maktum by saying, "Welcome to the one for whom my Lord rebuked me." The fact that Allah admonished the Prophet ﷺ on behalf of Abdullah, made the Prophet ﷺ treat him better, he ensured that he never felt excluded and he appointed Abdullah as the caller to prayer when they migrated to Madinah. The Prophet ﷺ also placed Madinah under Abdullah's authority when he was absent on several occasions.

What we learn here is that a disabled person should not be deprived of spiritual purification; acts of worship should be made accessible to them and they should not be forgotten. People should be given proper access to the Masjid, including the two Holy Mosques of Makkah and Madinah (*Haramain*) so that they can perform *umrah* and Hajj. We do not have the right to judge or decide who deserves spiritual nourishment. In another Hadith the Prophet ﷺ said, "The mosque is the house of every believer," and this also includes those with disabilities.

We can find another powerful example in the incident with 'Itban bin Maalik, who was also a blind man but belonged to the community of Madinah (*Ansar*). 'Itban said to the Prophet Muhammad ﷺ, "I wish that you Oh Messenger of Allah, would come and perform salah in my house so that I would take it as a place of prayer." In reply to this, the Prophet ﷺ promised to visit him and perform a prayer in his house saying, "I will do, if Allah so wills." 'Itban then reported, "Allah's Messenger and Abu Bakr came early in the morning. Allah's Messenger asked for permission to enter, which I gave. Without sitting, he immediately entered and said, 'In which part of your house would you like me to pray?' I pointed to a certain place in the house, so the Messenger of Allah stood and started praying, and we, in turn, stood and he lined us in a row. He performed two rak'ah prayer, ending it with taslim."[169]

The Prophet Muhammad ﷺ honoured the request of 'Itban as the lack of eyesight put 'Itban in a situation than made it difficult for him to go for prayer in the masjid on a regular basis. The response of Allah's Messenger ﷺ showed the love and attention that he gave to those who were disabled; he did not discount 'Itban's spiritualy or his access to spirituality, and accommodated his request for assistance.

Another lesson that Islam teaches us regarding those with special needs is that they are privileged and loved by Allah. There is a Hadith reported by Anas in Sahih Bukhari: The Messenger of Allah ﷺ said, "Allah said, 'If I afflict my servant in his two dear eyes and he remains patient, then he will be compensated for them with Paradise.'" Blindness was common during that time, and hearing that showing patience whilst being afflicted with blindness will lead to Paradise was a big comfort and motivation for people.

There is also a further Hadith reported by 'Ata bin Abi Rabah: "Ibn Abbas once said to me, 'Shall I show you a woman of the people of Paradise?' I said yes. He said, 'This Abyssinian lady came to the Prophet ﷺ and said, 'I get attacks of epilepsy and my body becomes uncovered, please invoke Allah for me.' The Prophet ﷺ said to her, 'If you wish, be patient and you will have Paradise, and if you wish, I will invoke Allah to cure you.' She said, 'I will remain patient,' and added, 'But I become uncovered, so please invoke Allah for me that I may not become uncovered.' So, he invoked Allah for her." In another narration of the same incident, the Prophet ﷺ said, "If you wish, be patient and you will not have any reckoning." To which she said, "I'll be patient, and not have any reckoning!"[170]

Society unfortunately, automatically treats those with special needs as inferior and the Prophet Muhammad ﷺ wanted to rid society of this approach. In one narration, Sa'ad bin Abi Waqqas felt that he was more entitled to the Prophet Muhammad ﷺ as he was so close to him, but the Prophet Muhammad ﷺ said, "If you want to find me, find me amongst the weak, because you are not given victory or aid from Allah except by the way that you treat those who are weak and oppressed." If we want the help of Allah, we must look at how we treat the weakest in our society; those who are oppressed or those with special needs. Often they are the most neglected, yet they are an asset to the Muslim community. The way in which we treat those with special needs reflects what we are able to receive from Allah. One Hadith is extremely powerful in getting across the message of mistreating someone with special needs, "Cursed is the one who misleads a blind person away from his path." This narration is both for the individual and a community; a community that does not respect or care for those with special needs, will ultimately be cursed.

Having a particular disability does not mean that a person is fully disabled or incompetent and that they should be disregarded. On the contrary, it may be that they have been blessed with a special ability in place of that disability. Many people with physical disabilities have a special and advanced form of comprehension; they can view matters from a light that others cannot. Making assumptions about people is wrong and we must not deem those with disabilities as worthless in society.

Muhammad Ali the boxer, may Allah have mercy on him, said that people assumed that his mind and mental capabilities deteriorated due to him suffering from Parkinson's disease, but he was in fact able to fully comprehend everything that occurred around him. The disease did not affect his cognitive function, but instead affected his speech and body, making him speak and move slowly, yet people were quick to assume that his mental capabilities had reduced. The Messenger of Allah ﷺ made this a specific point to mention to the Companions, and showed through his own actions that a person with a certain disability should not be seen as fully disabled; they can still have something to offer through other abilities.

Abu Hurairah reported: "A blind man once came to the Prophet ﷺ and said, 'Oh Messenger of Allah, I have no one to guide me to the masjid.' And so, he asked the Prophet ﷺ for a concession to pray in his home and he was given the concession. When he turned away, the Prophet ﷺ called him and said, 'Can you hear the call to prayer?' He said, 'Yes.' The Messenger of Allah replied, 'Then respond to it.'"[171]

We can see from this Hadith that the Messenger of Allah was gently saying to the blind man that he is still regarded as a full member of society and he would be rewarded for the extra struggle to answer the call to prayer in the mosque, but at the same time, the concession was still valid and he would get reward for praying at home. Having a disability does not put a person in a disadvantaged position in regard to gaining rewards, Islam caters for their needs and they do not become ineligible for the rewards that others gain. Another Hadith that further solidifies this is narrated by Zayd bin Thabit: "When the verse from *Surah an-Nisa* 4:95 was revealed, (*Those of the believers who sit behind… are not on an equality with those who strive in the way of Allah with their wealth and lives*), Abdullah bin Umm Maktum stepped forward as the Messenger of Allah ﷺ was dictating this verse, 'Oh Messenger of Allah, if I was capable of jihad. I certainly would have.'' Then Allah revealed, '*Except those who have a disability*.'"

Allah says clearly that those with a disability are not punished, nor are they exempt from receiving a reward, in fact they are fully rewarded.

Despite Abdullah bin Umm Maktum being specifically exempted due to his disability, and despite him being the one who earnestly asked Allah through the Prophet ﷺ for this exemption, his ambitious spirit was always driving him forward to seek greatness and to take part in battles. He was eventually martyred in battle against the Persians during the Caliphate of Umar bin al-Khattab, and he was found on the battlefield firmly grasping the banner of Islam.

Similarly, another Companion named 'Amr bin al-Jamuh had a crippled leg and so had difficulty walking. He once came to the Prophet Muhammad ﷺ before the Battle of Uhud to complain about his sons, "My sons want to prevent me from going out to fight with you, but by Allah, I wish to step with this crippled leg of mine into Paradise!" The Prophet ﷺ said to him, "Allah has excused you, you are not obligated to engage in Jihad." Then the Prophet ﷺ also turned to the sons of 'Amr to say, "Do not hold him back; perhaps Allah will grant him martyrdom." So, 'Amr went out to fight, barely being able to walk and was martyred during the Battle of Uhud. The Messenger of Allah ﷺ passed by his body and said, "It is as if I can see you walking with that leg of yours, and hearing it, in *Jannah*."

We find that the Prophet Muhammad ﷺ reassured his Companions and did not allow them to feel guilty for not being able to do things the same as others. We should also ensure that we are considerate towards others; a person may not be able to fast during the long summer days because of their old age or other health issues and they should not be made to feel guilty. They should also not be made to feel as though they are missing out on reward, rather we should reassure them that Allah has excused them due to their circumstances and they are not at a disadvantage. Allah is fully aware of what acts of worship a person would be doing had they been in better health.

Islam does not allow the burdening of people who are in difficult situations; we therefore, have no right to burden people or make them feel as though they are ineligible for reward. Under normal circumstances, we pray standing up, but the Prophet Muhammad ﷺ was aware that certain health or physical ailments could make it difficult for some people to pray standing up: "Whoever amongst you can pray standing up, should do so, and if you cannot pray standing up, then you can pray sitting down, and if you cannot pray sitting down, then you can pray lying down."[172] The Hadith clearly caters for people of different abilities and there is no difference mentioned in the reward that they will receive. However, in another narration the Prophet Muhammad ﷺ did make it a point to mention that there is a decrease in the reward for voluntary prayer if someone who is able to pray standing up, chooses to pray sitting down (for example the *Qiyam*, voluntary night prayer). The difference being in their ability to stand but choosing to sit down instead.

I also had a beautiful encounter with a brother who had unfortunately become paralysed from the nose down; he only lived for another nine days or so after becoming paralysed but he made every effort to offer his five daily prayers with the movement of his eyes. He was unable to even lift a finger, yet he was conscious of the time and he offered his prayers with his eyes. And knowing that Allah is the most Merciful and Compassionate, it is not far-fetched to hope and believe that such a person will be rewarded a lot more for his prayers because of his situation.

It is also worthwhile mentioning some jurisprudence (*fiqh*) issues in regard to this topic. We know that Allah does not burden a soul more than it can bear, and so He has absolved those who are blind from duties that necessitate eyesight. Allah has excused those who are sick or weak from fasting. Allah has excused people with specific conditions from certain obligations or actions that could make their condition worse. We find in the example of the life of the Prophet ﷺ (*Sunnah*) that the Prophet Muhammad ﷺ very clearly said that a person who is mentally incapable of fulfilling Islamic obligations is excused and that there are no sins written for them. This can bring a sense of comfort to those who are caring for or are related to individuals who not mentally capable of understanding their obligations as Muslims. Yet, the ease does not end at this point, those who are caring for others are also absolved from fulfilling certain obligations too, for example if you are helping someone with a disability to perform Hajj, both the disabled person and yourself, can leave Muzdalifah early. Another example would be someone unable to attend Friday (*Jumm'ah*) prayers due to sickness or disability, their caretaker can, and should, also stay home to look after them properly.

The Prophet Muhammad ﷺ did not limit this caring attitude for the disabled to the Muslim community, but he extended it to those who were not Muslim. One such example can be found in an incident reported by Ibn Kathir: When the Prophet ﷺ headed along with his army toward Uhud, intending to pass by a farm owned by a blind hypocrite, the hypocrite insulted the Messenger of Allah ﷺ by picking up a handful of dust and saying, "By Allah, if I am certain that none but you will be affected by it, I will definitely throw it at you." The Companions of the Prophet ﷺ were about to punish the blind hypocrite, but the Prophet ﷺ forbade them saying, "Leave him alone."

The Messenger of Allah ﷺ did not take advantage of the fact that the hypocrite was blind and punish him, in fact he ordered his Companions not to kill or even harm the man in any way. The situation at the time was very tense, emotions were running high as they were about to engage in a fierce battle, but the Prophet ﷺ showed calmness and did not allow anyone to take their anger out on the blind man, even though he was a hypocrite.

In a narration found in Bayhaqi, al-Hasan bin Muhammad said, "I entered upon Abu Zayd al-Ansari, who called out the *adhan* and *iqamah* whilst he was sitting." He added, "A man advanced and led us in prayer. That man was lame, whose leg was hit in the Cause of Allah, the Exalted." Such narrations give us a wonderful insight into the society that Prophet Muhammad ﷺ created, allowing those with illness, disabilities or special needs to take part in and even lead in acts of worship.

The Prophet's ﷺ society was one that was marked by mutual support and co-operation, as well as unity in honouring and respecting those with special needs. He led by example by showing mercy and compassion in the way that he dealt with those who had special needs. 'Ataa bin Abi Rabah was the first Mufti of Makkah, and not only was he black, but he was also blind and paralysed from the waist down. The fact that 'Ataa was the first Mufti speaks volumes about the culture of Islam. Neither racism nor prejudice towards his disabilities stopped him from becoming such a great scholar and renowned figure in that society.

When we look at the rule of Umar bin Abdul Aziz, we learn that he instructed his governors from each province to send him the names of all the people who were blind, or crippled, or too chronically ill to pray in congregation. After he had received the names of all these people, he ordered that every person be assigned an assistant to look after them, and that a servant would be assigned to every two people in order to ensure that they were taken care of properly.[173]

Another beautiful example is of al-Walid bin Abdul Maalik, he was the first person to establish care centres for people with special needs. He fixed stipends and hired doctors and caretakers in these care centres to look after those with special needs. Not only this, he also allocated special allowances for people with special needs, and assistance was sent to those who had a need such as the disabled, blind or ill.[174]

These changes were revolutionary and early Islamic culture paved the way for a more caring and just society towards those with special needs. It is then not an exaggeration to say that we should go out of our way to help those in need. When a person is ill, they are attended to by the angels. And a well-known Hadith of the Prophet ﷺ is that when we visit someone who is ill, we are accompanied by seventy-thousand angels, and they are still with us when we leave. Showing compassion to someone who is ill or disabled will reap many benefits and rewards, and if we want to have angels in our presence and our communities, we must dedicate ourselves to taking care of those who are ill or have special needs.

May Allah allow us to appreciate the ill and disabled in our families and wider communities and allow us to be of service to them. May Allah reward those with illnesses and disabilities for showing patience and strong-will. Amin.

36

DOCTORS OF THE PROPHET ﷺ AND ISLAM'S HISTORY OF HEALTHCARE

On the authority of Abu Hurayrah (may Allah be pleased with him), who said that the Messenger of Allah ﷺ said: Allah (mighty and sublime be He) will say on the Day of Resurrection: O son of Adam, I fell ill and you visited Me not. He will say: O Lord, and how should I visit You when You are the Lord of the worlds? He will say: Did you not know that My servant So-and-so had fallen ill and you visited him not? Did you not know that had you visited him you would have found Me with him? O son of Adam, I asked you for food and you fed Me not. He will say: O Lord, and how should I feed You when You are the Lord of the worlds? He will say: Did you not know that My servant So-and-so asked you for food and you fed him not? Did you not know that had you fed him you would surely have found that (the reward for doing so) with Me? O son of Adam, I asked you to give Me to drink and you gave Me not to drink. He will say: O Lord, how should I give You to drink when You are the Lord of the worlds? He will say: My servant so-and-so asked you to give him to drink and you gave him not to drink. Had you given him to drink you would have surely found that with Me.

WHILE IN THE previous chapter the focus was on how Islam treats those with disabilities and special needs, this chapter will centre on healthcare in general in the Islamic tradition. We will begin with a Hadith narrated by Abu Hurairah, who said that the Messenger of Allah ﷺ said: "Allah will say on the Day of Resurrection, 'Oh, son of Adam, I fell ill and you did not visit Me.' He will say, 'Oh Lord, and how should I visit You when You are the Lord of all the worlds?' Allah will say, 'Did you not know that My servant so-and-so had fallen ill, and you did not visit him? Did you not know that had you visited him you would have found Me with him? Oh, son of Adam, I asked you for food and you did not feed Me.' He will say, 'Oh Lord, and how should I feed You when You are the Lord of the worlds?' Allah will say, 'Did you not know that My servant so-and-so asked you for food and you did not feed him? Did you not know that had you fed him, you would surely have found that (the reward for doing so) with Me? Oh, son of Adam, I asked you to give Me drink and you gave Me not to drink.' He will say, 'Oh Lord, how should I give You to drink when You are the Lord of the worlds?' Allah will say, 'My servant so-and-so asked you to give him to drink and you gave him not to drink. Had you given him to drink you would have surely found the reward with Me.'"[175]

This Hadith sets the spiritual undertone behind the concept of healthcare; the major difference we can spot in this Hadith is how Allah addresses the sick person compared to the person who is hungry or thirsty. Allah says that we would find Him with the sick person, whereas we would find the reward for feeding or providing a drink to a hungry or thirsty person. It 'sets the stage' for how we should view those who are ill, and the importance that we should give them especially if we are operating out of an Islamic ethos.

There are many narrations throughout the Hadith that mention the importance of visiting the ill and the reward for doing so. One such narration I mentioned in the previous chapter which states that seventy thousand angels accompany a person who visits someone who is ill, and those seventy thousand angels continue to accompany that person even after they leave until they reach their home. Many scholars have commented on this narration and connected it to Bayt al-Ma'moor – the place in the Heavens which seventy thousand angels visit every day to glorify Allah and never get a chance to return. When we visit the sick, it is as if we are going to visit Allah accompanied by seventy thousand angels.

If we change our perspective and view the ill as a way to be in the company of Allah and the angels, as well as a source of reward, it will make us want to rush to visit and comfort the sick and direct resources towards them.

In order to get a clearer picture of how Islam views healthcare, there are several points to take into consideration:

1. We cannot discuss healthcare without first discussing the prevention of illness and disease.

2. Islam firstly advises us to eat and drink in moderation, and even to fast with moderation:

    - *Surah al-A'raaf 7:31: "And eat and drink but be not excessive. Indeed, He likes not those who commit excess."*
    - Looking at more recent times, the year 2016 was the first time in history that obesity became more common than being underweight.
    - People become ill because of eating too little, but they are now also increasingly becoming ill due to overeating.

3. It is a religious duty to seek treatment in Islam.

4. In many religious traditions, it is looked down upon to seek a cure for an illness as it is seen as a lack of trust and belief in God.

5. The Prophet Muhammad ﷺ said, "Seek treatment, oh servants of God, for Allah did not create a disease except that He created for it a cure, except ageing."[176]

6. Islam taught us about medical quarantine.

7. The Prophet Muhammad ﷺ said, "Do not enter a land in which there is a plague, nor exit a land fleeing from the plague."[177] Contagious diseases can be managed through quarantine and disallowing the movement of people entering and exiting that area; it protects society from becoming overwhelmed with illness.

8. There is a famous narration of Umar bin al-Khattab in which he decided not to enter a city with a plague, "We are running from the decree (*Qadr*) of Allah to the decree (*Qadr*) of Allah." The plague that was in the city was the decree of Allah and keeping away from the city was also the decree of Allah as Islam teaches societal preservation. Bad health compromises society, therefore taking the correct measures at the right time is vital for the welfare of society.

9. The Prophet Muhammad ﷺ said, "There is no harm allowed, nor any reciprocation of harm."[178]

10. The underlying message of this Hadith is societal preservation; Islam teaches us that society as a whole is to be protected and it is from this principle that concepts such as the importance of hygiene in Islam, the prohibition of intoxicants and prohibition of extramarital relationships, seemingly restrictive theological texts, are understood to have implications for the health of society as a whole.

11. The Prophet's example (*Sunnah*) covers everything from mouth hygiene (*miswaak* toothbrush) to bodily hygiene (for example washing after relieving oneself).

During the life of the Prophet Muhammad ﷺ, a Companion named Harith bin Kaladah, was employed to treat people by the Prophet ﷺ. Harith is the oldest known Arab physician and is said to have travelled to Gundeshapur – the intellectual centre of the Sassanid Empire – in search of medical knowledge, even before the advent of Islam.

When al-Muqawqas, the ruler of Egypt, sent a physician specifically for the care of the Prophet Muhammad ﷺ, the Messenger of Allah instead made the decision to commission the physician to treat people free of charge. We can see that free healthcare existed in Madinah over a millennia ago as health is something that is given great importance in Islam. During battles, the Prophet Muhammad ﷺ appointed field-medics such as the female Companion Rufayda al-Aslamiyyah who would tend to the wounded. Rufayda was given a share of the spoils of war by the Messenger of Allah ﷺ, he praised her and put her in charge of looking after those who were injured in battle. There are now scholarships named after her in some universities in the Muslim world – this was the legacy that she left.

Islamic history is filled with world-firsts regarding healthcare. The endowments (*awqaf*) in Damascus were the most prominent in early Islamic history; not only did they build the world's first hospitals, they also produced homes for 'retired' cats, dogs and cattle. They did not stop there however, there was also an endowment to hire people that would walk elderly people in the rain under an umbrella. The more charitable Muslims became, the more they had to search for endeavours to pursue in serving Allah's creation. They expanded without hesitation for the sake of seeking excellence (*ihsaan*).

The concept of an endowment (*waqf*), especially in early Islam, propelled the Muslim civilisation in every aspect of life, particularly the medical front. This endowment system continued until the end of the nineteenth century when unfortunately colonial interference let to it being dismantled. It was not the treasury or the generosity of a sultan that enabled Muslims to be at the forefront of medicine, but it was the endowment model which the masses were involved in as a result of their love for Islam.

The earliest pharmacists in history, such as Bayruni, were Muslims, just like the earliest doctors such as ar-Razi, Ibn Sina and Ibn Rushd – all of whom were world-leaders in their time. Access to healthcare was considered fundamental, irrespective of a person's social or religious status. Muslims did not limit healthcare to other Muslims, rather we can find many examples in history that prove otherwise. One such example is of Umar bin al-Khattab when he passed by a group of *dhimmis*, non-Muslims living under the protection of an Islamic caliphate, that had been afflicted with leprosy. He commanded that the collection of their tax (*jizya*) be suspended and that a medical stipend be granted to them from the treasury in order for them to seek treatment. Another example is of the Prophet Muhammad ﷺ sending Sa'ad bin Abi Waqqas to supplicate for and seek healing through recitation (*ruqya*) in the form of *Surah al-Fatihah* over a non-Muslim chief.

In the Islamic tradition of healthcare prisoners were also taken care of and were not left to suffer due to poor health. Ali bin Abi Talib would routinely check on the prisoners and would enquire about their health. Umar bin Abdul Aziz on the other hand would write to his governors to check on the prisoners and keep a close eye on those who are ill. The later Caliph al-Mu'tadid dedicated fifteen hundred dinars a month towards the needs and medical treatments of prisoners.

Other achievements in early Islamic history include the first hospital in Baghdad, built in the second century hijri by Haroon ar-Rashid, seven hundred years before the first hospital was built in Italy. Cordoba in Spain had fifty hospitals five hundred years before Italy had its first. The world's first 'medical board exams' were held in Baghdad as a result of the Prophet Muhammad ﷺ saying, "Whoever practices medicine while not being known to be proficient in it, is to be held accountable."[179]

Muslims were so advanced in the medical field that Willian Osler – a founder and the second president of the Medical Library Association – said, "The Canon (*Qanun*) of Avicenna (Ibn Sina) has remained a medical bible in Europe for a longer period than any other work."

The scale of what has been achieved throughout Islamic history in terms of healthcare is enormous, but I am only able to touch upon a few of these things in this chapter. However, even comparing the selected achievements mentioned above to healthcare systems today, we can find that many countries around the world do not provide easy access to healthcare. Numerous people die every day in America because they do not have access to healthcare; people cannot afford to get sick in America because of the extortionate costs implemented by the industry.

The right to healthcare is a moral issue; nobody should be denied access, nor should they be made to suffer because they cannot afford it or have different beliefs. The proliferation of the concept of *waqf*, of endowment, spearheaded the Muslim community's charitable activities in this regard in the past. Muslim communities should pave the way once again in creating charitable clinics and hospitals. Masjids should have free medical clinics on their premises and mobile clinics should be made so that people can have easier access to healthcare.

Islam teaches us to comfort people, to look out for them and to not make them feel like a burden upon us. There are two well-known Hadith that I wish to mention here, the first being, "Do not stare at those with leprosy", and the second being, "Smiling in the face of your brother is charity". Both of these Hadith teach us the importance of how we approach and treat people. Leprosy was a common illness during that time, and the Prophet Muhammad ﷺ knew that staring at someone with a physically visible ailment would make them self-conscious about the way they look. Staring at them could make them feel repulsed or awkward, and so the Prophet Muhammad ﷺ made it a point to mention that we should smile and act normally. The Messenger of Allah ﷺ emphasised that we should pay attention to the emotional wellbeing of people in addition to their physical health. We must show empathy towards people; empathy is a step beyond sympathy. Just like we feel positivity if we visit a doctor who smiles at us and treats us with respect, we should behave the same towards others.

May Allah instil compassion within us so that we may treat those who are ill with mercy and kindness, and may Allah show us compassion as we are spiritually ill and in need of Him. Amin.

WHEN ANIMALS INDICT HUMANS FOR CRUELTY

Abu Hurayra (ra) narrates: The Prophet ﷺ said, "As a man was walking along, his thirst became intense. He climbed down a well and drank from it, then emerged to find a panting dog licking the dirt from thirst. He said, 'There has certainly befallen this [dog] what has befallen me.' He [returned] to fill his shoe, then held it in his mouth, then climbed upwards and gave the dog drink. Allah appreciated him, and so He forgave him." They said, "O Messenger of Allah, is there reward in [kindness to] animals?" He said, "In every moist liver (i.e., living thing) is a [an opportunity for] reward."

THIS CHAPTER WILL focus on the rights of animals in Islam. There are countless narrations in the Hadith regarding the treatment of animals and it is worth remembering that if the Prophet Muhammad ﷺ had set such a high standard for animal rights, human rights would undoubtedly be given an even higher level of importance. The respect that the Prophet Muhammad ﷺ had for Allah's creation is clearly illustrated in the narration where the Prophet ﷺ stood up out of respect as the funeral procession for a Jewish man passed by them. He explained what he did by saying, "Isn't it a human soul?" The Messenger of Allah ﷺ highlighted the inherent value of a human being; the soul itself was enough to allow that to be a sanctified moment.

I want to begin by mentioning a Hadith narrated by Ibn Abbas: "The Prophet Muhammad ﷺ said, 'Do not take anything containing a soul as a target.'"[180] The Messenger of Allah ﷺ used this particular phraseology to draw attention, to make people think before taking the life of an animal because that animal too, has a soul. Sa'eed bin Jubayr also narrated that Ibn Umar passed by a group of people who had hung up a chicken and were shooting at it, when they saw Ibn Umar they quickly moved away because they knew they were doing something wrong. Ibn Umar asked, "Who did this?", but no one came forward. He said, "The Messenger of Allah ﷺ cursed those who do this act."[181]

Treating an animal with such heartlessness and disrespect equates to being cursed by the Prophet ﷺ and killing an animal for fun is simply not acceptable in Islam. In an authentic Hadith narrated by Abdullah bin Amar: "The Prophet Muhammad ﷺ said: 'Any person who kills even a tiny sparrow without right, will be questioned by Allah regarding it.' It was asked, 'Oh Messenger of Allah, what is the sparrow's right?' He replied, 'That it only be sacrificed to feed oneself, not to be thrown aside.'"

Killing or shooting even at a sparrow for the sake of enjoyment is impermissible in Islam; hunting can only be done for the sake of food and sustenance. We cannot assume that because hunting is permissible, that we can disregard the lives of animals and kill them at will. The implications of what is taught through the life and Hadith of the Prophet ﷺ requires a deeper understanding and appreciation of the spirit behind it; just because the saliva of a dog is impure it does not mean that we should hate dogs or mistreat them or that because killing a bird to eat is allowed, the life of a bird has no sanctity and it does not matter if they die. Abdullah bin Mas'ud said: "We were on a journey with the Messenger of Allah ﷺ and he went out to relieve himself. We saw a red sparrow that had two chicks with her, we took her chicks, so the sparrow started to flap her wings. The Prophet ﷺ came to us and he said, 'Who has devastated this one by taking her children? Return her children to her.' He also saw an ant colony which we had burned, and he said, 'Who burned this?' We said that we did it. The Prophet ﷺ said, 'No-one should punish with fire except the Lord of the fire.'"[182]

The wording that the Prophet Muhammad ﷺ chose to use for the bird was such that if we had only heard those words and did not know the context in which he spoke them, we would assume that he was speaking about a human being. Again he framed his words deliberately to make it clear that no human being has the right to take the children of a mother and cause her distress– even if she is an animal such as a bird. Furthermore, the journey that this Hadith relates to was a military expedition and thus shows us that even if there are more serious concerns that may require our attention it does not mean that we can neglect issues such as the rights of animals.

People may complain and ask why we speak about animal rights when the rights of humans are being violated all over the world, and then use this complaint as an excuse to be lazy towards the rights of animals. The Prophet Muhammad's ﷺ example shows us that every unique issue requires its own unique solution from a position of compassion; he showed a level of compassion for both animals and humans that people were not accustomed to. The fact that he paid such attention to the sparrow when his Companions took her children away from her, had shocked them. This shock was furthered when he admonished them for burning the ant colony; although they had their reasons, for example they were setting up camp in that area and did not want to be bitten by the ants. The Prophet Muhammad ﷺ told them clearly that nobody should punish any being by fire, as it is the right of Allah only to punish by fire.

In another Hadith, Abu Hurairah narrated: "The Prophet Muhammad ﷺ said, 'As a man was walking along, his thirst became intense. He climbed down a well and drank from it, then emerged to find a panting dog licking the dirt from thirst. He said, 'There has certainly befallen this dog what has befallen me.' He returned to fill his shoe, held it in his mouth, then climbed upwards and gave the dog a drink. Allah appreciated him, and so He forgave him.' They said, 'Oh Messenger of Allah ﷺ, is there reward in kindness to animals?' He said, 'In every moist liver (living thing) is an (opportunity for) reward.'"[183]

We learn here that the man did not do anything that would benefit Allah, but the fact that he cared for the creation of Allah, showed that he had appreciation for the Creator. And it is because of this attitude that Allah appreciated the actions of the man and forgave him. Another point is that the Prophet ﷺ used the phrase "every moist liver" to clarify that it does not matter which animal it is, or how impure or pure it is, that is all irrelevant. What is relevant is that they are all living creations of Allah and being good or charitable towards a living being provides an opportunity to gain reward from Allah.

Abu Hurairah also narrated another similar Hadith: "The Prophet Muhammad ﷺ said, 'As a dog was circling around a well, on the verge of dying from thirst, a prostitute from Banu Israel saw him. She removed her shoe (climbed into the well) and gave him drink from it. For that, she was forgiven.'"[184]

Allah forgave the woman for all the wrong that she had done for the act of giving a drink of water to a thirsty dog. Scholars have commented on this Hadith and said that the woman acted in a moment of sincerity, and Allah knows best, but this could have been a catalyst for other good in her life. It could have been a reminder to her that Allah will sustain her, just as she helped to sustain the dog, and she does not have to resort to something that is prohibited in order to sustain herself.

Islam is a religion that has established rights for animals, urged people to give animals food and drink, whilst threatening punishment for those who are cruel to animals and promised forgiveness, even for enormities, for those who take care of them. A drink of water can be enough to compensate for fornication, but the secret lies in what is behind the act; the sincerity of the act and the feeling of mercy that prompted it.

Abdullah bin Umar narrated that the Messenger of Allah ﷺ said: "A woman once tortured a cat; she trapped it until it died, and she entered the Hellfire as a result. Neither did she feed, nor give her a drink, nor did she leave her to eat from the insects of the earth."[185]

From a jurisprudence (*fiqh*) perspective, keeping a cat temporarily in a cage for a valid reason is permissible, however that does not give us the permission to keep it hungry or thirsty – we must take care of it. Outside of necessity, it is impermissible to keep a cat in a cage. The Prophet Muhammad ﷺ not only condemned the woman for imprisoning the cat, but also condemned her for starving it. We can see excellence (*ihsaan*) from the prostitute, and the epitome of cruelty in the form of the woman with the cat.

Our acts of kindness and cruelty define Paradise and Hellfire, and it is of utmost importance that we give the subject of animal rights its due. Many religious-minded Muslims will automatically feel disgusted at the sight of a dog and will try to maintain some distance so that they maintain their ablution (*wudhu*), very few will think of providing for a stray dog or showing kindness towards a dog. This is actually driven by culture and not Islam and it is important that we learn to separate the two.

The Prophet Muhammad ﷺ however, taught us many lessons about kindness towards animals. He also spoke about the sin of overburdening animals, and the importance of taking care of an animal which provides a service by feeding it and tending to its overall wellbeing. One powerful example is narrated by Abdullah bin Ja'far: "The Messenger of Allah ﷺ entered the garden of an *Ansari* man and found a camel therein. When the camel saw the Prophet ﷺ, it whimpered, and its eyes overflowed! The Prophet ﷺ came to it, wiped its tears, and asked, 'Whose camel is this?' A young man from the *Ansar* came and said, 'Mine, oh Messenger of Allah.' He said, 'Won't you fear Allah regarding these beasts which Allah has placed in your possession? For it has complained to me that you starve it and overwork it.'"[186]

A further example of the impermissibility of overburdening an animal can be found in a Hadith reported by Sahl bin al-Handhaliyya: "The Messenger of Allah ﷺ once passed by a camel whose back neared its stomach (showing clear signs of being overburdened), so he said, 'Fear Allah regarding these beasts who cannot speak for themselves; ride them healthy and eat them healthy (do not neglect them).'"

We should show mercy to animals when they are alive, and we must show mercy to them if we must slaughter them for our own sustenance. It is important for us to remember that on the Day of Judgement, everything will speak – animals which could otherwise not speak in this world, will be able to speak, and even our limbs which have no voice of their own, will speak if we used them for wrong. Even before slaughtering an animal, the Prophet Muhammad ﷺ advised that we sharpen our knife before bringing the animal forward and laying it down to be slaughtered. Showing an animal a knife, and worse, the knife being sharpened, will frighten it and cause it distress.

Mu'awiya bin Qurra narrated, from his father, that a man said, "Oh Messenger of Allah, I slaughter a lamb and feel mercy for it." The Prophet Muhammad ﷺ then said, "If you have mercy on the lamb, Allah will have mercy on you."[187]

In regards to using animals as a means of transport, Abu Hurairah narrated that the Prophet Muhammad ﷺ said: "Beware of taking the backs of your riding animals as pulpits, for Allah has only made them to deliver you to places that you would not otherwise reach without great exertion…" And in another narration, he said, "Ride them healthy and leave them healthy; do not take them as couches for your street and market conversations."[188]

The Messenger of Allah ﷺ made it clear in his speech that animals must be treated with respect and kindness and must not be burdened unnecessarily. The same society that did not think twice before burying its little girls alive, was now made to think about the well-being of its animals. They now feared that on the Day of Judgement, animals would testify against them. It was a big shift in the way that they approached people and animals; they went from being a society that viewed girls as less than human , to people who would treat animals with rights similar to those given to human beings.

I want to mention here a wonderful example of the Companion Tameem ad-Dari. A man once visited Tameem whilst he served as the governor of Bayt al-Maqdis (Jerusalem) and he found Tameem cleaning the wheat for his horse. The man said to Tameem, "Don't you have among your family someone who could suffice you this task?" Tameem said, "I do, but I heard the Messenger of Allah ﷺ say, 'No Muslim cleans his horse's wheat, then serves it to him, except that it is written for him one good deed for every grain.'"[189] Even for the governor of Jerusalem, the act of cleaning the wheat was not belittling, rather he hoped that the act would be a source of reward from Allah.

Similarly, in a lesser known but authentic Hadith narrated by Aisha, may Allah be pleased with her, it is said that the Messenger of Allah ﷺ used to tilt his vessel for a cat, and she would drink, and then he would perform ablution (*wudhu*) with its remains.[190] We can see from this Hadith that the Prophet ﷺ paid attention to the cat even at the time when he was going to perform ablution, so as not to keep the cat thirsty.

The Messenger of Allah ﷺ forbade cruelty towards all animals. Donkeys were not deemed prized animals, they were seen as the lowest of animals in terms of those that could transport, on one occasion Jabir bin Abdullah reported: "The Messenger of Allah ﷺ passed by a donkey whose face was branded. The Prophet Muhammad ﷺ said, 'Has it not reached you that I have cursed those who brand animals in their faces or strike them in their faces?' And he forbade them from doing this again."[191] In another narration, al-Abbas was riding with the Prophet ﷺ on a camel whose face was branded by fire. The Prophet Muhammad ﷺ said, "What is this branding, oh Abbas?" Abbas replied, "This is a branding we used to apply in the days of ignorance (*Jahiliyyah*)." The Prophet ﷺ said, "Do not brand with fire."[192]

Another form of cruelty that the Prophet ﷺ forbade was instigating fights between animals. Unfortunately, this act is still common today in various parts of the world and animals such as cockerels are pitted against each other and on-lookers place bets on which one will win. This also extends to bullfighting where people harm bulls mentally and physically in the name of entertainment.

The Prophet Muhammad ﷺ was also reported by Ibn Umar to have forbidden castrating animals, as it was common practice to do so in order to make male animals leaner, or bigger.[193] However, scholars have commented on this practice in regard to cats and have said that this is not a definitive prohibition in terms of a person not being able to take care of a large litter of cats which would come about if the male cat is not neutered. The scholars have also mentioned that whilst the Hadith was referring to larger animals, we should avoid neutering cats if possible and should not do it without a valid reason. Similarly, it is prohibited to declaw animals.

We are taught to be merciful towards animals when at home, and when travelling. Abu Hurairah narrated: "The Prophet ﷺ said, 'When you travel during a green pasture period, give the animals their share of grazing the earth.'"[194] We have been told through the teachings of the Prophet Muhammad ﷺ, that animals are entitled to mercy just as we are. The Companions and early Muslims understood this message very well and would take every care to ensure that they were being merciful and just towards animals. There are several beautiful narrations that document their understanding, some of which I would like to mention below:

- Abu Darda, whilst on his deathbed, said, "Oh camel, do not indict me with your Lord, for I never made you carry beyond your capacity."

- Adi bin Hatim would crush bread for the ants and say, "They are our neighbours, and so they have a right upon us."

- Umar bin al-Khattab once saw a man dragging a lamb by its foot to be slaughtered, and said to the man, "Woe to you, lead it to its death beautifully."

- Historians have documented that when 'Amr bin al-Aas conquered Egypt, a pigeon had landed on his tent (fustaat) and made its nest there, it had also laid an egg there. When 'Amr wanted to depart, he noticed the pigeon and decided not to dismantle his tent but leave it up. People started to build homes around that tent, thus creating a city which is today known as Fustat.

- Ibn Abdul Hakam narrated that Umar bin Abdul Aziz, during his caliphate, forbade anyone from kicking their horse except due to a need. His patrolmen were also given the duty of ensuring that nobody weighed their horses down with heavy reins or poked them with metal-tipped sticks. He also wrote to his governor in Egypt, "It has reached me that Egypt has delivery camels on which three-hundred and eighty kilograms are carried. If my message reaches you, let me not discover that any camel is carrying over two-hundred and twenty-eight kilograms."

When looking into Islamic history, we learn that laws of jurisprudence and endowments were strictly adhered to in terms of animal rights. Muslim jurists passed *fiqh* rulings that many people, even today, would find unbelieveable, for example they had ruled that if a blind cat strayed into a house, the members of the household must take it upon themselves to take care of the cat and spend on it because it cannot find its way home. My own mother, may Allah have mercy upon her, would take care of cats. We did not own any cats ourselves, but she would feed cats and show kindness towards them, and on several occasions we would have up to ten cats in our home. The mercy that she showed towards the cats made them feel welcome and comfortable enough to come and spend time in our home, sometimes even for a few weeks. Some of the cats would have a special bond with my mother and would only allow her to touch them.

We must seize these opportunities and do our best to earn rewards through good deeds. If a stray cat or other animal comes under our protection, even for a few hours or days, we must give it the care and love that it needs in order to remain happy and healthy.

Endowments (*awqaaf*) were a hallmark of Islamic Civilisation; no other nation throughout history could match up to the *awqaaf*. The endowments were not limited to humans and were extended to include the needs of animals. It has been documented that they had endowments for sick, elderly and handicapped animals.

One example of this the Madrasat al-Qattat in which hundreds of cats lived in Syria. It was referred to as a madrasah or school because they trained the cats to fend for and take care of themselves. There was also an endowment for stray dogs, giving them shelter and treatment if they were injured or poorly, known as Mahkayamat al-Kilaab.

Animals must be treated with dignity and patience, and we find the best examples of this from our Prophet Muhammad ﷺ. When the Prophet ﷺ came to Makkah from Madinah before the treaty of Hudaibiyah, his camel named Qaswah refused to move forward at one point. Some of the Companions said that Qaswah was stubborn, but the Prophet Muhammad ﷺ refuted their claim and said, "I swear by Allah, Qaswah is not stubborn and that is not a proper trait to attribute to her. What held her back is what held the elephants back (when Abraha came to destroy the Ka'abah)." Allah had stopped the camel for a specific reason, and the Messenger of Allah ﷺ stood up for Qaswah by admonishing his Companions and disallowing them from wronging the camel by accusing it of having a trait that was not true.

To conclude this chapter I would like to remind us that there are times when people or animals are completely at our mercy, we have full authority over them, they are just as much a test for us as we are a test for them. These times are actually opportunities for us to learn about the very purpose of our existence and this is where the spiritual incentive to treat them with justice and excellence (*ihsaan*) comes from. The spiritual aspect of it should propel us to go the extra mile in doing *ihsaan* for the sake of gaining reward from Allah.

The son of Imam Subki saw a dog outside and told it go away whilst calling it, "Dog, son of a dog." Imam Subki called his son and said, "Don't you know that the permissibility of speaking the truth is when there is no intention of an insult behind it?" Although there was truth in his son's statement, it was impermissible for him to insult the dog. Islam does not allow us to insult the creation of Allah as it shows bad character, and we will be held accountable for what we say.

The dependency we have on our Creator is far greater than the dependence that animals have on us, and just as we expect to receive mercy from Allah, we must also show mercy towards animals. If we understood and did the minimum by treating our friends in the way that the Prophet Muhammad ﷺ treated his enemies, our standards and actions would be greatly elevated. May Allah allow us to treat everyone and everything around us in the Prophetic way of excellence in whatever capacity we are capable of. And may Allah allow us to understand and implement the teachings of the Prophet ﷺ. Amin.

38

ENVIRONMENTALISM

It was narrated from 'Abdullah bin 'Amr that the Messenger of Allah passed by Sa'd when he was performing ablution, and he said: 'What is this extravagance?' He said: 'Can there be any extravagance in ablution?' He said: 'Yes, even if you are on the bank of a flowing river.'"

WHEN WE EXPLORE topics such as animal rights and environmentalism, the Islamic approach may seem overly idealistic to many people. It can seem difficult to apply these ideals, even though the Prophet Muhammad ﷺ taught us through his own actions how to deal with people, animals and the environment. We are unfortunately in such a state that we are unable to show compassion to other humans in the way that we should, making it difficult for us to achieve the high standards set by the example of the Prophet's life (*Sunnah*) in other areas. It is important to remind ourselves of the concept of *ihsan* - excellence and beauty - that we talked about earlier and how it is meant to define the overall character of a Muslim. A person with *ihsan* pays attention to things that other people typically do not pay attention to.

We can not be extremely beautiful in one aspect of our character while being ugly in another unless we are not understanding the text correctly, disconnecting or reading the text selectively.

In this chapter we will discuss the Islamic approach to how we should treat the environment, and how to apply this approach in the most practical way possible within the context of justice. I want to begin by mentioning a Hadith narrated by Abdullah bin 'Amr: "The Messenger of Allah ﷺ passed by Sa'ad when he was performing ablution, and he said, 'What is this extravagance?' He said, 'Can there be any extravagance in ablution?' He said, 'Yes, even if you are on the bank of a flowing river.'"[195] Extravagance here refers to the wasting of water, and the Prophet Muhammad ﷺ said that even if we have an abundance of a resource, we should not waste it. It is important to note in this Hadith that although the water was being used to purify for the purpose of prayer (a key pillar of a believer's daily life), the aim should be to use as little as possible without missing or keeping a single spot dry, and if wastefulness is possible with a noble purpose, this then speaks volumes for neutral or evil purposes.

In another well-known Hadith narrated by Abu Umamah, the Messenger of Allah ﷺ said: "The superiority of the learned over the devout worshipper is like my superiority over the most inferior amongst you (in good deeds)." He went on to say, "Allah, His angels, the dwellers of the heaven and the earth, and even the ant in its hole and the fish in water, supplicate in favour of those who teach people knowledge."[196] Ibn Rajab commented on this Hadith and said that a person who is knowledgeable pays attention to the rights of everything around him, and therefore does not transgress the rights of anyone or anything. Furthermore, it is interesting to note that things that most people deem insignificant, such as ants, will testify for or against us on the Day of Judgement. A knowledgeable person on the other hand, understands and remembers this, and will do their best to treat people, animals and the environment in a just manner.

A wonderful Hadith narrated by Anas gives a clear idea of the value of deeds that benefit the environment: "The Prophet Muhammad ﷺ said, 'There is no Muslim who plants a tree or sows a field for a human, bird, or a wild animal that eats from it, but it shall be reckoned as a charity from him.'"[197] Also, in another similar narration, the Prophet ﷺ

said: "No Muslim plants a shoot or sapling except that whatever is eaten or (even) stolen from it, or anyone obtains the least thing from it, except that it is considered charity on his behalf until the Day of Judgement."[198] The core message of these Hadith is that a Muslim should do their best to do things that will benefit the world and its inhabitants. A believer should optimise their stay on earth and find ways to be productive and make the world a better place. In fact, having this approach is so important and valued in Islam that Anas bin Malik reported that the Prophet Muhammad ﷺ said: "If the Final Hour comes while you have a palm-cutting in your hands and it is possible to plant it before the Hour comes, you should plant it."[199] This speaks to the idea of doing good irrespective of the circumstances around us; even in the face of an Earth that is about to be destroyed, if we have the opportunity to do good, we should do it.

Planting and growing for the sake of selling the produce is also rewarded in Islam as the produce becomes available only by growing it; the extinction of a plant makes it unpurchaseable. Cultivating the earth and not leaving it unattended or barren has rewards as the Prophet ﷺ said: "Whoever revives a barren land, it belongs to him." When a person intends good for others, this helps them to forgo incidents where they may have been dealt with unethically, for example someone stealing from their crop can still earn them reward as the Prophet Muhammad ﷺ mentioned in the Hadith quoted earlier. Whilst at the time they may feel that they are at a loss, in reality, the Hadith is telling us that they are actually gaining for the Hereafter. Loss is actually when a person behaves greedily and selfishly by hoarding and not allowing people to benefit from what they cultivate. The very first people that the tribe of *Quraysh* were likened to in the Qur'an were the people of a garden who plotted to *hoard* their produce, to pick their crops extremely early in the day so that the poor would not be able to take any of it and Allah pointed out that they were actually at a loss by this action.

Doing things with the right intention can guarantee us a place in Paradise even if it is just regarding a single tree. Planting trees and allowing people and animals to benefit from them, reaps great rewards. Likewise, those who cut down or uproot trees unnecessarily are condemned by Allah. We can find this condemnation in *Surah al-Hashr* 59:5: *"Whatever you have cut down of (their) palm trees or left standing on their trunks – it was by the permission of Allah and so He would disgrace the defiantly disobedient.*" We compare this with the Hadith mentioned earlier where the Prophet Muhammad ﷺ spoke about the importance of planting trees: "If the Hour is about to commence and one of you is holding a sapling, if he is able to plant it before it commences, then let him plant it." Scholars have commented on this and advised that it is not just about paying attention to good deeds and being productive it is also about not becoming destructive, neglecting to recognise our own destructive actions, just because selfishness and destructiveness are on the increase in the world around us. The Messenger of Allah ﷺ also told us the following: "Do not uproot or burn palms or cut down fruitful trees."[200] There is a lot of emphasis on trees, and it is important that we know how to deal with them. First and foremost, the Prophet ﷺ taught us that trees are living beings, we should reflect on them being a creation of Allah, and that we should empathise with them. There is a very famous Hadith in which we learn about the feelings of trees, it is narrated by Jabir bin Abdullah who said: "The Prophet Muhammad ﷺ used to go and stand next to a tree or palm-tree on Fridays. A woman or a man of the *Ansar* said, 'Oh Messenger of Allah, should we not make for you a pulpit?' He said, 'If you wish.' So, they made a pulpit (*minbar*) for him, and when the next Friday came, he was shown to the *minbar*. The tree cried like a small child, then the Prophet ﷺ came down from the pulpit and hugged the crying tree until it calmed down. It was crying because of the remembrance of Allah (*dhikr*) that it used to hear."[201]

The Prophet Muhammad ﷺ told us to reflect upon trees as one of the signs of Allah, Ibn Umar reported: "We were with the Prophet ﷺ and fresh dates of a palm tree were brought to him. On that he said, 'Amongst the trees, there is a tree which resembles a Muslim.' I wanted to say that it was the date-palm tree but as I was the youngest of all of them, I kept quiet. And then the Prophet ﷺ said, 'It is the date-palm tree. The date-palm tree is rooted, its branches reach high into the sky, and it produces fruit (benefit) throughout the year.'"

It is also worth noting that Allah says in *Surah al-Hajj* 22:18: *"Do you not see that to Allah prostrates whoever is in the heavens and whoever is on the earth, and the sun, the moon, the stars, the mountains, the trees, the moving creatures and many of the people?"* Scholars of exegesis (*tafseer*) mentioned that we are more likely to pay attention to things like the stars and the moon but we neglect the trees, and the wisdom behind Allah giving special mention to the trees is that we pause and reflect on their beauty and the blessings that they bring. Trees are one of the many signs of Allah's existence, and Allah has placed trees amongst the other more notable signs of His creation so that we can appreciate them and treat them as signs of Allah; therefore, be less likely to be destructive towards them.

Coming back to the topic of water, it is paramount that we do not waste water or contaminate it. Mu'adh reported in a Hadith that the Prophet Muhammad ﷺ warned: "Beware of the three acts that cause you to be cursed: relieving yourself in shaded places (that people utilise), in a walkway or in a watering place." Relieving oneself in certain areas was considered unjust, and still is to teach people not to disrespect public areas. The Prophet ﷺ forbade people from urinating in still water because it would cause unnecessary contamination. Whilst in most countries – especially the more developed – some of the rulings do not apply to us anymore in the literal sense of the wordings, we should still think carefully about our actions and whether we contaminate water unnecessarily. Modern warfare and even factories have contaminated large water supplies, and this is what the Prophet ﷺ forbade as the contamination of water affects the source of life for people.

Allah also calls on us to reflect on water in the Qur'an in *Surah al-Waq'iah* 56:68-70: *"And have you seen the water that you drink? Is it you who brought it down from the clouds, or is it We who bring it down? If We willed, We could make it bitter, so why are you not grateful?"* Islam teaches us to remember and thank Allah before and after drinking water with *Bismillah* and *Alhamdulillah*, the Prophet used to say *Alhamdulillah* with every sip. It teaches us to pay attention to the blessing of water and to be thankful for it. Ibn Umar would be reminded about the scarcity of water on the Day of Judgement when he read the above verse; it makes us realise the importance of water and how utterly in need we are of every drop of water that Allah sends to us.

Being grateful for water starts with us not violating Allah with this blessing, followed by showing humbleness. We may have a seemingly endless supply of water, but it is our duty not to violate Allah by wasting it or contaminating it. Allah calls on us to reflect on the blessing of water again in *Surah Mulk* 67:30: *"Say, 'Have you considered, if your water was to become sunken into the earth, then who could bring you flowing water?'"* Allah makes us contemplate on water to stop us from violating it, because if we violate it then we are automatically showing that we do not have appreciation for what Allah has blessed us with.

Appreciation does not end at plants or water, but we should also show appreciation for and take care of our local areas and streets. Earlier in the book, I mentioned the Hadith narrated by Abu Dharr in which we are told that removing harm from the road is a form of charity (*sadaqah*). The word *tareeq* refers to any road or path that people use, and the word *athaa* refers to even the lightest form of harm such as noise pollution, obscene sights or littering. Many of us do not think twice before throwing a wrapper, or piece of gum out of our car windows as we are driving but these are acts that cause pollution and harm. The Prophet Muhammad ﷺ told us that he saw a man strolling in Paradise because he removed a harmful thing from the road, and the word that he used was *athaa* to emphasise that it was a small form of harm. As Muslims we should aim to achieve this sense of excellence; other people may walk past something and think nothing of it, but we should pay attention to it and remove it as a form of *ihsaan*. Japanese people are renowned for their cleanliness; the Japanese fans put the entire world to shame by cleaning the entire stadium after watching a football game. Cleanliness is half of our faith and we as Muslims, should lead by example. Yet, unfortunately we see the state of the streets and roads after Hajj - there is unnecessary pollution caused by people littering.

During the Caliphate of Umar bin al-Khattab, Abu Musa was sent to Basra in Iraq as the new governor, and he introduced himself to the people by saying: "I was sent to you by Umar bin al-Khattab in order to teach you the Book of your Lord (Qur'an), the *Sunnah* (example of the Prophet), and to clean your streets." The importance of cleaning and looking after the streets was placed after the Qur'an and *Sunnah*, and this is something for us to reflect upon. Allah also says in the Qur'an in *Surah Mulk* 67:15: "*It is He who made the earth tame for you – so walk among its slopes and eat of His provision – and to Him is the resurrection.*" We should recognise the blessing that Allah gave us, and if we do not, we will not be able to show gratitude for it or give it its due right.

In *Surah al-A'raf* 7:31, Allah says: "*Oh children of Adam, take your adornment at every masjid, and eat and drink, but be not excessive. Indeed, He likes not those who commit excess.*" Allah and the Prophet Muhammad ﷺ teach us to seek balance and minimise our consumption; we are taught to be people who eat to live and not live to eat. We should not exceed what we need to function, overeating causes us to violate the blessings of Allah and ultimately, doing so can be a cause of testifying against us on the Day of Judgement. This idea extends beyond just food and speaks to overconsumption in every facet of life.

Allah also says in *Surah al-An'am* 6:165: *"And it is He who has made you successors upon the earth… that He may try you through what He has given you."* Allah appointed us as stewards on earth, making us responsible for the seemingly inferior creatures around us. This does not just mean feeding everyone or everything around us, it means we should make sure that the overall environment is as beneficial as possible for everyone.

Corruption, imbalance and inequality cause many people to suffer whilst others have more than they need to survive. We are told in *Surah Ar-Rum* 30:41: *"Corruption has appeared throughout the land and sea by reason of what the hands of people have earned so He may let them taste part of the consequence of what they have done that perhaps they will return to righteousness."* This verse has both spiritual and physical implications. If we take the topic of food, we can see how corruption creates an inequal society. There is enough food in the world for every person to have a healthy diet, but unfortunately millions of people die of starvation whilst millions of people overeat or waste food.

Maymoona, the wife of the Prophet ﷺ, saw a pomegranate pearl on the ground as she was walking and recited, *"Allah does not love corruption."* she connected corruption in the above verse to a person throwing away a pomegranate pearl instead of making use of it. It is a form of corruption when we disregard the signs and blessings of Allah, and we do not treat the environment in the way that it is meant to be treated.

Allah mentions in the Qur'an the way in which He set out the earth, the eco-system, to be of benefit to everyone, and He also mentions that He set the scales and balance of the universe so everything is in harmony. As stewards it is our responsibility not to transgress against the environment and the world around us. If a believer is to show that much care and attention to the environment, it undoubtedly indicates how much more careful we must be with the honour and dignity of human beings.

May Allah make us worthy stewards, allowing us to do right to everything and everyone around us. And may Allah forgive us for our transgressions in any capacity. Amin.

39

WITHOUT JUSTICE, THERE CAN BE NO PEACE

Ibn 'Abbas told Shahr (ibn Hawshab), "While the Prophet, may Allah grant him peace, was sitting in the courtyard of his house in Makkah, 'Uthman ibn Maz'un passed by and smiled at the Prophet, may Allah grant him peace. The Prophet, may Allah grant him peace, said to him, 'Why don't you sit down?' 'I will,' he said. So the Prophet, may Allah grant him peace, sat facing him. While he was conversing with him, the Prophet, may Allah grant him peace, stared at the sky and said, 'A messenger from Allah, 'Abdullah came to me just now when you sat down?' He asked, 'What did he say to you?' He said, 'Allah commands justice and doing good and giving to relatives. And He forbids indecency and doing wrong and tyranny. He warns you so that hopefully you will pay heed.' (16:90) 'Uthman said, 'That was when belief was established in my heart and I loved Muhammad.'"

As we are now nearing the end of this book, I want to return to a more general overview of justice and how it operates in Islam. Within the modern world, there is a different emphasis on justice and a different emphasis on peace. What we see is that the oppressed are usually told to forgo their rights for the sake of the bigger picture, and those with greater power and influence are not burdened in such a way. Quite often, movements for justice are shut down in the name of peace and reconcilliation, leaving justice unobtained.

There is a very famous slogan, "No justice, no peace", and whilst it is not taken from Islam directly, Islam is closer to this idea than any other system in the world – theological or otherwise. Islam highlights retributive justice and reiterates that there can be no peace without justice. One Hadith which covers this concept very well is narrated by Ibn Abbas: "While the Prophet ﷺ was sitting in the courtyard of his house in Makkah, 'Uthman bin Maz'un passed by and smiled at the Prophet ﷺ. The Prophet ﷺ said to him, 'Why don't you sit down?' He said, 'I will.' So, the Prophet ﷺ sat facing him. While he was conversing with him, the Prophet ﷺ stared up at the sky and said, 'A messenger from Allah came to me just now when you sat down.' He asked, 'What did he say to you?' The Prophet ﷺ said, '*Allah commands justice and doing good and giving to relatives. And He forbids indecency and doing wrong and tyranny. He warns you so that hopefully you will pay heed.*' 'Uthman said, 'That was when belief was established in my heart and I loved Muhammad.'"[202]

What is interesting about this Hadith is that the Prophet Muhammad ﷺ turned his attention away from 'Uthman – something that went against his reputation, as he was known for giving people his full attention. However, the reason for which he turned his attention away from 'Uthman was because he was delivered a revelation from Jibreel (*Surah an-Nahl* 16:90), and this revelation is described by Ibn Mas'ud as being the most comprehensive verse that was revealed to the Prophet Muhammad ﷺ. The entirety of the religion or faith is encompassed within this one verse, and it was given so much importance that Umar bin Abdul Aziz would recite this verse at the end of every Friday sermon, which then became a tradition that has carried on until today.

One thing that we should keep in mind is that Allah does not command us to do something that He does not do Himself in His own capacity. For example, Allah commands us to be just and merciful whilst He is the most

Just and most Merciful. Allah also says that He has forbidden oppression for Himself and that He has made it forbidden amongst us all. Ibn al-Qayyim has also commented on this and said that the three components of our natural disposition (*fitrah*) are monotheism, justice and mercy. If a child is alone in the desert with no other external influences, they would undoubtedly develop a natural belief in One God. Children are born with a sense of justice and a sense of mercy; they realise if an act is oppressive and will instinctively know that it is wrong.

Justice is the minimum that we should aim for, whilst excellence (*ihsaan*) is the maximum. Justice begins with justice towards Allah and it requires us to be consistent in honouring His rights in private and in public. To achieve *ihsaan* with Allah, our relationship with Him in private should be better than our public relationship with Him. It would be unjust to only honour Allah when we are around other people and forget about Him when we are alone; we should at the very least, honour Allah the same both in public and private, but to do *ihsaan* is to honour Him more in private. The Prophet Muhammad ﷺ also taught us that we should worship Allah as if we can see Him, and if we cannot see Him then we should know that He sees us. Discrepancy in any way leads towards hypocrisy, and hypocrisy is hated.

Allah also forbids indecency, wrongdoing and tyranny – publicly and privately. Any act of indecency is forbidden in Islam, even if done privately. Proudly boasting about a sin in public shows shamelessness on our part and is a level above indecency, whilst being unjust towards the creation of Allah is an act of tyranny.

In regards to peace and justice, Martin Luther King Jr. made a very powerful statement saying, "Peace is not the absence of tension, but the presence of justice." Peace holds huge importance in Islam, and the word peace (*salaam*) literally means freedom from chaos. The Prophet Muhammad ﷺ also said, "A Muslim is the one from whose tongue and hands people are safe." When we say *Assalaamu Alaikum*, we are saying that no harm will come to the other person from us as we are sending peace upon them.

Paradise is referred to as *Dar-us-salaam* because it is free from any imperfections and anything that could disturb the peace. Allah, Himself is as-Salaam – the source of peace as He is free from any defect or flaw. The core of Islam revolves around peace; it asks for the absence of harm towards the entire creation of Allah, which brings about the question, can there truly be peace in the presence of injustice? The simple answer to this is no, there cannot be true peace whilst there is injustice in the world. True peace will exist in Paradise, where nobody can be harmed or bothered by anything negative.

The verse from Surah an-Nahl explains that we cannot achieve excellence (*ihsaan*) without justice (*adl*). When we see that people's rights are being taken away, we do not focus on embellishing privileges, rather we must focus on removing oppression. The priority in Islam is to restore the rights of people and to remove whatever disturbed the peace.

One of the greatest scholars in Islam named Fudayl, said that he prioritised seeking forgiveness (*istighfaar*) over glorification (*tasbeeh*) in his remembrance of Allah because if we have a garment that is dirty, we must clean the stain before we accessorize the garment. Ibn Abbas also said that justice is to remove ugliness from society and excellence is to promote virtue. Looking at it from a societal perspective of restorative justice, we cannot tell a person who is facing injustice to show excellence (*ihsaan*) by relinquishing their rights, instead we must establish their rights and put them in a position where they feel enabled to show *ihsaan*.

Islam has the concept of both retribution (*Qisas*) and forgiveness (*Afw*), while retribution is the right of the one who has been wronged, to show benevolence is encouraged. However, they can not be pressurised or bullied into forgiveness and *ihsaan*. Society should be structured whereby the person who is wronged is in a position to freely choose between justice and excellence. Excellence (*ihsaan*) is the standard that we hold ourselves to it is not something that we force upon someone else. Once that right to free choice has been established and the oppressed feels truly free to choose between justice or forgivenss can we remind them that in showing benevolence and *ihassn* we can expect to receive even greater benevolence and *ihsaan* from Allah. Allah says in *Surah ash-Shura* 42:39: *"And those who, when tyranny strikes them, they defend themselves"* meaning, that when a person is being oppressed, they should defend themselves. If we do not defend ourselves, we are enabling the oppressor to oppress others which can cause injustice on a larger, societal level. Allah praises self-defence, and even when we show benevolence, the oppressor should have the tools of oppression removed from them so that they can not cause injustice to others.

Malcolm X never used violence, nor called to violence, however he found it wrong that those who are oppressed should have to commit to passiveness, in principle, whilst the oppressors commit to violence. Allah also says in the Qur'an in *Surah ash-Shura* 42:40: *"And the retribution for an evil act is an evil one like it, but whoever pardons and makes reconciliation – his reward is due from Allah. Indeed, He does not like wrongdoers."* We should not look down upon those who choose retribution over forgiveness, as Allah has given them the choice and they will not be blamed. Allah mentions this in the following verse of *Surah ash-Shura* 42:41: *"And whoever avenges himself after being wronged – those have not upon them any cause for blame."* Blame should only be put upon the oppressor, whilst the oppressed are given a genuine option of choosing retribution or forgiveness.

Jesse Williams made a powerful statement during a famous speech, "If you don't have an established critique of my oppression, you don't have a right to an opinion on my resistance." This is also the stance of Islam regarding this matter; no blame on the oppressed but rather, it is on the one causing the injustice.

Imam Zaid Shakir writes: "This social aspect of justice has been beautifully summarised by Imam al-Qurtubi. He says, discussing the relationship between two words that are usually translated as justice (*al-adl*) and distributive justice (*al-qist*), 'Justice is the basis of all human relations and the foundation of Islamic rule.' This saying is illustrative of the meaning conveyed by the saying of God, *'Verily, We have sent Our Messengers with clear proofs, and we have revealed unto them the Scripture and the Balance in order that they lead people with justice'* (*Qur'an 57:25*)"

Imam al-Mawardi also summarised the social implications of distributive justice by saying that one of the things that is able to reform worldly affairs, is the principle of distributive justice. It facilitates amicable relations between people, engenders obedience to the Divine Law, and brings about the prosperity of countries. It is the basis of a thriving economy, stable governments and strong family systems. Nothing corrupts the mind or nations as quickly as tyranny. That is because there are no acceptable limits (to regulate tyranny). It is for this reason that Ibn Taymiyyah saw the responsibilities of a successful Islamic government emanating from a single Qur'anic verse, (4: 58), in which Allah enjoins that we deliver trusts to their rightful possessors and when we rule or judge between people, we do so with justice.

If a person is called to judge between people, they must judge with justice and this begins with distributive justice before restorative justice.

A person in that position of power must do their part to ensure that everyone is in a fair place first, only after that can they take things back to their original framework. It is due to this reason, that in current times, it is unfair to complain about immigrants arriving in the United States without talking about what the United States has done to their countries of origin. Those people were put in unfortunate and horrible positions, forcing them to flee their home to seek protection in other countries. It is also unfair to expect that the crime rate will be the same for people in poverty and people that are rich or to punish poor people more when it comes to crimes compared to rich people, but unfortunately this is the case in the majority of places around the world. It is important to understand that we must be just towards all people equally, and only after restoring justice can we promote virtue and begin promoting *ihsaan*.

May Allah allow us to be just and allow us to create societies in which justice is easily accessed. May Allah also allow to be from those who aim to achieve excellence in our lives. Amin.

40

GRADUAL CHANGE VERSUS RADICAL REFORM

'Abdullâh b. Mas'ud (ra) narrates: The Prophet ﷺ said: "There is no Prophet whom Allah sent to any nation before me, but he had disciples and companions from among his nation who followed his path and obeyed his commands. Then after them came generations who said what they did not do and did what they were not commanded to do. Whoever strives against them with his hand is a believer; whoever strives against them with his tongue is a believer; whoever strives against them with his heart is a believer. Beyond that there is not even a mustard-seed's worth of faith."

Alhamdulillah, we are at the end of this book and I hope that you have benefited from it as much as I have Insha'Allah.

In the previous chapter I discussed the concept of there being no justice without peace; the presence of justice is an essential requirement for peace. This leads me to the topic for this final chapter in which we ask, at what point do we disrupt peace for the sake of justice? How can we enact meaningful change in society? We will answer these questions Insha'Allah by looking at the Prophetic way of enacting change within society.

Whilst in the previous chapters it may have seemed as though the approaches were too idealistic; it is in fact due to us not being able to achieve a basic level of decency in how we treat those around us with justice that makes those approaches seem idealistic and unattainable. This brings about the need to understand the Prophetic approach to enacting change and I want to discuss the concept of gradual change versus radical reform. The word radical, however, needs clarification, should not be understood under the connotation of violence; rather, it should be understood in the true definition of the word which is rapid and transformative.

There are a few things that I want to address regarding this topic before going into more detail:

- There is a difference between a goal and a process. What this means it that there may be someone who acts in accordance with a 'radical agenda' in the sense that they want to take rapid and meaningful steps towards a positive change.

- Some people see gradual change as being escapist or too passive, or even as a form of cowardice.

- Every prophet was sent to correct the deviations of the people before him. The Prophet Muhammad ﷺ explained that every prophet was given disciples or companions who would follow and obey everything that they taught. Most prophets also encountered hypocrites during their own lives, and then Allah sent a prophet to rectify what was twisted and changed from the teachings of the prophet before them, one such example is of the Prophet Isa coming to solidify the teachings of the Prophet Musa, may the blessings of Allah be upon them both.

- Regarding hypocrites, the Prophet Muhammad ﷺ said: "Whoever strives against them with his hand is a believer, whoever strives against them with his tongue is a believer, and whoever strives against them with his heart is a believer. Beyond that there is not even a mustard seed worth of faith."[203]

The main Hadith that I want to quote is one that provides a very good foundation when discussing change. Abu Sa'eed al-Khudri, may Allah be pleased with him, narrated: "The Prophet Muhammad ﷺ said, 'Whoever of you sees an evil, let him change it with his hand, if he cannot, then with his tongue. If he cannot, then with his heart – and that would be the weakest of faith.'"[204]

The first thing that we learn here is that the Prophet ﷺ connected faith directly with how we respond to evil. We are also taught by the Prophet Muhammad ﷺ that just because a certain matter may seem overwhelming, and we may not be able to make a dramatic change, it does not excuse us from doing whatever is within our capacity. Allah will not ask about the things that we were incapable of changing, but He will ask if we internally felt a desire to change them. Not everyone can make physical changes to situations, however the Prophet ﷺ told us that having the desire to change or feeling revulsion towards these things should be the very least that we do. Evil should not be normalised, nor should we just accept it.

Another lesson that we learn is that all of the one-hundred and twenty-four thousand prophets came to establish a singular message and the essentials of this message were monotheism, spirituality and morality. Any differences were in the smaller details of legislation and jurisprudence, but the overall standard of their message on morality and monotheism was the same. For example, every prophet and his nation would practice fasting, it was prescribed upon all of them. However, the method of fasting varied from nation to nation.

When looking into the prophets and their messages, some may ask why did Allah not send one prophet for the entirety of humanity, or if prophets were such great and perfect people, why did people keep going astray after they had come and gone? Each and every prophet was chosen by Allah to deliver His message to the people, and they came to right the wrong that people had committed by failing to adhere to the principles of the previous prophet. The Prophet Muhammad ﷺ too, came to undo the evil that had been done by those who did not follow the belief and values that the prophets before him had taught. The Prophet ﷺ also described himself as being like the last brick in a house, and this is because gradualism is a tradition (*Sunnah*) of Allah.

When speaking about gradualism, scholars have said that Allah is capable of creating everything in an instant, but He wished to establish the gradualism of events as a tradition in His universe. Allah could have made conception and birth instantaneous but wished for humans to understand the wisdom by which their lives must be governed. Allah could have chosen for everyone to be created in the same way that the Prophet Isa, may the blessings of Allah be upon him, was created, but there is a process and there is wisdom behind this process. Allah could also have sent His angels to eradicate the opponents of the Prophet Muhammad ﷺ before they even resisted, but He wished the example of the Prophet ﷺ to be as human and replicable as possible. Through the Prophet Muhammad ﷺ, Allah teaches us prudence, perseverance and steadfastness.

One of the greatest teachings in the Qur'an is that with hardship comes ease. The way or tradition in which Allah allows things to happen clearly shows that there is gradualism in the creation of Allah. There is also gradualism in our personal acts of worship, for example the Prophet Muhammad ﷺ said: "This religion is one of ease, and none will overburden himself with religion except that it overwhelms him. So, seek a middle path and draw near to perfection as much as you can, and be hopeful of Allah and seek help in being consistent through the morning hours, the afternoon and parts of late night."[205] The Messenger of Allah ﷺ taught us that we should develop our relationship with Allah in a gradual sense. Our relationship with Allah should be meaningful and calculated, rather than being overzealous and burning out quickly. We should slowly increase in our acts of worship, to strengthen our relationship with Allah and increase our love for Him.

The religion is not wrong or difficult, but it is our own approach that makes it hard for ourselves. We should not try to do everything at once, which is why the Prophet ﷺ taught us to seek the middle path, and then progress slowly towards perfection whilst remaining hopeful of Allah. We are told to take steps suitable for us, to focus on our personal progress and to keep hope even if we see someone who is ahead of us in worship. Part of overburdening yourself with Islam is undertaking what is not currently sustainable or achievable for you. The Prophet Muhammad ﷺ also said, "Undertake actions that you can bear, for Allah does not give up (rewarding you) until you give up (seeking it)."[206]

There is also gradualism in the way that the religion is taught, for example we find that Ali bin Abi Talib, may Allah be pleased with him, said: "Do not give them things they are not ready for, do you want them to disbelieve in Allah?" Regarding this, the scholar Ibn Taymiyyah said, "If the person being commanded or prohibited is currently incapable, whether due to his ignorance or his negligence, and removing that ignorance or negligence is not possible, perhaps it would be better to abstain from commanding or prohibiting him. As some have said, silence is the best response to some issues, just as the Law-Giver (Allah) initially kept silent regarding certain commands and prohibitions until Islam grew and became dominant. Likewise, the scholar can defer the conveyance and explanation of certain matters until he is able, just as Allah deferred revealing some verses and explaining some rulings until the Messenger of Allah ﷺ became empowered, in order to ensure its adequate understanding."

The prophets all came with their messages in a calculated manner; the Prophet Isa did not overturn the tables as his first approach to the corruption amongst the people, nor did the Prophet Musa split the sea right away. Allah first commanded Prophet Musa to speak words of gentleness, lenience and wisdom so that the Pharaoh may comprehend. Allah was giving Musa hope, that although the Pharaoh was the most evil person created, he may think about the message that Musa is giving him. The Prophets Musa and Haroon were not responsible for the reaction of the Pharaoh, but they were responsible for inviting him to see the truth. They came with Divine commands, to teach Divine commands with Divine wisdom, and it is known that the Prophet Muhammad ﷺ would only convey that which could be comprehended and practiced by the people.

There is also a well-known saying in Islam which says, 'If you wish to be obeyed, only instruct that which is feasible.' This is why the Messengers of God would teach and command that which was feasible; they would not ask people to do more than they were capable of otherwise they would run the risk of being disobeyed rather than obeyed. When a person accepts Islam, there is a gradual acceptance and carrying out of responsibilities – they cannot take it all in at once. A person cannot and should not become overwhelmed with religion because 'a believer is guided by the light and an extremist is blinded by the light'. If a person tries to take it all in and practice everything at once, they will become overwhelmed and unable to comprehend matters properly whilst also negatively impacting others.

The Prophet Muhammad ﷺ would allow temporary concessions for new Muslims in order to let them grow closer to Islam gradually. One example of this can be found with the tribe of Banu Hanifa; when they accepted Islam, they said that they could not pray five times a day from the very beginning and so the Prophet ﷺ allowed them to pray however many times was feasible for them at that point. Umar bin al-Khattab asked the Prophet Muhammad ﷺ why he allowed this and the Messenger of Allah ﷺ replied that they would eventually reach the five daily prayers, because once they tasted the sweetness of faith, they would adopt the ways of Islam with maturity.

There are also examples of political gradualism in Islam; the Treaty of Hudaybiyya being one of them. When the treaty was being written, the Makkans would not accept the phrase "Messenger of God" and demanded that they be erased in order for the treaty to move forward. Ali bin Abi Talib did not want to erase these words but the Prophet Muhammad ﷺ asked him to erase them for the sake of the treaty. The Prophet ﷺ also accepted some unfair terms of the treaty which included Abu Jandal being sent back with his persecutors, but this was all done for the sake of bringing about the justice of Islam in the long run. Umar, known for voicing himself without fear, outright objected to this by saying, "We should not compromise. Are we not on the truth? Are they not on falsehood? Our martyrs are in Paradise whilst their dead are in the fire."

However, in the grander scheme of things, the treaty brought about more good for Islam. Even after eighteen years of calling to the faith, the number of Muslims was only three-thousand, but after the treaty had been signed with the setback terms, the number of Muslims increased to ten-thousand in under two years. There was no longer any persecution, and Muslims were able to show the beauty of Islam without fearing for their lives, thus leading to what Allah called a clear victory (*Fathan Mubeena*).

There was always wisdom behind the choices that the Prophet ﷺ made, as he was looking to deal with the situation at hand in the best way possible. One example of this is the way in which the Prophet Muhammad ﷺ dealt with the hypocrite Abdullah ibn Ubayy ibn Saloul. Abdullah ibn Saloul was actively plotting against the Prophet ﷺ and trying to destabilise Madinah by pitting people against one another. The Companions – especially Umar bin al-Khattab – asked the Prophet ﷺ to deal with him and punish him for what he was doing, however, the

Prophet ﷺ chose not to hold Abdullah accountable because of the *fitnah* and division that it would cause in the city. Abdullah ibn Saloul died a natural death, and the Messenger of Allah ﷺ clothed him with his own cloth, even though he was the chief of the hypocrites. The Prophet ﷺ then said to Umar, "Oh Umar, now the very same people that would have risen up against us for killing him (Abdullah ibn Saloul) would now willingly do it themselves." What he meant by this was that the people now realised the evils that he had committed in their society.

The Messenger of Allah ﷺ responded to everything with wisdom, and when his Companions such as Khabbab, may Allah be pleased with him, vented his frustration regarding the persecution and torture that he had to face in Makkah and asked for something to be done about it, the Prophet ﷺ told him that he was being hasty and that people before him had also been tested. This approach teaches us that evil does not justify evil, nor can evil be changed or stopped by another evil. When terrorist groups kill children, some governments retaliate by killing their children or children in that area which is not justified. Evil is made worse by retaliating with evil, and the Prophet ﷺ was teaching Khabbab that their situation will change, but they must not become impatient; they will fight against the persecution when the time is right.

If we sacrifice our principles as a result of impulsive decisions and partake in evil whilst saying that we are changing or getting rid of evil, we are in fact becoming a product of that which we claim to despise. Hastiness is directly tied to a lack of trust in Allah, whilst sometimes trust in Allah is used as an excuse to shut down legitimate means of change.

There are two extremes; on one hand people who are impatient can make wrong decisions and involve themselves in actions that will cause more harm than good, whilst on the other hand, some people believe that everything comes from Allah and so choose to just sit back and pray. However, the Prophet Muhammad ﷺ did neither. He was not hasty, nor did he just pray. He, like the previous prophets, did not lose hope in Allah, and they did whatever was right and, in their capacity, to change the situation.

Scholars, when discussing this subject, have said that it is important to look at the greater benefits and harms. If we do not make the correct calculations and act accordingly, we can end up causing more harm than good, even if we have legitimate concerns and grievances. Being unprpared can result in more damage to our community, even though we did not partake in any evil, which is why it is important for us to remember the teaching of the Prophet ﷺ in which he told us to undertake that which we are capable of.

One of the greatest revivers or reformers in Islamic history is Umar bin Abdul Aziz. He removed a lot of injustice and corruption from society at the young age of thirty-eight, when he was given the leadership position of Caliph. Umar bin Abdul Aziz had a very pious son named Abdul Malik who would press him to accelerate the decisions of reform. Abdul Malik would say, "My father, why are you not executing matters? You are delaying things that I imagined you would have completed on the day of your inauguration before nightfall. By Allah, I wish you would do this, even if it meant that you and I would boil for it in the kettles." He wanted his father to do more, even if it meant that people would revolt against them and kill them.

Umar bin Abdul Aziz said to his son, "My son, alongside the great share Allah has portioned to you (i.e. righteousness), you still carry some of the qualities of the young. My son do not be hasty, for Allah has dispraised wine twice in the Qur'an, then prohibited it on the third occasion. I fear committing them to the truth (justice) altogether, lest they reject it altogether. I cannot present them with any part of the religion, except while offering some worldly benefit alongside it, in order to soften their hearts – out of fear that they would erupt against me in a way that I cannot repel. Does it not please you that not a day passes by your father, except that he revives a Prophetic tradition (*Sunnah*) and destroys an innovation (*bid'ah*) during it?"

Umar bin Abdul Aziz understood the importance of not being hasty, and he explained to his son that hastiness and fearlessness, hallmarks of youth, are sometimes the greatest disruptors of reform. Although Umar did not want to reintroduce the authentic *Sunnah* on his first day, he did in a sense change the world overnight. His Caliphate only lasted two and a half years, and in these two and a half years he reinstated pure justice which was the hallmark of Islam in its earliest years. Nobody could find anyone to give charity to because he had eliminated corruption and disparity. However, his leadership came to an abrupt end when he was poisoned and killed. He was not radical enough for his son, but he was too radical for others which is why he was killed.

The verdict is always going to be subjective to the type of change that we are making. The example that Umar bin Abdul Aziz gave in regard to the gradual prohibition of alcohol is very important for us to remember, because Allah knows best of all that reforming society is not like reforming an individual. Even individuals vary in the way that they accept change; whilst some people will have the will and strength to accept a bigger change, others accept baby steps and it is important to choose the right methodology in the light of repelling a greater evil with a lesser evil.

Umar bin Abdul Aziz did ruffle feathers in society, just as the Prophet Muhammad ﷺ and his morality made people uncomfortable. However, we must understand that the aim is not to trigger a reaction that we cannot handle at that particular time. For example, the Prophet Muhammad ﷺ spoke up against idolatry, female infanticide and tribalism, all of which had a lot of backlash from people, however he did not allow his Companions to take up arms in self-defence in Makkah or allow them to curse the idols (although he did later take up arms for the sake of justice and tear down the idols himself at the conquest of Makkah).

In conclusion of this chapter, I would like to mention some final lessons:

- The standard should always be maintained, and there should be no ambiguity even as we take baby steps towards that which is right, people should always know what the truth is. This is especially important for people that have a set of principles that they are bound by because they believe those principles to be Divine.

- We cannot be ambiguous about our principles; however, we can prioritise and make wise decisions about how we are going to carry out certain actions or agendas to enact a meaningful change in society.

- Before the Muhammad ﷺ was given prophethood at the age of forty, people already knew that he did not believe in idol worshipping. However, they did not feel threatened by this until he began preaching against idol worshipping.

- In order to achieve a holistic agenda of reform, hearts must also be reformed. The hearts and minds of people must be willing to accept societal policies, and so moral rectification and justice go hand in hand.

- People could trust the Prophet Muhammad ﷺ regarding what was bad for their Hereafter, because he would also seek to protect them from that which was bad for them in this life.

- Imam al-Ghazali, may Allah be pleased with him, wrote a monumental piece on spirituality which is named *Ihya Ulum ad-Deen*. This was written during the crusades and attacks from the Mongols; oppression was being fought against, yet the Qur'an and *Sunnah* were still being taught.

- Some people do not actively participate in any reform, but when they see someone else working to achieve a certain aspect of reform, they will criticise them for leaving out other aspects and try to stop the reform altogether. This is the same attitude that the hypocrites had at the time of the Prophet ﷺ - they would complain about issues whilst trying to keep people away from accepting the truth of Islam.

- It is important for us to remember that no individual is tasked with everything at the same time. We can specialise in certain areas, and we should not undermine or tear each other down for doing what we are capable of.

- Gradualism cannot be used as an excuse for inaction or laziness, and at the same time hastiness or foolishness can be mistaken for courage but that urgency can cause more harm than good.

- Allah says in *Surah ash-Shura* 42:38: "*…Who conduct their affairs by mutual consultation…*" Working together to think about what actions to take to enact a meaningful change in society is something that Allah has praised.

I seek refuge in Allah from any mistakes and shortcomings, and if I have said anything wrong then it is from myself and Shaytan, and if any good has been said then all praises are due to Allah. May Allah allow us to aspire towards the examples and teachings of the Prophet Muhammad ﷺ. May Allah allow us all to benefit from the Hadith and lessons that have been covered in this book. Amin.

ENDNOTES

1. at-Tirmidhi
2. al-Bukhari & Muslim
3. Muslim
4. Muslim
5. Muslim
6. Abu Dawud
7. al-Bukhari
8. at-Tirmidhi
9. Abu Dawud
10. Abu Dawud
11. al-Bukhari
12. Muslim
13. al-Bukhari
14. Muslim
15. al-Bukhari & Muslim
16. at-Tirmidhi
17. at-Tirmidhi
18. at-Tirmidhi & Abu Dawud
19. Muslim
20. Muslim
21. Al-Haakim
22. al-Bukhari
23. Al-Haakim
24. Abu Dawud
25. Umar bin Abdul Aziz
26. Ahmad
27. Abu Dawud
28. Abu Darda
29. al-Bukhari & Muslim
30. Muslim
31. Musnad Ahmad
32. Ibn Majah
33. Musnad Ahmad
34. Ahmad
35. Abu Dawud & Tirmidhi
36. Ibn Majah
37. Muslim
38. at-Tirmidhi
39. at-Tirmidhi
40. al-Bukhari
41. at-Tirmidhi
42. at-Tirmidhi
43. Ibn Majah
44. al-Bukhari
45. at-Tirmidhi
46. al-Bukhari
47. al-Bukhari
48. Abu Dawud

49.	Tafsir Al-Tabari & Qurtubi	90.	Bukhari & Muslim
50.	Abu Dawud	91.	al-Bukhari
51.	Al-Haakim	92.	Muslim
52.	at-Tirmidhi	93.	al-Bukhari
53.	Musnad Ahmad	94.	al-Bukhari
54.	Tafsir Al-Tabari	95.	Ahmad
55.	Abu Dawud	96.	al-Tabarani
56.	Abu Dawud & at-Tirmidhi	97.	Muslim
57.	al-Bukhari	98.	al-Bukhari
58.	Muwatta Malik	99.	Muslim
59.	al-Bukhari & Muslim	100.	al-Bukhari
60.	al-Bukhari & Muslim	101.	al-Bukhari
61.	Ahmad	102.	Ahmad
62.	Bukhari	103.	Ibn Majah
63.	at-Tirmidhi	104.	Ibn Majah
64.	Abu Dawud	105.	Baihaqi
65.	al-Bukhari	106.	Abu Dawud
66.	Abu Dawud	107.	al-Bukhari
67.	at-Tirmidhi	108.	al-Bukhari & Muslim
68.	al-Bukhari	109.	al-Bukhari
69.	al-Bukhari & Muslim	110.	al-Bukhari
70.	al-Bukhari	111.	Abu Dawud
71.	Al-Haakim & Ibn Hishaam	112.	Muslim
72.	Ahmad	113.	at-Tirmidhi
73.	al-Bukhari	114.	al-Bukhari
74.	Muslim	115.	al-Bukhari
75.	al-Bukhari	116.	al-Bukhari
76.	at-Tirmidhi	117.	al-Bukhari
77.	al-Bukhari	118.	Nasa'i
78.	al-Bukhari & Muslim	119.	al-Bukhari
79.	al-Bukhari	120.	Muslim
80.	Ahmad	121.	Ibn Majah
81.	Muslim	122.	at-Tabaraani
82.	al-Bukhari	123.	Ibn Majah
83.	al-Bukhari	124.	Musnad Ahmad
84.	at-Tirmidhi	125.	Musnad Ahmad
85.	Muslim	126.	al-Bukhari
86.	Muslim	127.	Muslim
87.	Muslim	128.	al-Bukhari & Muslim
88.	al-Bukhari	129.	Muslim
89.	Abu Dawud	130.	Abu Dawud

131. Abu Dawud
132. al-Bukhari
133. Sharh Ma'ani al-Athar
134. al-Bukhari
135. Muslim
136. Abu Dawud
137. al-Bukhari
138. at-Tirmidhi
139. al-Bukhari
140. Abu Dawud
141. Abu Dawud
142. Sahih Targhib
143. at-Tirmidhi
144. al-Bukhari
145. al-Bukhari
146. Muslim
147. Abu Dawud
148. Abu Dawud & at-Tirmidhi
149. Musnad Ahmad
150. Ibn Abi Dunya
151. al-Bukhari
152. al-Bukhari
153. al-Bukhari
154. Muslim
155. Muslim
156. at-Tirmidhi
157. Abu Dawud
158. at-Tirmidhi
159. at-Tirmidhi
160. at-Tirmidhi
161. at-Tirmidhi
162. Abu Dawud
163. al-Bukhari
164. Ibn Majah
165. Nasa'i
166. Ibn Majah
167. at-Tirmidhi
168. Muslim
169. al-Bukhari & Muslim
170. al-Bukhari
171. Muslim
172. al-Bukhari
173. Ibn al-Jawzi
174. Ibn Kathir
175. Muslim
176. al-Bukhari & Muslim
177. al-Bukhari
178. Ibn Majah
179. Abu Dawud
180. Muslim
181. al-Bukhari & Muslim
182. Abu Dawud
183. al-Bukhari & Muslim
184. al-Bukhari & Muslim
185. al-Bukhari & Muslim
186. Abu Dawud
187. Ahmad
188. Abu Dawud
189. Ahmad
190. at-Tabarani
191. Abu Dawud
192. at-Tabarani
193. as-Sayuti
194. Muslim
195. Ibn Majah
196. at-Tirmidhi
197. al-Bukhari & Muslim
198. Muslim
199. al-Bukhari
200. Muwatta Malik
201. al-Bukhari
202. al-Bukhari
203. Muslim
204. Muslim
205. al-Bukhari
206. Abu Dawud

INDEX

A
Abdullah bin az-Zubair
 verse recite, 73
Abdullah bin Mas'ud
 enjoining or doing good, 39
 first defect that destroyed Banu Isra'il, 81
 mentioned about forbid evil, 39
Abdullah bin Mubarak
 great scholar as, 129–130
 rights of neighbour, 144–145
Abdullah bin Umar, 50–51
 ghulool, 161
 shepherd, conversation on fast, 164
Abdullah bin Zubair bin Aslam
 conversation with father, 83–84
 Hadith narrated by, 83
Abu Bakr, 45
 ayah from *Surah al-Ma'ida*, 55
 reminding people, 54
Abu Dawud
 acceptance of Islam, 27
 narrated Hadith, 3–4

Abu Dhar
 advice by Prophet, 38–40
 assistance, 40
 belonged to Ghiffaar, 26
 compared with Mu'adh, 27
 deeds Prophet taught, 37–40
 enjoining, 39
 genuine intention, 27
 Hadith narration by, 19–20
 inquisitive nature, 36
 leadership and trust, 30
 Prophet testified, 27
 questions to Prophet Muhammad, 41, 42, 43
 reply to Prophet, 27
 strict attitude with himself, 29
 teaching by Prophet Muhammad, 42
 what Prophet told to, 29
 why Prophet referred as weak, 28
Abu Huraira (ra)
 Hadith by, 98
 Hadith narrated, 7, 94–95, 139
 said about messenger of Allah, 94
 saying about three people, 23–24

Abu Jahl
  man of great physical strength, 127
  supplication *(du'a)*, 126–127
Abu Saeed
  Hadith narrated, 51–52
  narrates about silence, 60
Abu Sayeed al-Khudri
  Hadith narrated by, 61
  lessons learnt from Hadith narrated by, 48–49
  two narrations, 47
Abu Umamah
  shyness and guilelessness, 107–108
acts of injustice, 14, 79
  example of Allen Brooks, 79
adultery, 143–144
afzal-ul-jihad, 49
Aisha
  Hadith narrated by, 131–132
  Imam Bayhaqi commented on Hadith, 132
  narrated Hadith, 112, 113
ajar. *See* reward
ajeer, 165
akhira, 28
al aman, 21, 24
Al 'Urs bin 'Amirat al-Kind
  narrated about sins, 81
Al-Adab Al-Mufrad
  collection of mannerisms, 73
  characteristics, 73
Al-Birr wa Taqwa, 122
Al-Ghish, 98
al-Hurr bin al-Qayys, 72–73
Ali bin Abi Talib
  story about, 107
Al-Ihsaan, 73
Allah, 9, 160
  consistency in message, 20
  incident of Aisha, 13
  infinite, 3
  loves muqsiteen, 21
  messenger of, 161
  no love for dhaalim, 21
  punishment to oppressors, 114–115
  supplication, 24
  Surah Al-Qasas, 28:83, 30
  trait of people of excellence, 38
  wants us to remember, 93
al'ly, 108
amal, 13
amanah, 160
ambiguity with injustice, 50
Ammar bin Yasir
  representing Muslim, 58–59
Anas
  narrated Hadith, 140
anger, 133
  argument between Abu Bakr and Umar, 135–136
  concept of righteous, 133–134
  example narrated by Anas, 135
  Ibn Abi Mulaika, 134–135
  Prophet Muhammad's character, 136
  Umar bin al-Khattab, connection with, 133
aqsaam. *See* capacities
Ar-Rahman, 20
Ash-Shakoor, 87
at-Tabaraani
  story of sincerity and fear of cheating, 95–96
At-Taqseer, 73
authority, 24
  position, 40
ayah, 54
Azhar bin Abdullah al-Harari
  torture in Islam, 151

B

backbiting, 12, 42, 59–60, 62, 80, 154
Battle against Persians
    courage of the Muslims, 129
Battle of Badr
    connection with Abdullah bin Mas'ud, 127
    torture in Islam, 150
Battle of Siffin, 107
Battle of Uhud
    strength and Islam, 128
beating, 11, 14
belittling sins, 80
betrayal, 97
Bible
    Matthew 23:23, complaint of Isa, 115
Bukhari
    Hadith narrated, 141
burda, 17

C

Caliph, 45
Caliphate, 31
capabilities, 35
capacities, 40
capitalism, 20
charity, 38–39, 43, 44, 65, 66, 68, 69, 96, 141, 143, 161, 162, 163, 170, 74, 75, 201, 214, 219, 235, 298
Christians, 17–18
    Pope Urban II, 58
clothing
    importance explained by Prophet, 68–69
community, 32
companions, 28, 55, 60-61, 67, 72, 88-89, 107, 152, 128-129, 137, 138, 143, 150, 153, 162, 163, 194, 217, 225, 240, 250, 260, 272, 274, 289, 291, 311
    discussion about strange things, 55
    female, 260
    no support, 61
    second Hadith, 55–56
compassion, 156
comprehensiveness of *tatfeef*, 85–93
connotations, 75, 173, 200, 204, 226
corrupt lawyers and unserved justice
    Abdullah bin Umm Maktum, 268
    Allah
        disability act, 271
        excused people, 273
        Surah 'Abasa 80:1-4, 268
    al-Walid bin Abdul Maalik
        care centres for people, 274
    Amr bin al-Jamuh
        Companion, 272
    Anas reports, 267–268
    Battle of Uhud, 272
    Bayhaqi
        narration found in, 274
    blind man rights, 271
    burdening of people, 272
    Hadith
        beautiful encounter, 273
        caters for people of different abilities, 272–273
        of Prophet, 275
        reported by Ata bin Abi Rabah, 270
    Islamic obligations, 273
    jurisprudence *(fiqh)* issues, 273
    killing of disabled babies, 267
    Messenger of Allah, 273–274
        people with disabilities, 267
        rak'ah prayer, 269
    mosque, 269
    physical disabilities, people with, 271

Prophet Muhammad
    reassured his Companions, 272
    revolutionary and early Islamic
        culture, 275
    society, 270
    Umar bin Abdul Aziz
        rule of, 274
    woman with mental disability, 267

D
darakaat, 15
Da'wah, 42. *See* supplication
Day of Judgement
    pulpits of light, 21
    seven groups of people, 21
    Umar, 24
Day of Resurrection, 42
deception, 97, 108, 110, 180
    Al-Ghish by Zahr al-Shahree, 98
    business transactions, 98–100
    cheating on job applications,
        102–104
    legal ruling, 101–102
    marriage, 100–101
    scholars tells about problems,
        103–104
    sincere advice, 101–102
    worst type, 97
dictators, 58, 204
dhaalim, 21
dhulm, 10
    greater forms, 14
    meaning, 4
    no justification, 14
    types, 4
doubtful income, 163
Dr Hatem
    commented on Hadith, 140

E
ego, 29
e'lam, 12

connection with Qur'ran, 13
e'lamu, 13
eloquence, 108, 110
enjoining or doing good, 39, 208
environmentalism
    Allah
        Qur'an in *Surah al-Waq'iah*
            56:68-70, 297
        says in *Surah al-Hajj* 22:18,
            296
        Surah al-An'am 6:165, 299
    Bismillah and *Alhamdulillah*, 297
    blessing of water
        in *Surah Mulk* 67:30, 297
    Caliphate of Umar bin al-Khattab,
        298
    corruption, imbalance and
        inequality, 299
    cultivating, earth, 295
    Day of Judgement, 298
    Hadith
        narrated by Anas, 294
    ihsaan, 298
    Islamic approach, 294
    Maymoona, 299
    Messenger of Allah
        superiority of learned, 294
    No Muslim plants, 294
    palm-cutting, 295
    planting and growing trees, 295
    remembrance of Allah *(dhikr)*, 296
    scholars of exegesis *(tafseer)*, 296
    Surah al-A'raf 7:31, 298
    tareeq, 298
    three acts, 297
    tribe of Quraish, 295
extended family, rights
    Abu Huraira
        narration, 211
    aunts and uncles, 211
    benefits of, 212–214

child custody
    maternal aunt or paternal uncle responsibility, 211
    en route to Makkah, 214–215
    grandparents, 211
    Hadith
        orphan, concept of custody, 210
    Hamza
        daughter custody of, 210
    Khadijah's sister, 215
    kunya, 210
    mothers and maternal aunts, 210–211
    Prophet Muhammad
        ruled in the favour of Ja'far, 210
    Surah Baqarah 2:133, 212
    ties of kinship, 214

F
fairness
    examples in Islam, 115
faith, 61
    al-haya, 105
    al-'iy, 105
false testimony
    Islam, 111
family realm of social justice. *See* parents and children, justice
fard, 59
father, 11, 22, 91, 107, 110, 127, 171, 186, 189
    presented as leader (imam) of children, 22
fear, 51, 52, 59, 81, 96, 109, 127, 175, 176, 207, 222
    persecution, 51
    subjective, 51
fiqh, 74

fitna. *See* rebellion
fitrah, 4
followers, 6, 8, 29, 44, 52, 95, 121155, 268
forgiveness, 74

G
giving advice, 48
ghani, 32
gharar in Islam
    Allah
        Ibn Taymiyyah, 180
    availability and deliverability uncertainty in ownership, 181
    claims, 183
    contract of excessive risk, 180
    financial benefit, 183
    function, 182
    gharar, 179
        Arabic version, 180
        business transaction, 180
        deceptive uncertainty, 180
        literal translation, 180
        prohibition of, 180
        selling someone, 181
        three rules, 181–182
    Hadith, 181
        narrated by Abu Musa al-Ashari, 182
    Islam, 179
        goal in, 180
        innovative models, 182
    Islamic
        finance or insurance models, 184
        model of insurance, 183
        Western insurance models, 184
    Islamisation, 184
    Joe Bradford
        Fatwah and its Role in Regulatory Capture, 184

Messenger of Allah, 180
    cooperative insurance, 182
    forbade transactions, 180
    prohibited, purchase of fruits, 180
natural disasters or unforeseen circumstances, 182
policies, 183
Prophet Muhammad
    pooling resources and mutual co-operation, 182
Qayyim, 181
schemes, 183
social security
    concept of government, 182
Takaful, 184
technically speaking, 181
warranties, 184
gharrah, 86
Ghawrath
    conversation with Prophet Muhammad, 76
gheebah, 59
gheerah, 132. *See* righteous anger
ghish. *See* deception
God-consciousness, 35, 111, 204
goodness, 30
good mannerisms and characteristics, 73
grace, 3, 9
guardian, 22, 23, 73, 74, 100, 204, 213

H
Hadith
    Abdullah ibn Umar, narrated by, 19
    Abu Dhar, 37
    balance in character of Prophet Muhammad, 132
    consistent message, 38
    difficult one, 72
    giving hand, 126
    Ibn Abbas, 65
    lessons learnt from, 20–22
    nurturing of companions and children, 73
    poverty, 38
    related in Sunan Bayhaqi, 23
    revenge, 132
    Sahih Ibn Hibban, 19
    spend on, 75
    strong believer, 125
    Umair, 13–14
    Uthman bin Affan, 63–64
Hadith Qudsi, 2
    Abu Dawud, 3–4
    Abu Mas'ud al-Badri, 11
    Ibn Rajab, by, 3
    Imam Ahmad, defined by, 2
    Imam Ibn Taymiyyah, defined by, 3
    lessons, 2–3
    lessons learnt from, 11–15
    Mas'ud al-Ansari, 11
    meanings of referring ya ibadi, 4–5
    Prophet Muhammad, 2
Hafs bin Abdul Rahman
    partner of Imam Abu Hanifa, 96
Hakeem bin Hizam
    narrated about retaining goodness, 109
haq. *See* truth
Haramain, 41
hayaa, 108
hayaah, 108
hellfire
    tongue, 47
healthcare prisoners
    Islamic tradition, 280–281
hidden corruption, 33
hikmah. *See* wisdom
Hilf Al-Fadool

building coalition of justice
  al-Muqawqas, 279
  battles, 279
  Bayt al-Ma'moor, 277
  Caliph al-Mu'tadid, 281
  The Canon *(Qanun)* of
    Avicenna (Ibn Sina),
    281
  Companion Rufayda al-
    Aslamiyyah, 279
  Day of Resurrection, 277
  endowment *(waqf)*, 280
  Haroon ar-Rashid, 281
  healthcare prisoners, 280
  healthcare, views, 278–279
  Islamic history, 280
  leprosy, 281
  Messenger of Allah, 282
  Muslim communities, 281
  narrations throughout, 277
  pharmacists in, 280
  right to healthcare, 281
  Sa'ad bin Abi Waqqas, 280
  spiritual undertone, 277
  Surah al- Fatihah, 280
  Umar bin al-Khattab, 280
Hilf al-Fadool, 120
  lessons learnt, 121–124
Hind came to Prophet, 74
homelessness, 68
honour killings
  article by Dr Jonathon Brown, 259,
    264. *See* murder
housing and food
  Abu Hurairah, 67–68
  importance explained by Prophet,
    67–68
  people of Suffah, 67
Hudhaifa
  narrated what Messenger of Allah
    said, 78, 79
  no "yes men," 79

Hurmuzan, 24
  connection with Umar, 24
hypocrisy
  al-badha, 105, 108
  al-bayaan, 105, 108
  eloquence, 108
hypocrites
  described by Messenger of Allah,
    134

I
Ibn Abbas, 41
  Hadith narrated by, 65
  revelation of verse, narrated in
    Bukhari, 72
  statement about companions, 16
  torture in Islam, 150
Ibn al Qayyim
  explaining *Surah al-Ma'ida*, Verse
    8, 7
  justice, 7
Ibn Hajar
  worst type of deception, 97
Ibn Hajr
  father, leader (imam) of children,
    22
  Hadith reported by Ibn Umar,
    22–23
Ibn Jareer at-Tabari, 162
Ibn Katheer
  statement about tatfeef, 87
Ibn Majah
  Hadith narrated by, 85–86
Ibn Mas'ud
  accustom yourself, 80
Ibn Qayyim
  commented on Quraysh, 76
  destruction of nation, 8
  excellence/deficiency, 77
Ibn Rajab
  defined Hadith Qudsi, 3

grace, 3
justice, 3
transgression, 3
Ibn Taymiyyah
    Hadith narrated by, 83
    hearing or listening, 82
    Ibn Qayyim, destruction of nation, 8
    statement about Allah and nation, 8
ihsaan, 38, 73, 76, 77, 90, 154, 156, 158, 159, 189–190192, 200, 202–203, 207–2, 165185, 186187
ill treatment., 15
ilm, 13
imam, 22. *See* leadership
Imam Abu Hanifa
    creating link, 58
    rights of neighbour, 144
    son, 96–97
    stories about, 96–97
    wealthy and honest merchants in Madinah, 96
Imam Ahmad
    defined Hadith Qudsi, 2
    faced testing situation, 58
Imam al-Bayhaqi
    mother and Aisha, 25
Imam al-Bughawi, 161
Imam al-Ghazali
    believers and completion of the things, 91
    major sins of the scholars, 58
    statement about position, 33
Imam al-Haraawi
    statement, 59
Imam Al-Qutayba
    saying about oppression, 23
Imam al-Shawkani
    commented on Hadith, 163

Imam As-Safarini, 37
Imam Ghazali
    referring to believers, 133
Imam Hasan al-Basri, 15
Imam Hussain
    silence, 60–61
Imam Ibn Qudama
    Mukhtasar Minhaj al-Qasideen, 80
Imam Ibn Taymiyyah
    defined by Hadith Qudsi, 3
    orphans, 74
Imam Khattabi
    said about truth, 48
Imam Maalik
    spoke about clothes of power, 129
Imam Nawawi
    human condition, 132–133
Imam Shawkani
    beautiful saying, 110–111
imamah, 22
imams, 30
iman. *See* faith
indecency. *See* vulgarity
injustice, 28
insurance, 183
inquisitive nature, 39
intoxicating, 14
investigative
    torture in Islam, 151
Islam
    central and agreed-upon legal maxim, 8–9
    examples of fairness and mercy, 115
    false testimony, 111
    form of oppression, 4
    justice and, 1–2
    shooting for sake of enjoyment, 284
    strength and Battle of Uhud, 128
    Suhayl accepted, 116

Surah Luqman, verse 13, 4
wrongdoing and supporters, 118
Islamic court
   murder/honour killing, 264
Islamic ethics
   Allah
      Surah al-Hashr 59:9, 234
      Surah at-Tawbah 9:6, 235
   Allah will shelter, 232
   concept of migration, 236
   essence of Islam, 232
   first migration, 233
   gender equity
      Arab tribes, 261
      Aristotle, 261
      authentic narration, 260
      Council of Macon, 261
      female Companions, 260
      feminism, 258
      honour killings article by Dr Jonathon Brown, 259, 264
      iddah, 262
      ideologies, 259
      iftidaad, 262
      Islamic reform, 257
      law of inheritance, 264
      liberation of women, 257
      menstruation or *hayd*, 263
      Messenger of Allah, 262
      Muslim community *(ummah)*, 265
      Nation of Islam, 258
      New Testament, 264
      Niddah laws, 261
      Prophethood of Muhammad, 262
      socio-historic influences, 259
      Surah al-Ahzab 33:35, 260
      Surah an-Nahl 16:58, 262
      Surah at-Takwir 81:8-9, 261
      topic of feminism, 259
      views, 259
      women empowerment, 258
   group of refugees, 233
   Hadiths
      verses Qur'an, 261
   human rights, 232
   Ibn ad-Daghinah, 233
   Imam Awza'i
      Muslim, 235
   Madinah *(Ansaar)*, 234–235
   migrants, care, 235
   Modern refugee law, 236
   non-Muslim refugees and migrants, 235–236
   refugees, 234
   right in Islam, 236
   right to migration, 233
   stereotyping and collective guilt
      Allah, created people, 251
      Angels, assumption of, 250
      Battle of Badr, 254
      Companions, 250
      groups of people, 253
      Hadith is *hijaa*, 252
      hesitation to fight, 254–255
      Hudhayfa, 252
      Ikrima accepted Islam, 250
      Muslims, 256
      Prophet, wording of, 250
      Qur'an and Prophetic tradition, lessons, 250
      Safiyyah, 255
      unfair policies, 252
      violence and terrorism, 252–253
   Sunnah, 232
   tribal system, 232
   Umar bin Abdul Aziz
      refugee camps, 234

Islamic history, 29, 280
Islam's position on slavery
   Abdullah Hamid Ali
      article *'Beyond Race'*, 238
   Al-Muqawqis delegation, 246
      companions, 247
   Amr bin al-'Aas sent a delegation, 246
   anti-racist, 237
   anti-racist society, 244
   Bible saying, 228
   black Muslims, 245
   Caliphate of Umar, 246
   Companions of Prophet, 240
   customs and beliefs, 239
   Days of Ignorance *(jahiliyyah)*, 239
   descent of Arabs, 240
   Egyptian ruler
      al-Muqawqis, called for Muslim delegation, 246
   Exodus 21:20, 228
   Hadith
      modern-day slavery, 229
      themes, 238
   images from Libya, 228
   ISIS, 229
   Julaybeeb, 247, 248, 267
   manifestations, 240
   Messenger of Allah
      days of ignorance *(jahiliyyah)*, 239
   Michael Zeuske
      comments, 227
   Muslim countries, 227
   Muslim history
      ease and respect, 245
   partition causes, 239
   people of Makkah, 238
   Prophet and Caliphs, 248
   Prophet Muhammad
      laws of slavery, 230
      Muslim community *(ummah)*, 239
      piety *(taqwa)* exists, 241
      pre-Islamic period, 238
      views, 224–225
   Qur'an statement in, 228
   racism, 38, 172, 237-238, 239, 241, 242, 243–244, 248, 249, 257, 274
      bigotry or discrimination, 243–244
      Malcolm X, 244
      nationalism or tribalism in, 242–243
      structural, 239
   Rib'ee bin 'Aamir, 225–226
   slaveowners, 226
   structural racism, 239
   Surah *Al-Hujurat* 49:13, 240
   transatlantic slave trade, 226
   Umar bin Khattab, 246
   Umm Mihjan
      black woman, 248
   Usama bin Zayd
      black Companion of the Prophet, 245–246
   The Walking Qur'an by Rudolf Ware, 226
   white supremacy, 241

J

Jabbar
   Hadith narrated, 141
Jabir, 71
Jannah, 27. *See* paradise
Jareer bin Abdullah al-Ba
   story of sincerity and fear of cheating, 95–96
jihad, 49
jurisprudence, 74, 81–82

justice
    defined by Ibn Rajab, 3
    Ibn al Qayyim, 7
    Islam and, 1–2
    Prophet Muhammad, 1–2
    Surah al-Ma'ida, Verse 8, 7
just ruler, 22, 24, 29

K
khafi. *See* public sight
khayr. *See* goodness
khiya, 74
killing, 6–7, 54, 58, 60, 75, 76, 149
    animal for fun, 284
    disabled babies, 267
    article by Dr Jonathon Brown, 259, 264
    unlawful, 188
    prostration, in, 59
    shooting for sake of enjoyment, 284
kinship, 75

L
labour ethics, 156
leader, 22
leadership, 29
    Abu Dhar, 30
    examples, 30
    permissible time to seek, 33
    position, 31–34, 58, 248, 250, 313
    Prophet Sulayman, 30
    questions about, 34
    role, 34, 204
    spirituality, 32
    trust, 29
legislation, 9, 20, 308
Luqman Hakeem, 46–47

M
Madinah, 17, 41
    Muslims migrated to, 64
    non-Muslim resident, 64
    story about inhabitants and Prophet, 106
Makkah, 41, 44
    Muslims, in, 57
    Zubaid, businessman, 119–120
Malik ibn Murthad
    narrated Hadith, 36
marital relationship, 204
marriage, 4, 16–17, 83
    deception, 100–101
    decision to delay, 187
    contract, 189
    rights work in, 199–207
    aspects changed, 200
    long lasting, happy and successful, 207
    excellence *(ihsaan)* in, 207–208
    arranged, 212
    forced, 229
mercy, 78, 87, 111, 115, 120, 132, 140–141, 187, 195, 206216, 216
    examples in Islam, 115
Messenger of Allah, 161, 164
    trust and, 165
mimbar. *See* pulpit
mother, 25, 188, 193, 210, 214, 245
    as parent, 24
    great right over us, 15
    leader *(imamah)* of household, 22
    man carrying on back for hajj, 187

Mount Saf, 76
Mu'adh, 7
muaith, 155
Mubeen, 108
muhaajireen. *See* Makkah
muhabbah, 4
Mukhtasar Minhaj al-Qasideen
    Imam Ibn Qudama, 80

muqsiteen, 20, 21
murder
    Islamic court, 264
Muslim Community, 52
Muslims, 42
    Abyssinia, in, 57
    Al-Birr wa Taqwa, 122
    Hadith narrated, 141
    Makkah, in, 57
    migrated to Madinah, 64
    water, 65
    would be like Ammar bin Yasir, 58–59

N
Nafsi, nafsi!, 93
Noam Chomsky
    quote, 117–118
Nu'man bin Bashir
    torture in Islam, 151

O
obligatory, 59
oppression, 5, 9, 13, 14, 47, 48, 51, 54, 56, 226, 230. *See also* dhulm
    economic, 121
    first level, 15
    forbidden, 147
    form, 4
    greater forms, 14
    meaning, 4
    no justification, 14
    Prophet Muhammad's warning, 6
    reason for, 20
    ruins society, 123
    second level, 15
    Surah Luqman, verse 13, 4
    third and worst level, 16
oppressor
    opposite of, 21
orphan, 16

Imam Ibn-Taymiyyah, 74
Yusuf bin Malik al-Makki, 73–74

P
paradise, 43
    tongue, 47
parents and children, justice
    Allah, 186
        Qur'an, 188
        special mercy, 187
    Arab culture, 188
    child of their rights, 190
    Hadith, 189
    Ibn Abbas
        unlawful killing, approached by man, 188
    Ibn Umar
        reply, 187
    ihsaan, 185–186
    Imam Ahmad
        circumstances, 187
    Islam in Louisiana (USA), 190
    Islamic texts
        rights and responsibilities, 185
    Messenger of Allah, 186
        disobey of Creator, 189
    Paradise *(Jannah)*, 187–188
    Prophet Ibrahim
        Dua with Allah, 189
    Prophet Muhammad
        expression to convey message, 186
        humility, 188
        obedience, 189
        Sa'ad bin Abu Waqas, 189–190
    Qur'an
        treatment of parents, 186
    relationship between, 186, 190
    righteous children, 191
    scholars, 186, 187
    Umar bin al-Khattab, 186

Zain al-Abideen
  great-grandson, 187
people of Shaam, 2
people of Suffah, 67
people of Ukdhood
  torture in Islam, 148
people punished by, 57
personality issues (flaws), 34
pious employee
  Abdullah bin Umar
    ghulool, 161
    shepherd, conversation on fast, 164
  ajeer, 165
  Allah, 160
    messenger of, 161
  amanah, 160
  ameen, 165
  Day of Judgement, 161
  doubtful income, 163
  Hakeem bin Hizam, 162
  Ibn Jareer at-Tabari, 162
  Imam al-Bughawi, 161
  Imam al-Shawkani
    commented on Hadith, 163
  Messenger of Allah, 161, 164
    trust and, 165
  Prophet Muhammad, 160
    Hadith, 161
    recited Bismillah, 164
    (Sirah) serve as lessons regarding, 163
  Rights of employee
    Abdullah bin Umar, 161
  shareek, 165
  Umar bin al-Khattab
    Muslims to Persia, 162
  urwa, 162
  wakeel, 165
position
  authority, 40

questions about, 34
statement by Imam al-Ghazali, 33
poverty, 29, 38, 111, 175, 177, 211, 234, 255, 305
prayers, 32
prisoner, 68, 75, 116, 149, 150, 227, 229, 280
privilege, 112–113
Prophet Ibrahim
  supplication, 30
Prophet Muhammad, 160
  Abu Dhar and two explanations to choose him, 28
  anger management, 136
  belittling sins, 80
  betrayal, 97
  conversation with Usamah, 113–114
  Day of Judgement, 6, 97
  depth of wording, 41
  discussion about strange things, 55
  do not sit silently, 60
  example of trust, 75
  Ghawrath, 76
  Hadith, 161
    about tolerating people, 61–62
    mentioned to Ibn Khidam, 52
  Hadith Qudsi, narrated by, 2
  help both oppressed/oppressor, 59
  importance of the pact, 123
  incident of Aisha, 13
  incident of young man laughing, 8
  justice, 1–2
  learning from, 28–30
  message narrated by Abdullah ibn Amr ibn al-As, 6–7
  Mount Saf, 76
  no justification of hitting of slave, 14
  pulpits of light, 21
  questions of Abu Dhar, 41

Quraysh, 76
   recited Bismillah, 164
   Sahih Bukhari, 7
   saying reported by Safwan, 6
   sayings reported by Abu Dharr, 2
   second Hadith, 55–56
   serve as lessons regarding, 163
   story of Fatima bint al-Aswad, 114–115
   Surah al-Kahf, 18:6, 54–55
   talked about assistance, 40
   talks about people in general, 22
   third Hadith, 56
   warning against oppression, 6
protecting or supporting, 42
Prophet Sulayman
   leadership, 30
prostration, 59
protecting/supporting, 42
public sight, 32
pulpits of light, 21, 25, 31, 197
punishment, 12

Q

Qadhi Al-Iyyad
   importance of hearing both sides of story, 110
qadi, 23
qa'ida, 8
Qays bin Abi Hazm
   Hadith narrated, 53–54
Qur'an
   punishment to oppressors, 114–115
   Surah al-An'am 6:116, 79–80
   Surah al-Ma'idah 5:8, 65
   Surah al-Qalam, 68:17, 65
   Surah Al-Qasas, 28:83, 30
Quraysh, 76
   suffers, Messenger of Allah and companions, 77

R

radkh, 37
Raja'a bin Khaiwa, 31
Ramadan, 8–9, 41
   lessons learnt from, 42
rebellion, 32
recklessness, 50
responding to evil with good, 71-77
reward, 40
righteous anger, 133–134
   cursing people, 134
   determining factors, 134
   example of Musa, 136–137
   incident narrated in Sahih Muslim, 137
   Isa, showed controlled, 137
   Mu'adh bin Jabal al-Ansari, 136
   points to help in finding and channelling, 137–138
rights of animals, 283
   acts of kindness and cruelty, 287
   appreciation for Creator, 286
   beautiful narrations, 289–290
   Companion Tameem ad-Dari, 288
   cruelty
      whilst threatening punishment, 286
   endowments *(awqaaf)*, 291
   Hadith
      Sahl bin al-Handhaliyya, 287
   Ibn Umar, 284
   ihsaan, 291–292
   jurisprudence *(fiqh)*, 286
   Madrasat al-Qattat, 291
   Messenger of Allah
      forbade cruelty towards all animals, 289
      sparrow's right, 284
   Mu'awiya bin Qurra, 288
   Prophet Muhammad
      merciful towards animals, 289
      wordings, 285

reward in kindness to animals, 285
son of Imam Subki, 292
treatment, heartlessness and
    disrespect, 284
rights of elderly within society
    companions, 217
    generations gap, 217
    Hadith
        Glorifying Allah, 216
        taken care of by Allah, 217
    Prophetic guidance, 222
    specific lessons, 218–222
rights of neighbour
    Abdullah bin Mubarak, 144–145
    Abu Dhar, 142–143
    Abu Hurairah, Hadith by, 142, 143
    Aisha, Hadith by, 142
    Allah, 301
        merciful, 302
        says in *Surah ash-Shura* 42:39, 303
    Dr Muhammad Ismail al-
        Muqaddam, example
        by, 141
    example is of Muslim sister, 142
    excellence, 303
    Hadith, 301
    Hadith by Samura bin Jundab, 141
    Ibn Abdil Barr, commented on
        hadith, 143
    Ibn Mas'ud about sins, 143–144
    ihsaan with Allah, 302
    Imam Abu Hanifa, 144
    Imam al-Mawardi
        social implications, 304
    Imam Zaid Shakir
        book, 304
    Islam
        retribution *(Qisas)* and
            forgiveness, 303
        judge between people, 304
    justice, 302
    Malcolm X, 303
    narration from Jabbar, 141
    no justice, no peace, 301
    paradise is referred to *Dar-us-salaam*, 302
    peace and justice, 302
    pointed by Messenger of Allah, 143
    Qur'an
        in *Surah ash-Shura* 42:40, 304
    Surah an-Nahl, 303
    three worst types of people, 144
    Uthman, 301
rights work in marriage
    aiming for excellence, 207
    Book of Ephesians, 208
    Day of Judgement, 200–210
    emotional voids and needs, 207
    excellence in a marriage
        Hadith narrated, 203
    God-consciousness *(taqwa)*, 204
    husband
        emotional rights, 205–206
        right to intimacy, 205
        upon wife, 204–205
    Ibn Katheer, commented on, 200
    Imam Ahmad, case, 207
    morning prayer *(Fajr)*, 208
    Surah Baqarah, 2:228, 200
    wife
        fourth right, 202–203
        second right, 202
        technical rights of, 201–203
        third right, 202
        upon husband, 200
        worship at night *(Qiyam al-Layl)*, 208
Road of Zubaida, 69
rulings of jurisprudence, 60
ruling on silence and injustice, 53-62

S

sadaqah, 39
Saeed bin Jubair
    killed in prostration, 59
    showed no fear, 59
Sahih Bukhari, 7
Sahih Muslim, 105–106
    prohibition of desiring position, 32–33
salah. *See* prayers
salawat, 3
satan
    biggest tricks, 32
scholars, 11, 15
    Abdullah bin Mubarak, 129–130
    commented on saying, 15
    ego, 29
    form of striving, 49
    Ibn Hajar on Hadith, 40
    mentioned, why other nations destroyed, 56
    objectives of law, 116
    oppression, 15
    private sins *versus* public oppression, 56
    problems that come with deception, 103–104
    rulers, 49
    struggle, 49
    Sufyan Ath-Thawri, 22
    tafseer, 13
    talks about dhaalim, 21
    torture in Islam, 150
    two explanations and Abu Dhar, 28
    ulema awaam, 49
    Umar bin Abdul Aziz on, 130
security posts, 69
selflessness, 92
sense of greed, 66
sense of security, 21, 24
shareek, 165

shar'iah, 48
    meaning, 118
Shaykh Abul Abed
    statement, 54
Shaykh Salman
    interesting observation, 57
short-changing, 88, 111
    brotherhood in, 91–92
    family context, 89–90
    Hadith, 88
    Ibn Qayyim and his teacher, 92
    Imam Shafi, 92
    Muhammad bin Sireen, 91
    scholars, 92
    teachers and students, 88–89
    workplace in, 90
    your lord, 88
short-changing/cheating, 85
Shuraih to judge, 107
shyness, 110
silence, 57, 60
    Abu Saeed narrates about, 60
    evil was committed, 57
    examples, 59
    Imam Hussain, 60–61
    mandatory but when, 60
    permissible, 60
    prohibited, being evil, 57
    situations not supporting, 59–60
    speaking up, 58
    when it is sinful, 60
sin of favouritism
    Companions, 194
    competitiveness, 196
    daughters
        preferential treatment to, 198
    Hadith
        Nouman bin Bashir, 194
        tone, 193
    Hassan and Hussain
        grandsons of Prophet, 195

Imam Ahmad
  pleased with Allah, 195
Islam
  religion of balance, 193
Messenger of Allah
  attention, 194
  daughters as gift, 197
  parents, expectations, 194
  treated Usama, 195
  words, 193
  permissible exceptions to child, 195–196
Prophet Muhammad
  position, 193
  scholars, 195
  studies effects of, 196
  treating children differently, 193
  Umar bin Abdul Aziz, 195
skilled, 40, 41
slave, 4, 5, 9, 11, 12, 14, 17, 206. *See also* ya ibadi
  beating, 47
  Christian, 17–18
  freed slave, 13, 68, 95, 113
  Umair, 13
small acts of kindness, 44
social justice and injustice
  beware of greed, 167
  Bukhal, 169
  cause of Allah, 168
  Day of Judgement, 167
  entire circumambulation (*tawaf*), 168
  fitna of *ummah*, 169
  greed, 166–167
    afflicts, 169
  guest of Allah's Messenger, 169
  Ibn Qayyim, 169
  iman, 168
  Messenger of Allah
    man, worst two qualities, 170

prepare the meal, 169
shuh, 168, 169
Surah al-'Adiyat 100:6, 170
Surah al-Hashr 59:9, 170
trial *(fitna)*, 167
ummah, 167
speaking, 49, 58
  when, harmful and ineffective, 61
speech, 46–47, 50, 58, 108, 109, 143, 205, 206–207
struggle, 47, 48, 49, 51, 244, 271
Sufyan Ath-Thawri, 22
  statement about two categories of people, 30
sujood, 59
Sulayman ibn Abdul Malik
  will and Umar, 31–32
Sunan al-Bayhaqi al-Kubra, 120
Sunan Bayhaqi, 22–23
Sunnah, 48
supplication, 24
  example as incident, 24
  Prophet Ibrahim, 30
superiority, 204, 241, 244, 261, 294
Surah al-Anfal 8:60, 128
Surah al-A'raf 7:199, 71
Surah al-Baqarah 2:228, 90
Surah al-Hashr 59:9, 92–93
Surah al-Insan 76:8, 150
Surah al-Ma'idah 5:2, 122
Surah al-Ma'idah, Verse 8
  justice, about, 7
Surah al-Mutaffifeen
  opening passage of, 87
Surah al-Mutaffifeen 83:4-6, 87
Surah an-Nisaa 4:105-112, 109
Surah ash-Shu'ara 26:183, 157
Surah Fatihah, 5
Surah Israa, verse 23, 15

T

tafseer, 13, 54, 86
tahneek, 50
taqi, 32
taqwa. *See* God-consciousness
tarbiyyah, 55
tashr'ee, 20
tatfeef, 85
    brotherhood, 91-92
    family context, 89-90
    regards to teachers and students, 88-89
    scholars, 92
    statement by Ibn Katheer, 87 (*See also* short-changing)
    workplace, 90-91
    your Lord, 88
tawakul, 49
The Essence of Islam
    quote from, 1
tongue, 47
torture in Islam
    Azhar bin Abdullah al-Harari, 151
    Battle of Badr, 150
    definition by United Nations, 152
    forbade torturing prisoners, 149
    forbidden oppression, 147
    forced confessions, 150–151
    Hadith, 146
    Ibn Abbas, 150
    Ibn al-Qayyim commented, 148
    investigative, 151
    Mujahid, 150
    narrated about Hisham bin Hakim bin Hizam, 146
    not limited to humans, 148
    Nu'man bin Bashir, 151
    people of Ukdhood, 147
    scholars, 150
    Surah al-Insan 76:8, 150
    Thumama, 149–150

torture in islam
    prohibition
        Caliphate, 313
        Companions, 312
        entirety of humanity, 308
        fitnah Abdullah accountable, 312
        gradualism, 309, 310
        grander scheme of things, 311
        greatest revivers, 313
        hypocrite Abdullah ibn Ubayy ibn Saloul, 311
        Law-Giver (Allah), 310
        Messenger of Allah, 309
        political gradualism in Islam, 311
        Prophet Muhammad
            new Muslims, temporary concessions, 311
        Prophet Musa, 310
        prophetic approach, 307
        prophets and their messages, 308
        Qur'an
            greatest teachings in, 309
        sacrifice our principles, 312
        scholars, 312–313
        Umar bin Abdul Aziz, 313
transgression, 3, 55, 80, 160
    defined by Ibn Rajab, 3
    like an evil, 79
    no transgression justification for, 14
    Prophet Muhammad, raised voice against, 13
    thankful to Allah, 77
treachery, 74
true repentance, 12
trust, 75, 158, 160, 165, 186, 315
truth, 47
    form of objection, 48
    giving advice, 48

Imam Khattabi, 48
ways to speak, 48

U
ulema awaam, 49
ulema sultan, 49
Umar al-Khattab, 48
Umar bin Abdul Aziz
    private sins *versus* public oppression, 56
Umar bin al-Khattab
    became Muslim, 127
    connection with anger, 133
    conversation with son, 83–84
    incident in Caliphate, 91
    Muslims to Persia, 162
    supplication (du'a), 126–127
    wise, learned and physically fit, 127
Umar bin Khattab
    punishment to son and Amr, 116–117
    faith, 61, 62
Umar ibn Abdul Aziz
    example set by, 45
    how appointed as Caliph, 31
    successor of Sulayman ibn Abdul Malik, 31
Umar ibn al-Khattaab
    advice to Sa'ad ibn Abi Waqas, 32
    connection with Christian, 17–18
Umar Mukhtar
    example of ethics, 75
Umm Salama
    Hadith is narrated by, 7, 106
umma, 11
ummah, 22–23, 29. *See* community; followers
umrah, 150
unjust rulers, 58
unskilled, 40
    example of what to do, 41
    lessons learnt from, 42

urwa, 162
Usamah
    beloved of Prophet Muhammad, 113–114
usury or interest *(riba)*, 171
    Abdullah bin Umar
        types of loans, 175
    Abrahamic faiths, 176
    Al-Baghawi, 174
    Allah
        thirty-six acts of adultery *(zina)*, 174
    case of, 172
    Day of Judgement, 175, 178
    debt crisis in Nigeria, 177
    dirham, 173
    global economy collapse, 175
    gravity of, 174
    Hadith
        powerful and horrifying, 178
    Imam Abu Hanifah
        lent, money, 175
    individual level, 174
    inequality, 174
    Islam, 173, 176
    making money from money, 176
    Messenger of Allah, 176
    Muslim community, 172
    Prophet Muhammad
        farewell sermon of, 172
        no-one left, 177
        pass a ruling *(fatwa)*, 177
        swimmer, 178
    Qur'an
        connotations, 173
        Surah al-Hashr 59:7, 173
    Surah al-Baqarah, 174
    Surah al-Baqarah, 174
    zakah, 176
Uthman
    assassinated Ali, 74

Uthman bin Affan
    Hadith narrated by, 63–64
Uthman ibn Abi al-Aas
    leader or not, 33

V
verses, 66, 86, 110, 174, 251, 261
violation, 14, 159
vulgarity, 108

W
wakeel, 165
water, 64, 66, 69, 83, 92, 99, 108, 148, 169, 286, 294
    meaning in Hadith, 65
    what Prophet emphasises on, 66
    Zubair and dispute, 66
wisdom, 12, 41, 50, 76, 115, 170, 197, 217, 296
work conditions and employee treatment, 153–158
    Abdullah bin Umar, 153, 157–158
    Abu Dawud, 154
    Abu Saeed al-Khudri narrated, 155
    becoming lazy, 155
    compassion, 156
    form of excellence, 154
    fulfilling and returning trust, 158
    labour ethics, 156
    muaith, 155
    no proud, 157
    show appreciation, 157
    Surah ash-Shu'ara 26:183, 157

Y
ya ibadi
    meanings of referring, 4–5
Yahya bin Maeen
    teaching statement, 15–16
Yemen, 7, 27, 34, 68
yunfiq, 37
Yusuf bin Malik al-Makki
    orphans, 73–74

Z
Zayd bin Amr bin an-Nufayl
    amazed Prophet, 82–83
    son Saeed, 82
Zubaid
    business in Makkah, 119–120
Zubaida
    example of Road of Zubaida, 69–70